THE
LAND
OF
CAIN

THE LAND OF CAIN
Class and Nationalism
In English Canada 1945-1975

Philip Resnick

New Star Books • Vancouver

New Star Books
2504 York Avenue
Vancouver, B.C.   V6K 1E3
Canada

Canadian Cataloguing in Publication Data

Resnick, Philip, 1944-
  The land of Cain

    Bibliography: p.
    Includes index
    ISBN 0-919888-68-2 bd.
    ISBN 0-919888-67-4 pa.

    1. Nationalism — Canada. 2. Social classes —
Canada. 3. Canada — History — 1945-
4. Canada — Relations (general) with the United
States. I. Title.
FC97.R48   320.9'71'064   C77-002229-4
F1034.2.R48

CONTENTS

ACKNOWLEDGEMENTS

I began thinking about this topic more than a decade ago. As an adolescent in my native Montreal in the early 1960s, I was dimly aware of the upsurge of nationalism in the new Quebec of the Quiet Revolution. Moving to Toronto in the late 1960s, I found myself caught up in some of the nationalistic agitation surfacing in the media, universities, and student movement.

My first attempt to explore some of the ideas in this study was in a radio program entitled "Nationalism and Socialism," which I produced in early 1971 as part of a series on CBC Ideas, "The Idea of Nation."

Since moving to Vancouver in 1971, I have continued to follow Canadian nationalism "from the hinterland," particularly with reference to breakaway and similar movements for Canadian unions.

I presented an exploratory paper on "The Ideology of English Canadian Nationalism 1945-1975" at the 1975 Canadian Political Science meetings in Edmonton, and have benefited from the criticism and comments of Phyllis Clarke, Danny Drache and Denis Smith.

I would like to thank Louis Le Borgne and my good friends Hugh Armstrong and Koula Mellos for making their theses available to me for purposes of this study.

I would also like to thank a number of people who made themselves available for interviews, including Joe Morris, President of the Canadian Labour Congress, Ron Lang, Legislative Director of the CLC, Norm Simon, publicity director of the Canadian Union of Public Employees, Daryl Logan, National Director of the Committee for an Independent Canada, and most especially Michael Barkway of

The Financial Times of Canada and Abe Rotstein, University of Toronto. The latter two's comments and suggestions proved most valuable.

I would also like to thank Jim Conrad of the Canadian Federation of Independent Business for being most helpful with information and material about his organization.

I would like to acknowledge the help of Maureen Boyd, who worked as a research assistant for three months during the summer of 1975, particularly in sifting through *Hansard* and the Norman Mackenzie Collection, UBC. I would also like to publicly thank the B.C. NDP government, which paid her salary under the Careers 75 program.

A special debt is owed my colleague in the Department of Political Science, UBC, Alan Cairns, whose helpful and trenchant comments at various stages in the writing made this a more careful study than it might otherwise have been; to C.B. Macpherson, Department of Political Economy, University of Toronto, whose advice has been most precious; and to Ivan Avakumovic, Department of History, UBC, whose criticisms were invaluable in helping me turn what was originally a Ph.D. thesis into a more publishable manuscript.

To be sure, none of the above, or others who helped me in one way or another, bear any responsibility for the conclusions and arguments contained herein. Some, indeed, will be most unhappy with them. At the minimum, however, I hope all will acknowledge the seriousness of the endeavour.

I have a great debt to a number of libraries, including the Library, Department of Labour, Ottawa, the library of the Association of Universities and Colleges of Canada, Ottawa, the clippings library of *The Financial Times of Canada*, then still in Montreal, the subject files of the Canadian Institute of International Affairs library, Toronto, the Vancouver Public Library, and most especially the UBC Library—Special Collections, Government Documents and Newspapers, and the General Collection.

Four final acknowledgements. First to the Canada Council for its generous financial support to me as a Ph.D. student. Having sent me out to Europe some years ago on a different quest, it will no doubt be surprised by the quarry with which I have returned. Second, to UBC, for a small research grant which allowed me to travel east in May, 1975 and consult a good deal of material, as well as interview most of the respondents mentioned above. Third to Esther McDonald for her original typing of the manuscript. Finally, to Andromache for her intellectual support, and to Amos and Jonah for their promise.

P.R.
Vancouver, B.C.

. . . the land should not be called the New Land, being composed of stones and horrible rugged rocks; for along the whole of the north shore, I did not see one cart-load of earth and yet I landed in many places. Except at Blanc Sablon there is nothing but moss and short stunted shrub. In fine I am rather inclined to believe that this is the land God gave to Cain.

Jacques Cartier

Another such war, and the hope of Socialism will be buried under the ruins of imperialistic barbarism . . . Here capitalism reveals its death hand, here it betrays that it has sacrificed its historical right of existence, that its rule is no longer compatible with the progress of humanity . . . Socialism or barbarism!

Rosa Luxemburg

FOR A SOCIALIST CANADA
AND A SOCIALIST QUEBEC

Chapter One
AN APPROACH TO
ENGLISH CANADIAN NATIONALISM

What constitutes a nation, and is there an English Canadian, as distinct from a Canadian, nation? How has English Canada's national consciousness developed in the thirty years since World War II? What is the connection between English Canadian nationalism and the changing fortunes of American imperialism and Quebec nationalism? How have the different class forces within English Canada reacted to nationalism, and how would one characterize the dominant forms of nationalism that have emerged in recent years? What is the significance of English Canadian nationalism in a world of multinational corporations and national liberation movements, and how is it likely to develop in the years to come?

If we begin this study with a series of questions, not assertions, it is because nationalism, more than any other political ideology, lends itself to a myriad of contradictory interpretations. There is no single definition of nationalism, while nationalist movements in this century have run the whole gamut from fascism through conservatism, liberalism, socialism, and Marxism to speak only of the more important political credos. What is significant is just how great the staying power of nationalism has been, and how in societies as divergent as the advanced capitalist ones of the western world, the emerging countries of the third world, and the centrally-planned ones that term themselves socialist, nationalism has been a recurrent force.

It is our position that nationalism can only be studied meaningfully in relation to concrete material forces in different societies. There is no single ideal-type of nationalism universally applicable, and there is no point debating abstractly whether nationalism in general is a good, bad, or indifferent thing. Yet much of liberal theory does precisely this, and even socialist theory, all too often, does scarcely any better. Hence the need for considerable modesty in undertaking a study such as this,[1] and no less importantly, the need for a good deal of care in analysing the specific nature of English Canadian nationalism.

Though certain Tory historians shudder at the very questioning of a single Canadian nationality,[2] both liberal and social democratic writers in recent years have been willing to recognize, at a minimum, the bi-national character of Canada. To be sure, whether arguing for co-operative federalism, partnership between the two founding peoples, or bilingualism and biculturalism across the boards,[3] most English Canadian writers stopped short, at least until 1970, of accepting a fundamentally political, as opposed to cultural, basis for Canada's national duality.[4] Indeed, there is a whole school of writing deriving from that arch-progressive Lord Acton and epitomized in the work of Pierre Elliott Trudeau and his palace intellectual, Ramsay Cook, praising the multinational state as the embodiment of divine reason on earth.[5]

Quebecois, on their side, have not been so reticent in asserting their own claims to nationhood. The historical origins of this claim are hardly recent,[6] but the last fifteen years have witnessed the take-off of the idea of Quebec independence among intellectuals, students, the new petty bourgeoisie of professionals and civil servants, and elements of both the blue collar and white collar working class.[7] The Parti Quebecois, now in power in Quebec, is committed to the idea of independence, and even those French Canadians who stop short of espousing separation have little difficulty in seeing French Canadians, and more specifically Quebecois, as "a distinct race or people characterized by common descent, language, or history," to use the Shorter Oxford definition of the nation.

For English-speaking Canadians, however, the problem is reversed. If Quebec nationalism starts from a common origin, history, and language, now setting itself political and economic objectives that may culminate in the establishment of a separate political state, English Canadian nationalists begin with the latter. Or more accurately, the concept of nation for English-speaking Canadians since 1867 begins with a political unit called Canada and a territory stretching from sea to sea. There has up to now been little formal recognition by most English-speaking Canadians of their separate national character within what is called Canada; indeed the dominant strain in English Canadian thought is probably to reject such distinctions.

> We in Ontario have never thought of ourselves, or of English-speaking Canada, as a nation because we thought that there was one nation, Canada, to which both we and our compatriots in French Canada belonged.[8]

The problems with the term English Canada are many. For one, it seems to suggest a common ancestry of the non-French speaking people of Canada, which Canadian demography, particularly in this century, belies. The multiplicity of ethnic origins among Canadians from other than the British Isles or France, more than 25 per cent of the total population and more than 35 per cent of the non-French-speaking population of the country,[9] makes such a short-hand expression suspect. Secondly, there is the heterogeneous character of the nine predominantly English-speaking provinces plus the territories, which makes them a quite different entity from the relatively compact and somewhat more homogeneous Quebec. English Canada is an unnatural amalgam of distinct regions. Thirdly, and most importantly, the political and emotional loyalty that English-speaking Canadians have invested into national symbols, have hitherto been into pan-Canadian symbols and structures, including Quebec. The nationalism of English Canadians, as LePan argued, has essentially been Canadian nationalism.

In its favour, one can say that the term English Canada points to the one element the non-French speaking population of Canada (other than some native people and recent immigrants) have in common, namely language. As long as the federal structure of Canada is maintained, we must be able to make distinctions between the term Canadian pertaining to both English-speaking and French-speaking Canada and the term English Canada pertaining to the non-French Canadian/Quebecois population of Canada. If Quebec, the homeland of most French Canadians, were to become independent and the rest of the country to continue as an independent political unit, the latter would undoubtedly still be called Canada (not English Canada) and its citizens Canadians (not English Canadians). But this latter Canadian nation is as yet only potential, not real, and for the moment there will continue to be confusion between the specifically English Canadian and pan-Canadian strands in the term Canadian. Throughout this study, therefore, we will be using the terms Canadian and English Canadian interchangeably to refer to the non-French Canadian population of the country, concentrated, as it happens, outside Quebec. Though there is a significant Anglophone minority in Quebec and a Francophone minority in the other nine provinces, the rough correlation between language and territory in Canada means that the ultimate national expression of its two principal linguistic groups coincides with the two areas where each is in the overwhelming majority—Quebec for the Francophones, English Canada for the Anglophones.

If Canada as a whole is a distinct political entity, if both the language and territory of the country, and of the English-speaking parts in particular, can be delineated easily enough, its nationhood is not thereby a sure thing. As one critical observer of the Canadian scene noted in 1953:

> Broadly speaking, one may say that no nation can foster among its people a consciousness of national identity unless one at least of the following conditions is fulfilled: either the country must be sufficiently small and compact to permit easy and frequent access to any of its parts; or its inhabitants must be of approximately the same descent, sharing a similar *Weltanschauung* and cherishing a common cultural heritage; or they must be united from without by allegiance to some ideal—whether it be the concept of national destiny as in the Third Reich, or simply an inchoate way of life, as in the United States. The first two requirements are both

present in Britain, the second alone in France, the third in America. None of them is to be found in Canada.[10]

There is no shared history common to United Empire Loyalist and Ukrainian farmer, Chinese coolie or central European proletarian. The Canadian economy, as a whole generation of economic historians tells us, was cradled in the bosom of two empires, and has depended throughout its short history on external, as much as internal, developments.[11] The founding *Weltanschauung* on the English Canadian side was counter-revolution,[12] and there has been relatively little in the political history of the country to generate the kind of loyalty and fervour of countries with heady political traditions. "Peace, order, and good government" is not the stuff for which people mount barricades (though it does not preclude participating in larger wars in which the imperial power is engaged); the tawdry trappings of a foreign monarchy are no substitute for an indigenous Canadian value system. Lacking that history of political struggle or revolution (save the abortive 1837 revolt) that characterizes most nations of Europe and the Western Hemisphere, or the experience of conquest and alien domination that long underlay Quebec nationalism, English Canada, not surprisingly, has had a weak sense of identity. The Canadian state, in no small part, was created to serve imperial interests, while different regions were unequal and often unwilling participants in an arrangement which benefited central Canadian capital and its outside allies first. The lack of strong loyalty to the centre felt by many with regional loyalties, the weakness of Canadian nationalism on the scale of world nationalisms, betray the external constraints that underlay the original Dominion of Canada and have underlain much of Canadian history since.

Yet there is potentially a Canadian nation, no less than a nation of Quebec. If one of the definitions of nationalism is the desire to maintain or preserve a particular nation, there has been no lack of this throughout Canadian history.[13] The very survival of Canada as a separate entity on the northern half of the North American continent, despite the tremendous attraction and power of the United States, is evidence enough of what Renan called "a plebiscite of every day."[14] The persistence of Canadian national feeling, more marginally during the years of Cold War, more strongly now that American imperialism has been weakened, is in fact the subject of this study.

What nationalism has meant in the English Canadian context since 1945 can perhaps be best defined as follows:

> *Nationalism is a concern that the political, economic, and cultural affairs of a territorially-defined polity be controlled and directed by individuals and/or corporations that are members of that polity, rather than by forces outside it.*

This is not necessarily the nationalism of a classical colony striving for formal political independence from the mother country. That type of nationalism may have existed in the Upper Canada of the 1830s; it was a factor, though not the dominant one, in the move to home rule, i.e., Confederation, of the 1860s; it figured in moves to imperial devolution and dominion status during the first decades of this century. It is not, however, the leitmotif of the American Empire which emerges after World War II, which recognizes its subordinate members as formally independent. In fact, it is precisely because Canada is formally independent after 1945, that such large sections of its leadership and population reject the earlier concept of nationalism, i.e., political independence, as obsolete, turning their backs on nationalism *tout court*.

In this, English Canadian politicians and businessmen, intellectuals and workers were following the dominant liberal thinking of the time. Had not nationalism, or at least its intransigent forms, been held responsible for the economic crisis of the 1930s, with its protectionism, autarchy, and depression? Had nationalism not been used by power-hungry politicians, e.g., Mussolini and Hitler, to rally support to their regimes, "lending an increasingly self-assertive and hostile colour to the national attitude to the outside world."[15] Was nationalism not a root cause of war?

Coupled with these sentiments was the contrast between nationalism and the higher principles of liberalism, "the promise of the dignity of man, of his rights as an individual, of his duties to his fellow men."[16] The new liberal internationalism of the war and immediate post-World War II years had little patience with nationalism, which it saw as only a passing form of integration, beneficial and vitalizing, yet by its exaggeration and dynamism easily destructive of human liberty.[17]

No wonder a Lester Pearson could dismiss the nationalism of the nation state and a Pierre Elliott Trudeau lay all the crimes of humanity at its doorstep.[18]

The new nationalism which we define above is all the more interesting because it develops despite widespread anti-nationalism in post-war Canada. Concern with political, economic, and cultural control and direction is an uneven, even uncertain one, during the two decades of Cold War, roughly 1945-1965. As we shall try to show, different classes and sections of Canadian society resented *specific aspects* of American cultural or economic domination, while accepting a subordinate/neo-colonial role within the American empire. This began to change fairly dramatically in the decade 1965-75, owing to developments in the political economy of American imperialism and of Canadian capitalism. Where minority voices on the right or left spoke out in the 1940s, where there was only episodical concern with American domination in the 1950s, the 1960s and 1970s, a period of waning American power, saw nationalism coming home to important sectors of the intelligentsia, students, middle class professionals, the trade union movement, political parties, small businessmen, and more exceptionally, large. Chapters 3-5 will sketch this historical development.

What we must now set out more clearly is the approach we shall be adopting in this study. The reader may recall the reference at the beginning of this chapter to the need to study nationalism in relation to concrete material forces. What this suggests at a minimum is that we will be attempting something more than an intellectual history of post-war Canadian nationalism. Rather, we shall be stressing the role of social class, that is class defined in the Marxist sense of the *position people occupy in relationship to the means of production,* in explaining both support for and opposition to nationalism. At the same time we shall have to take account of the relations between Canada and the United States over the thirty-year period, essentially those of dependency, as limiting factors on an exclusively class focus.

Class analysis must be mediated through the larger prism of imperialist relations in the post-World War II period, particularly where a country like Canada is concerned.

Let us reassure the sceptics that we do not hold that Marxism has the only valid thing to say on the subject of nationalism. There are too many contradictions in the writings of Marx and Engels themselves, not to speak of such important later theoreticians as Kautsky, Bauer, Luxemburg, Lenin, Stalin, or Mao to speak of a *single* Marxist interpretation of nationalism. Nor does our favouring class as a category for analysis mean that we rule out other phenomena such as regionalism, political culture, ethnic origin, or even such purely stochastic variables as personality, as without any bearing. We hold that a materialist explanation grounded in class and imperialist analysis can explain more about such social and political phenomena as nationalism than rival approaches. But it may not explain everything. Similarly, a Marxist theory of imperialism that takes into account the transformations which capitalism has undergone since Marx's time—the internationalization of capital, the emergence of the so-called multi-national corporation, the interpenetration of finance and industrial capital, unequal relations between first world industrialized and third world resource producers—is more relevant than rival sociological or economic approaches, without necessarily being the last word. We remain non-dogmatic in our application of Marxist categories, but convinced of their political and intellectual cogency.

What is especially important in the Marxist approach to nationalism is its recognition that in class-divided societies, such as our own, political ideas are rooted in economic relations.

> The ideas of the ruling class are in every epoch the ruling ideas, i.e., the class which is the ruling *material* force of society, is at the same time its ruling *intellectual* force. The class which has the means of material production at its disposal, has control at the same time over the means of mental production, so that thereby, generally speaking, the ideas of those who lack the means of mental production are subject to it.[19]

Even as the rising bourgeoisie of the 17th, 18th, and 19th centuries was revolutionizing the basis of economic production, so in the political sphere it was overturning absolutist and autarchic forms of government, rooted in the feudal period. It was natural that the bourgeoisie, in challenging the old ruling class for power, reformulate the concept of nation to more closely correspond to its own class interests. Hence the use of nationalism by the Parliamentary side of the 1640s and 50s,[20] by the "sober" revolutionaries of America in the 1770s and 80s,[21] or the claim staked out by the French third estate in 1789 to represent the nation.[22] Hence the more general appeal to nationalism by the bourgeoisies of countries such as Germany or Italy in the 19th century, and its extension outwards to the rest of the world since.

To be sure, nationalism is not solely a bourgeois phenomenon. There are examples enough of its use by aristocratic or landowning elements in the 19th and early 20th centuries, and its invocation by the peasantry and working class in many different countries. Still, in capitalist societies nationalism was first and foremost an ideological weapon in the hands of the rising capitalist class.

It was this fact which led Marx, Engels, and many other early socialists to be critical of the bourgeoisie's use of nationalism and to argue that class loyalty was more important than national loyalty. "The working men have no country," Marx and Engels declared in the Communist Manifesto,[23] and throughout their writings, nowhere more than in Marx's discussion of the Paris Commune, they pointed to a proletarian consciousness that transcended the narrow limits of the bourgeois nation state.[24]

This internationalist strand in socialism and Marxism is extremely important, and has led at least some socialist theoreticians to a blanket condemnation of nationalism little different from that we have already encountered in several liberal writers. Where the latter, from Lord Acton to Pierre Elliott Trudeau saw in nationalism, particularly once other classes than the bourgeoisie became involved, a threat to what Isaiah Berlin terms "negative liberty,"[25] internationalists like Rosa Luxemburg or Anton Pannekoek saw nationalism as an example of bourgeois ideology, and a direct obstacle to the class struggle.[26] Even social democrats of the Fabian variety, e.g., the authors of the League for Social Reconstruction's *Social Planning for Canada* of 1935, usually had few kind words for nationalism, which they assumed must necessarily take a bourgeois form:

> That foreigners control this or that *particular* industry will trouble none but those earnest patriots who, in defiance of all the evidence, persist in believing that the Canadian capitalist is a different kind of being from the foreign, that the one is a philanthropist, the other a robber and a cheat.[27]

Yet such a reading of nationalism is neither very dialectical nor profound. For if nationalism poses a challenge to socialist theory and even a threat, as the wholesale collaboration of social democratic parties with their respective governments at the outbreak of World War I illustrated, it also provides an opportunity. In the case of an oppressed or dominated society, the struggle for national liberation can be at the same time the opening wedge for social revolution. The experience of China or Vietnam in this century bears this out, as, in a European context, does the history of Tito's Partisans during the Nazi occupation of Yugoslavia in World War II. In the case of developed capitalist societies, nationalism is more likely to be the preserve of a dominant bourgeoisie. Yet even here, the possibility often exists for an alternative conception of the nation based on the interests of the working class or elements of the petty bourgeoisie. A quite careful analysis of the class structure of a particular capitalist society and its interactions with the larger capitalist system is therefore called for, especially in what Lenin referred to as the age of imperialism.

It is important to recall that Marx and Engels in the very quotation claiming that the working class have no country go on to say:

> We cannot take from them what they have not got. Since the proletariat must first of all acquire political supremacy, must rise to be the leading class of the nation, must constitute itself *the* nation, it is, so far itself national, though not in the bourgeois sense of the word.[28]

This suggests the possibility of a working class, as opposed to bourgeois, form of nationalism, and a working class concept of the nation. Marx and Engels, moreover, were prepared to support certain national struggles, e.g., in Poland and Ireland, not necessarily led by the working class. "No nation can be free if it oppresses another nation."[29] To be fair, Engels, for one, had little sympathy for the nationalism of most small peoples,[30] while Marx shared many of the prejudices of 19th century metropolitan Europe where colonialism was concerned.[31] But it is far too simple to categorize Marx and Engels as enemies of any and all nationalisms.

Similarly, the heated debates within the Second International around the national question, the attempts by such different theorists as Karl Kautsky or Otto Bauer to frame a socialist position on nationalism[32] attest to the intractability of the problem. It remained for such twentieth century practitioners of revolution as Lenin or Mao Tsetung to come up with some of the more interesting formulations, and even these are by no means perfect.

Lenin's writings on nationalism stressed the principle of self-determination for nations oppressed by other nations,[33] while expressing preference for proletarian leadership of the national struggle within an oppressed nation.[34] Lenin was willing to support any anti-imperialist struggle not led by a reactionary class.[35] At the same time, he was critical of great nation chauvinism, including Russian chauvinism within the USSR.[36]

Mao Tsetung, for his part, was quite prepared to use nationalism as a weapon against the Japanese invader, distinguishing between the nationalism of an aggressor and of his victim.[37] Moreover, Mao was flexible enough to support a broad democratic coalition, including the so-called national bourgeoisie, alongside the peasants, workers, and intellectuals, in the larger struggle against the Kuomintang.[38] Many other third world liberation movements have followed similar principles.

The direct relationship of all this to a developed capitalist society such as Canada is far from clear. A Marxist theory of nationalism might, however, pose the following questions:

1) What is the nature of English Canadian nationalism, i.e.,

is it oppressive, e.g., of Quebec, progressive, e.g., that of an oppressed or colonized nation in the age of American imperialism, or potentially a combination of both?

2) What is the class nature of English Canadian nationalism, e.g., bourgeois, petty bourgeois or working class?

3) Is a coalition of anti-imperialist forces led by the working class desirable or possible?

Let us discuss each of these in turn.

Regarding 1, it would, for example, be important to see the extent to which English Canadian nationalism is willing to recognize Quebec's right to self-determination. A Canadian nationalism based on the permanent subordination of Quebec in the name of a united Canada could hardly be considered progressive. One based on recognizing the specificity of Quebec, up to and including its right to form a separate political entity, if it so chooses, would be another matter.

Further, it would be all-important to assess the development of English Canadian nationalism within the larger framework of post-war capitalism. On the assumption that American imperialism is the dominant force through much of this period, we must examine whether Canada can properly be considered either a colony or a neo-colony. If it is, we will expect the more important economic, cultural, and even political questions to be decided in the metropolitan centre, the United States. This would then give English Canadian nationalism a potentially anti-imperialist dimension, though conceivably Canada *herself* is in an imperialist relationship with parts of the third world.

Regarding 2, the more classical Marxist criteria of class come into play. But when we talk about Canada being a capitalist society, or of classes being determined by people's relationship to the means of production, we must face two further facts.

Firstly, English Canada as already noted is divided into several distinct regions, and there may be regional differences of opinion on such a question as nationalism, even among members of the same class. English Canadian nationalism seen from British Columbia or Nova Scotia is not necessarily the same as seen from Ontario, just as in earlier periods of Canadian history the national tariff sharply divided the hinterland regions of Canada from the centre.

At the minimum, then, we will have to pay attention to regional viewpoints in our examination of class attitudes to nationalism over a thirty year period. We shall attempt to do this both in our choice of regional spokesmen for the different classes and in our use of public opinion data.

Nonetheless, regionalism does *not* vitiate our concern with classes as a whole. Capitalism does not differ in any fundamental way from one region of English Canada to another. Institutional arrangements at the national level link the members of different social classes, e.g., regional capitalists sit on the boards of the largest chartered banks, professional bodies draw their membership from across the country, the Canadian Labour Congress groups most of organized labour outside Quebec. *As long as one does not mistake the Canadian political economy for the more centralized ones of Europe or Japan,* there is everything to be gained from speaking of classes in global terms throughout this study.

Secondly, capitalism today is not the capitalism of Marx's or Luxemburg's or Lenin's day, and our use of class categories must take this into account. In the capitalist sector, the movement to imperialism and monopoly of the early part of this century has gone a stage further with the so-called multinational corporation. The big bourgeoisie in Canada, who own the principal means of production, e.g., industry, banks, resource companies with assets in excess of $25 million, or often $100 million,[39] are based on a combination of indigenous and foreign-owned capital, as every serious study of the last decade or so has underlined.[40] While we might expect some tension between different fractions of the big bourgeoisie where nationalism is concerned, we might no less expect a fusion of interests in defence of a close alliance with the most powerful capitalist power, the United States. We shall be exploring both tendencies at work.

Where smaller business interests are concerned, let us say enterprises with assets of less than $25 million, and more typically less than $5 million, we might expect deference to the big bourgeoisie on the one hand, and somewhat greater sensitivity to indigenous as opposed to foreign control on the other. At its lower reaches, the smaller bourgeoisie shades over into what can more classically be described as the traditional petty bourgeoisie. Those enterpreneurs who are essentially self-employed, employing no or only a handful of employees, resemble self-employed farmers or self-employed professiónals, such as most doctors, lawyers, architects or writers in terms of their relations to the means of production. For purposes of our study it may prove difficult to distinguish between the smaller bourgeoisie employing significant amounts of labour and hence appropriating significant amounts of surplus value, and the essentially self-employed business element. In the real world of ideological perception, differences between the two are probably not that consequential.

The reaction of self-employed professionals or farmers to an issue such as nationalism may, on the other hand, differ from that of the self-employed business element. Moreover, the politics of the traditional petty bourgeoisie as a whole, as past experience tells us, is vacillating and contradictory in the extreme, and there is no necessary identity of views amongst the members of its different components.

The most significant change in post-war Canadian capitalism has been the take-off of the state sector, by which is meant the combined activities of governments at the federal, provincial, and municipal levels. This increase has coincided with the changeover from a still largely primary and secondary industry-oriented economy at the war's end, to a more service-oriented one thirty years later. The implications of this have to be taken into account in any class analysis of Canadian nationalism. More to the point, we will be interested in the attitude of that component of the tertiary or service sector—the intelligentsia and the salaried professions, for the large part university-trained—who are sometimes termed new middle class and whom we shall be categorizing as a new petty bourgeoisie.

Unlike the old petty bourgeoisie of self-employed farmers, businessmen, or professionals, members of the newer group do not own their means of production. Like the salaried working class, they are directly dependent on the sale of their labour power in the market place. Yet unlike the manual working class or white collar workers, members of the new petty bourgeoisie are overwhelmingly professionals. Moreover, in many cases their employer is not the private capitalist or corporation, but the state, or state-funded institutions. Teachers, university professors, hydro engineers, public administrators, or urban planners are good examples of this newer category, whose class interests cannot be directly assimilated to those of the big bourgeoisie, the smaller bourgeoisie, or even much of the traditional petty bourgeoisie. (They are, however, much closer in outlook to the self-employed professionals—doctors, lawyers, architects—of this latter class.)

What differentiates the new petty bourgeoisie from the working class is the fact that the former is at best only indirectly productive of economic wealth. Furthermore, its members absorb, at least in part, some of the surplus value which capitalism appropriates from the labour power of the working class. While Marx was thinking more of the old petty bourgeoisie than of the new when he penned the following comments, they are not without relevance to the latter.

> The great mass of so-called "higher grade" workers—such as state officials, military people, artists, doctors, priests, judges, lawyers, etc.—some of whom are not only not productive but in essence destructive, but who know how to appropriate to themselves a very great part of the "material" wealth partly through the sale of their "immaterial" commodities and partly by forcibly imposing the latter on other people—found it not at all pleasant . . . to appear merely as people partaking in consumption, parasites on the actual producers.[41]

Or again,

> All these illustrious and time-honoured occupations—sovereign, judge, officer, priest, etc.,—with all the old ideological professions to which they give rise, their men of letters, their teachers and priests are *from an economic standpoint* put on the same level as the swarm of their own lackeys and jesters maintained by the bourgeoisie and by idle wealth . . . They are mere *servants* of the public, just as others are their servants. They live on the produce of *other* people's industry . . .[42]

That Marx was also aware of the potentially productive role of elements of the new petty bourgeoisie, e.g., the scientific estate, is evident from certain passages in the *Grundrisse*:

> In the productive process of large-scale industry . . .the conquest of the forces of nature by the social intellect is the precondition of the productive power of the means of labour as developed into the automatic process . . .[43]

The fact remains that in any Marxist theory of class, the new petty bourgeoisie like the old finds itself somewhere between the working class and the big bourgeoisie. Though most of the new petty bourgeoisie's income is derived from salaries, members of this class usually have access to higher salaries and greater benefits, e.g., travel, leisure time, than workers. This difference can be traced back to the element of surplus value in a petty bourgeois' income, something a recent study of the petty bourgeoisie in France does very carefully for that country.[44]

> A social group is petty bourgeois when it occupies a position in the relations of production which allows it legally (through commercial benefits, honoraria, "salary," or payment) to benefit from part of the surplus value which the capitalists appropriate from the proletariat.[45]

It follows that the politics of the new petty bourgeoisie will be as ambiguous as is their class position. Since many of its members, moreover, are in the business of manipulating ideas, one may expect quite a range of opinion and great internal fractionalization, going from right to left on the spectrum.

Finally, any discussion of classes in contemporary Canadian capitalism must deal with the working class, that overwhelming majority of the population who do not own their means of production and who, in Marxist economic theory, are producers of surplus value.[46] This class category includes today not only workers in primary or secondary industry, directly productive of surplus value, but many of the so-called tertiary sector workers, who are in fact doing disguised proletarian labour.[47] Waitresses and janitors, stewardesses or day care workers are examples of so-called service sector employees who are descendants of the old capitalist servant class, now selling their labour power on the market place. At the same time, the army of office workers—secretaries, clerks, stenographers, sales or advertising personnel—arises as a consequence of the increasing division of labour in late capitalist society, and of the need to externalize certain tasks which once would have been performed within the small family firm, or for that matter, farm. How directly productive some of these white collar tasks are is open to question, yet they are indirectly crucial to the successful operation of the capitalist system. Indirectly, therefore, white collar workers are contributors to the production of surplus value, (in contradistinction to members of the new petty bourgeoisie, however, they are not, in aggregate, appropriators of surplus value).

In examining the attitude of the English Canadian working class towards nationalism, we will be looking at both blue and white collar workers. We will take into account, however, not only possible differences in class consciousness among different types of workers, but also the larger hegemony of liberal capitalist ideas over the working class in North America. The trade union movement of Canada, for example, is at best lukewarmly social democratic, and only passingly critical of capitalism as a system. At the same time, the organic links between many unions in the Canadian Labour Congress and American unions, especially in the primary and secondary sectors, pose similar analytical problems to those raised by the mixed foreign-indigenous capital base of the big bourgeoisie. How independent, in fact, is the mainstream Canadian labour movement, and what are the implications of close links with the AFL-CIO for its position on the national question?

Once we have analyzed the class nature of English Canadian nationalism since the war, and some of the movements it has given rise to in recent years, we should be in a position to assess the desirability and possibility of a working class-based nationalist movement (Question 3 above).

To recapitulate the principal objectives of this study, we shall be looking at nationalism in an advanced capitalist society, Canada, and more particularly at the nationalism of the dominant element within the country, English-speaking Canadians. We have defined nationalism in the post-World War II context as *a concern that the political, economic, and cultural affairs of a territorially-defined polity be controlled and directed by individuals and/or corporations that are members of that polity, rather than by forces outside it.* In and of itself, such a nationalism can be articulated by different class forces, e.g., the bourgeoisie, the petty bourgeoisie, the working class, and can have a reactionary, neutral, or progressive character. By examining the differing positions of these classes over time and relating their attitudes to changes in Canada's position within the American sphere, it should be possible to evaluate the nature of English Canadian nationalism, and its possible future interaction with both capitalist and socialist ideologies.

CHART 1.1
The Class Structure of English Canada and of Quebec

CANADA

ENGLISH CANADA	QUEBEC
Big bourgeoisie: Foreign-control, e.g., manufacturing, resources	**Big bourgeoisie:** Foreign control, e.g., manufacturing, resources
(Assets in excess of $25 million)	(Assets in excess of $25 million)
Indigenous-control, e.g., manufacturing, finance, transportation	English Canadian control, e.g., manufacturing, finance, transportation, resources.
	Indigenous control: some manufacturing, finance, transportation
Smaller bourgeoisie: Foreign control as above	**Smaller bourgeoisie:** Foreign control as above
(Assets under $25 million)	(Assets under $25 million)
Indigenous control as above	English Canadian control as above
	Indigenous control as above
Traditional petty bourgeoisie:	**Traditional petty bourgeoisie:** identical to English Canada
Farmers, i.e., independent commodity producers	
self-employed business	
self-employed professionals	
New petty bourgeoisie: teachers/professors	**New petty bourgeoisie:** identical to English Canada
civil servants	
other salaried professionals	
Working class: white collar	**Working class:** identical to English Canada
blue collar	
unemployed	

Chapter Two
THE POLITICAL ECONOMY
OF NATIONALISM

The purpose of this chapter is to set forth as clearly as possible the principal developments in the political economy of Canada in the period of 1945-75. Since for a Marxist analysis material relations are of the very essence, if we are to properly understand the development of English Canadian nationalism we must first determine what were the main changes in both the external relationships and internal class structure of the country.

The logical place to begin is not with Canada itself but with the dominant capitalist power of the post-war period, the United States. One does not have to be a Marxist to recognize just how overwhelming was the political, military and economic power of the United States at the end of World War II, and just how rapidly the U.S. came to impose its *Pax Americana* over most of the non-communist globe.[1] *The rise of American imperialism and its subsequent weakening can be taken as the main independent variable for our study.*

Economically, Europe and much of Asia lay in ruins after 1945, while the United States had a productive capacity that far exceeded the remainder of the non-communist industrialized nations for well over a decade.

TABLE 2.1
Gross National Products at Market Prices
(At Current Prices and Current Exchange Rates in U.S. Dollars)
(Billions of Dollars)

	1947	1950	1955
Organization of European Economic Cooperation Member countries combined, (i.e., Western Europe)	141.2	138.8	219.1
Canada (Canadian Dollars)	13.1	18.0	27.1
Japan	3.6	11.0	24.6
United States	231.1	284.8	398.0

Sources: OEEC, *Statistics of National Product and Expenditure 1938, 1947-55*, Paris, 1957, p. 195; M.C. Urquhart & K.A.H. Buckley, eds., *Historical Statistics of Canada*, Cambridge & Toronto, 1965, Series E 1-12, p. 130; *Economic Survey of Japan 1970-1*, Tokyo, 1971, Statistical Appendix, pp. 152-3. Yen converted to dollars at 360 Y to the dollar; Emma S. Woytinsky, *Profile of the U.S. Economy*, N.Y., 1969, Table VI.1, p. 131.

The U.S. dollar was *the* international reserve currency, and despite the Marshall Plan, remained in short supply well into the 1950s. Militarily, the United States alone possessed the atom bomb until 1949, and through the decades of Cold War was the principal military power on the non-communist side. Politically and ideologically, the American commitment to anti-communism knew few bounds, and its messianism set the tone for other powers, large and small, allied to it in NATO, SEATO and a host of other treaties and pacts.

There was one particular area of weakness, however, where the U.S. economy was concerned, which had already become a matter of public concern during the Korean War. Its very size and productive capacity made the United States the largest consumer of raw materials in the world.

The President's Materials Policy Commission (the Paley Commission) of 1952 listed 22 key materials where U.S. reserves were either inadequate or non-existent, stressing the need to mobilize foreign supplies.

We believe that the destinies of the United States and the

rest of the free non-Communist world are inextricably bound together. This belief we hope will colour everything we have to say about the Materials Problem . . . *The overall objective of a national materials policy for the United States should be to insure an adequate and dependable flow of materials at the lowest cost consistent with national security and with the welfare of friendly nations.*[2]

Of the 22 materials potentially in short supply, Canada was an important supplier of nickel, copper, lead, zinc and asbestos, and potentially of iron, sulphur, titanium, cobalt and petroleum.[3] Nor was the hydroelectric potential of the St. Lawrence, Niagara and Columbia River areas ignored "which are among the best sites remaining to the Nation for developing hydropower in the lower cost range."[4] Continentalism was one aspect of a larger American drive for resources.

The figures on trade and investment seen from the United States underline Canada's post-war importance to her.

TABLE 2.2
Canada's Percentage Share of U.S. Exports and Imports

	1938	1948	1958	1971
U.S. Exports to Canada as a Percentage of all U.S. Exports	15	15	20	23
U.S. Imports from Canada as a Percentage of all U.S. Imports	14	23	23	27

Sources: Thomas E. Weisskopf, *American Economic Interests in Foreign Countries: An Empirical Survey*, Center for Research on Economic Development, The University of Michigan, Discussion Paper 35, Ann Arbor, Michigan 1974, Tables 2 and 3, pp. 22-3. The statistics in these tables were in turn taken from United Nations, *Statistical Yearbooks, 1962* and *1972*.

TABLE 2.3

Distribution of U.S. Direct Foreign Private Investment Assets by Area and Sector

	1950		1959		1972	
	Value ($billion)	%	Value ($ b.)	%	Value ($ b.)	%
All Areas	11.8	100	29.7	100	94.0	100
Canada	3.6	31	10.2	34	25.8	27
Europe	1.7	15	5.3	18	30.7	33
Latin America and Caribbean	4.6	39	9.0	30	16.6	18
Developed Economies (i.e., Canada, Europe, Japan, Australia, New Zealand and S. Africa)	5.7	100	16.9	100	64.1	100
Mining and Smelting	0.4	7	1.3	7	4.4	7
Petroleum	1.0	18	4.5	27	14.2	22
Manufacturing	3.0	52	8.1	48	32.8	51
Other Sectors	1.3	23	3.0	18	12.7	20

Source: Weisskopf, *American Economic Interests in Foreign Countries*, Table 8. p. 28, with data taken from S. Pizer and F. Cutler, *U.S. Business Investments in Foreign Countries* (1960) and U.S. Department of Commerce, *Survey of Current Business*, September, 1973.

Canada in the 1940s and 1950s became a prime area for American investment, reflecting the growing importance of Alberta oil, Ungava and Labrador iron ore, Ontario nickel and much besides. A chart from a Canadian source further illustrates this (next page).

It would be wrong, however, to downplay the importance of American investment in manufacturing in both Canada and Europe in the post-war period. As Table 2.3 shows, fully 52 per cent of U.S. direct foreign private investment in developed economies was in this sector, and the figure 22 years later remained at 51 per cent. As Chart 1 indicates, 43.7 per cent of U.S. direct investment in Canada in 1967 was in manufacturing, compared to 38.9 per cent in petroleum, natural gas, mining and smelting. Indeed, a more recent calculation in the Corporations and Labour Unions Returns Act (CALURA) for 1972 indicates that 52.7 per cent of the assets of foreign-controlled non-financial

CHART 2.1

UNITED STATES DIRECT INVESTMENT IN CANADA
BY INDUSTRY GROUP

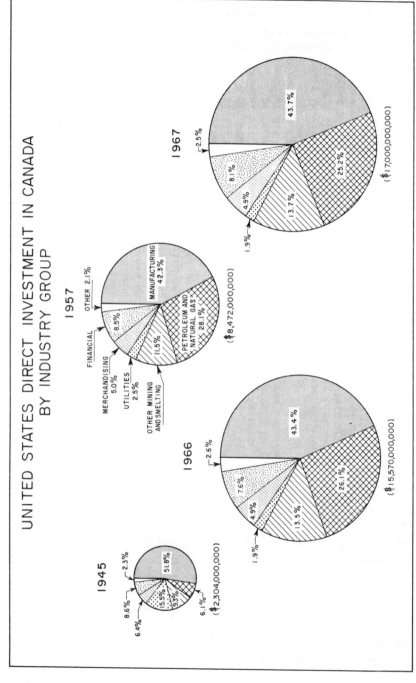

corporations in Canada were in manufacturing, though great caution is called for since more than one-fifth of this "manufacturing" was in petroleum and coal products.[5] The fact remains that a significant amount of American-controlled investment in Canada was and is in manufacturing, something which undercuts a too simplistic analysis of Canada as a resource hinterland to an American industrial metropolis.

To continue our discussion of America's international position through to the 1960s and into the 1970s is to point to a decline in American hegemony. By 1964, for example, the American share of Western GNP was no longer the roughly 60-65 per cent it had been in the immediate post-war years.

TABLE 2.4

Relative Weight of Gross National Product or Gross Domestic Product as a Percentage of that of all OECD Countries in 1964

United States GNP	52.9
Canada GNP	3.6
France GDP	7.3
West Germany GDP	8.6
Italy GDP	4.1
United Kingdom GDP	7.6
Other Europe GDP	10.2
Japan GNP	5.7
Total OECD	100.0
of which OECD without the U.S.	47.1
OECD Europe	37.8

Source: Organization for Economic Cooperation and Development *Economic Outlook*, Paris, July, 1967, No. 1, Table 1, p. 6.

Politically, de Gaulle had begun his policy of defiance within the so-called Western Alliance, Cuba had survived American-sponsored invasion, the United States was becoming ever more deeply involved in its most fateful post-war imperial venture, the Vietnam War (to end a decade later in ignominious defeat). Nationalism was in the air in scores of newly independent states, while the old Cold War conflicts were giving way to a more complicated, less easily managed, multi-polar world.

By the late 1960s, the international monetary system had begun to creak; by August 1971 Nixon had been forced to impose a 10 per cent surcharge on imports and a *de facto* devaluation of the American dollar; by the autumn of 1973, the Arab oil boycott had brought home the fragility of both the U.S. and other Western economies. (Interestingly the Paley Report of 1952 had foreseen some of this: "The capacity of the free world to meet its expanded needs for the next quarter of a century presents a very mixed picture. The more indusrialized nations, with such notable exceptions as the United States and Canada, are faced with serious energy deficits. Like Western Europe, Japan and some parts of Latin America must obtain key energy supplies from imports."[6])

What this added up to for the United States in the economic sphere is evident from the following tables.

TABLE 2.5

United States Balance of Payments (in millions of dollars)

	1968	1969	1970	1971	1972
Exports	33,588	36,473	41,980	42,769	49,650
Imports	32,964	35,835	39,870	45,648	53,950
Trade Balance	624	638	2,110	−2,879	−4,300
Change in Reserves	880	1,187	−2,477	−2,348	

Source: OECD *Economic Outlook*, July, 1970. No. 7, p. 66; July, 1972, No. 11, p. 60.

TABLE 2.6

Relative Weight of Gross National Product or Gross Domestic Product as a Percentage of that of all OECD Countries in 1973

Canada GNP	3.7
United States GNP	40.0
Japan GNP	12.9
France GDP	8.0
West Germany GNP	10.9
Italy GDP	4.3
United Kingdom GDP	5.4
Other OECD countries	14.8
Total	100.0
of which OECD Europe	41.0

Source: OECD *Economic Outlook*, No. 17, July 1975, Table 1, p. 13.

In 1973, the Gross National or Domestic Products for Western Europe exceeded that of the United States for the first time since 1945. Canadian GNP was approaching 10 per cent of the American total, roughly proportionate to the ratio of the two populations. Japan had better than doubled its position in less than ten years. As another OECD study indicated, *the growth in the real GNP* of all the OECD countries excluding the United States had *averaged* 6.3 per cent annually over the period 1959-60 to 1971-2, while the United States had only averaged 4.1 per cent.[7]

To be sure, America's role as the principal capitalist power was not to end overnight. Indeed, there was a certain continuity in change, to paraphrase Gunder Frank,[8] where U.S. resource requirements were concerned and where Canada's role as supplier came in.

TABLE 2.7
Canada's Share of Selected U.S. Mineral Imports in 1970 from all Countries (In per cent)

Natural Gas	95
Petroleum (Crude)	51
Iron Ore	53
Nickel	89
Tungsten	95
Copper Ore	25
Lead	29
Zinc	53
Mercury	81
Titanium: Ilmenite	58
Asbestos	93
Gypsum	77
Potash	86
Sulphur	65

Source: Weisskopf, *American Economic Interests in Foreign Countries*, Table 16, pp. 36-43, in turn calculated from figures in U.S. Department of the Interior, *Minerals Yearbook, 1971*, Volumes I and II.

Of the 211 multinational corporations in manufacturing with sales of more than $1 billion in 1971, 127 were still American.[9]

Yet in the United Nations study just mentioned, 84 of the top 211 multinational corporations were *not* American. In a more

recent study by *Fortune* magazine of the fifty largest industrial
corporations in the world in 1974, non-American corporations
numbered twenty-six.[10] And though Canada did not figure on
this list, it came off fairly well where the 300 largest industrial
corporations and fifty largest commercial banks outside the
United States were concerned.

With 20 of the 300 largest industrial corporations, Canada was
in fifth place after Japan, Britain, West Germany and France.[11]
True, at least six of these twenty, including such giants as Ford
Motors of Canada, Imperial Oil and Gulf Oil Canada were
foreign-controlled, and two others, Alcan and International
Nickel, while having significant Canadian investment,[12] were
also American-controlled. Still, the remaining twelve, including
Massey-Ferguson, Canada Packers, MacMillan Bloedel, Noranda
Mines, Stelco, Moore Corp., Northern Electric, Domtar,
Seagrams and Cominco, are Canadian-controlled and have
considerable clout both in Canada and internationally. In the
banking sector, the Royal Bank of Canada, Candian Imperial
Bank of Commerce, Bank of Montreal and Bank of Nova Scotia
ranked respectively 19th, 26th, 28th and 42nd among non-
American banks.[13]

*The overall importance of the changes in America's
international position for Canadian nationalism cannot be too
greatly emphasized.* No country in the post-war period
experienced as high a percentage of American investment and
control, none was as politically, culturally and psychologically
influenced by every nuance of American behavior, in none were
objective conditions less favourable to the development of an
anti-imperialist consciousness. True, anti-Americanism in English Canada was as old as the hills and valleys in which the United
Empire Loyalists had settled. But much water had flowed under
the bridge since the 18th century, and in the conditions of the
post-World War II world, one polarized between the United
States and the Soviet Union, there were few Canadians prepared
to oppose American imperialism head on. One might add that the
United States itself had little reason to challenge the existence of
a *politically* independent Canada. The American empire could
afford to be more supple than the Soviet—its overwhelming
economic strength made its yoke more tolerable, even attractive,
to its dependencies.

If some opposition to aspects of American domination was to surface in the late 1940s or mid-1950s, it would take a vastly different context such as the late 1960s, when American imperialism was economically weakened and politically and militarily under attack, for anti-Americanism to become widespread in English Canada. Such are the changes in the ideological sphere resulting from changing material relations, in this case between an imperialist power, the United States, and subordinate states.

These material relations come home more directly when we begin to analyze internal changes in the Canadian political economy over the thirty year period. One important factor we have already pointed to is the large American stake in Canada. The increased importance of American investment in the post-war period is evident from Statement 1, though its exact significance is another matter (see next page).

It is one thing to compare the major characteristics of foreign controlled and Canadian-controlled non-financial corporations as the CALURA Reports do and come up with concrete figures (see Statement 2, next page).

One can further break this down by industrial sector, underlining the predominantly foreign stake in mining and manufacturing and the predominantly Canadian one in construction, utilities, wholesale trade, retail trade, finance and services (see Table 2.8, page 43).

Where finance, in particular, is concerned, one can agree with E.P. Neufeld that this is a sector with only a relatively small degree of foreign ownership (the major exception being fire insurance companies).[14] Are we therefore justified to assume that there is a so-called comprador and a so-called indigenous fraction of the Canadian bourgeoisie, as Wallace Clement tends to do,[15] and that, by implication, their politics may differ fundamentally on such questions as nationalism?

We tend to think that too rigid a distinction between foreign-controlled and indigenous fractions of the Canadian bourgeoisie minimizes their common interests, indeed the fusion of interests that takes place between their most important members over the post-war period. Though there are nuances in the positions of different capitalist spokesmen, and some are

Statement 1

Foreign Long-Term Investment in Canada, Selected Year Ends, 1914-67

Owned in	1914	1926	1939	1945	1957	1962	1967
				millions of dollars			
United States	881	3,196	4,151	4,990	13,264	19,155	28,030
United Kingdom	2,778	2,637	2,476	1,750	2,917	3,399	3,576
All Other Countries	178	170	286	352	1,283	2,336	3,096
Totals	3,837	6,003	6,913	7,092	17,464	24,890	34,702

Source: Statistics Canada, *Canada's International Investment Position 1926 to 1967*, p. 25, Statement 7.

Statement 2

Major Characteristics of Corporations by Control, 1972, Non-Financial Industries — Total

	Foreign	Canadian	Unclassified[1]	Total
No. of corporations	5,845	39,431	115,271	160,547
		millions of dollars		
Assets	56,351	96,924	8,085	161,360
Equity	27,905	35,290	2,659	65,854
Sales	60,171	90,789	13,972	164,933
Profits	4,418	5,267	305	9,990

1 Unclassified corporations are those with less than $250,000 in assets or $500,000 in sales, and hence not required to report under CALURA.

Source: Corporations and Labour Unions Returns Act, *Report for 1972, Part I, Corporations*, Ottawa, 1975, Statement 1A, p. 17.

TABLE 2.8

Degree of Foreign Ownership
in Major Industry Groups, 1972
Assets in millions of dollars

Major Industry Group	Degree of Foreign Ownership		Government Enterprise	Unclassified
	50%-100%	0-49.9%		
Mining	11,821	6,087	190	160
Manufacturing	29,538	21,784	591	1,007
(including Petroleum)				
Construction	1,031	5,837	–	1,147
Utilities	3,410	16,415	26,039	489
Wholesale Trade	5,004	8,799	854	1,162
Retail Trade	2,241	5,787	221	1,895
Finance	14,803	45,276	11,659	72,935
Services	1,845	4,413	24	1,701

Source: Corporations and Labour Unions Returns Act, 1972, *Part I, Corporations*, Table 2, pp. 132-3.

more sypathetic to forms of Canadian nationalism than others, by and large all accept an important measure of continentalism provided a *minimum area* of Canadian sovereignty is maintained. On this score, American branch plant presidents and Canadian bankers see eye to eye, just as Tory spokesmen differ *but in degree* from Liberal.

There are, to be sure, different interpretations of just what degree of American investment control or ownership is desirable, with concern being more strongly articulated in specific areas, e.g., culture, or sectors of the economy, e.g., banking, natural resources, than in others. More rarely, there may be a philosophical division in the ranks of the big bourgeoisie, e.g., over the Abbott Plan of 1947 or the Trans-Canada Pipeline of 1956, which seems to correspond to formal fractionalization. Yet the divisions are never hard and fast, so that to speak of a nationalist-oriented fraction of the Canadian bourgeoisie permanently pitted against an American-oriented fraction rooted in the branch plants would be mistaken. As Harold Innis observed long ago, American branch plants themselves have a vested interest in a form of Canadian nationalism:

Branch plants of American industries were built in Canada in order to take advantage of the Canadian-European system and British imperialism . . . Paradoxically, the stoutest defenders of the Canadian tariff against the United States were the representatives of American capital investors. Canadian nationalism was systematically encouraged and exploited by American capital. [16]

Conversely, Canadian banks and other large corporations have been active co-participants in the Americanization of the country.

The Canadian bourgeoisie we are talking about can be said to include the directors (though also the principal executive officers and shareholders) of the 170 dominant corporations John Porter discusses in *The Vertical Mosaic*. [17] It would certainly include the directors of the 113 dominant corporations Wallace Clement singles out in his more recent *The Canadian Corporate Elite*. [18] More pertinently, we would include in our definition the directors and *principal* executive officers and shareholders of the more important banks, insurance and trust companies, and 669 non-financial corporations, both foreign- and Canadian-controlled, that in 1972 had assets in excess of $25 million each. Combined, these corporations controlled some $102 billion or 65.4 per cent of the total assets of all non-financial corporations reporting under the Corporations and Labour Unions Returns Act. [19] The exact numbers involved are not easily calculated; but at the outside, we are speaking of a class that today might number upwards of ten thousand. (Not sharing Porter's or Clement's concern with elite as opposed to class analysis, we see little point, however, in trying to define the Canadian bourgeoisie as an exceedingly small, almost conspiratorial group, hovering around a thousand members.)

Let us now turn to examine other classes in Canada. A note of caution to the reader is in order here, since we have been forced to use statistics which apply to Canada as a whole, including Quebec, rather than to English Canada alone. The main reason is the difficulty of finding *comprehensive* tax data for English Canada alone going back to the 1940s. (Tax returns do provide such a breakdown for taxable returns, but not for *all* returns, which is our main concern.) Census data, for its part, does not provide some of the detailed information on occupation available from tax returns, and the need for comparability between these two main sources necessitates figures for Canada as a whole. A check of the taxable returns for 1972, however, does allow one to conclude that Quebec's percentage of the various occupational categories is in rough proportion to its share of Canada's population as a whole.[20] We are not, therefore, in most areas risking very much to assume that the absolute figures for English Canada are between 70 per cent and 75 per cent of those cited here for Canada as a whole, and that the percentage ratios among the various classes and sub-groups are essentially the same for English Canada and Canada. Still, some deviation is possible, and in at least one case, the figures on international vs. national unions, will have to be taken into account.

The small business sector would include the vast majority of the business proprietors who have filed income tax returns since 1945, and a good number of those classified as investors and property owners (see Table 2.9, next page).

A small percentage of those listed in Table 2.9 were really members of the big bourgeoisie, but the overwhelming majority were owners of small or medium-sized businesses and companies, small or medium amounts of equity, property, etc. The exact ratio between smaller bourgeoisie and self-employed petty bourgeoisie in Table 2.9 is difficult to determine. The CALURA data cited in Statement 2, however, shows roughly 45,000 corporations with asset size ranging from $250,000 to $25 million and 115,000 corporations with assets under $250,000. A majority of the entrepreneurs in our Table 2.9 would fall into the latter category or would be unincorporated, and most of these would be employers of no or very few wage-earners. It is possible then to argue that the majority of entrepreneurs listed in Table 2.9 probably belong to our petty bourgeois category, with most of the remainder constituting the smaller bourgeoisie.

Analytically, however, as was argued in Chapter 1, it is all but impossible to distinguish accurately between the views of smaller bourgeois and self-employed petty bourgeois businessmen. Throughout this study, then, we shall be using the term small business to describe the two types of entrepreneurs that must be distinguished from the big bourgeoisie. The relative increase in the number of investors and property owners as compared to

TABLE 2.9

The Smaller Bourgeoisie *and* Self-Employed Business Fraction of the Traditional Petty Bourgeoisie

	1946		1950		1955		1960	
	Nos.	%	Nos.	%	Nos.	%	Nos.	%
Business Proprietors	178,294	5.6	268,070	6.9	294,960	6.0	320,487	5.4
Investors and Property Owners	81,617	2.6	95,070	2.4	124,110	2.5	171,610	2.9
Combined	259,911	8.2	363,140	9.3	419,070	8.5	492,097	8.3
Total taxable and non-taxable returns by occupation	3,162,032	100.0	3,866,160	100.0	4,923,700	100.0	5,850,611	100.0

	1965		1970		1972	
	Nos.	%	Nos.	%	Nos.	%
Business Proprietors	337,664	4.7	362,021	3.9	377,736	3.6
Investors and Property Owners	247,469	3.1	428,813	4.7	479,991	4.6
Combined	585,133	7.8	790,834	8.6	857,727	8.2
Total taxable and non-taxable returns by occupation	7,163,160	100.0	9,183,407	100.0	10,382,005	100.0

Source: Canada, Department of National Revenue, *Taxation Statistics for 1946*, Ottawa, 1948, Table C, pp. 122-5; *Taxation Statistics for 1950*, Ottawa, 1952, Table C, pp. 84-7; *Taxation Statistics for 1955*, Ottawa, 1957, Table 3, pp. 36-40; *Taxation Statistics for 1960*, Ottawa, 1962, Table 3, pp. 40-45; *Taxation Statistics for 1965*, Ottawa, 1967, Table 3, pp. 26-31; *Taxation Statistics for 1970*, Ottawa, 1972, Table 3, pp. 40-51; *Taxation Statistics for 1972*, Ottawa, 1974, Table 3, pp. 40-51.

actual entrepreneurs indicated in Table 2.9 may have some long-term significance, e.g., small business may be becoming an increasingly parasitical rentier class. What is important to our study is the relative stability of the small business sector as a whole over a twenty-five year period.

Using taxation data, the total number of farmers in Canada, long the backbone of the traditional petty bourgeoisie, has evolved as shown in Table 2.10 (next page).

More significant statistically, and this underlines one of the weaknesses of taxation data, are the figures derived from censuses and labour force studies showing a long-term decline in agriculture as a percentage of the labour force (see Table 2.11, next page).

Taxation data can only measure those filing returns, whether taxable or not. It cannot measure those not filing returns at all, a not insignificant number in the case of farmers, and perhaps other self-employed. Where farmers are concerned, their importance for an issue like English Canadian nationalism would obviously be greater when they were 15.9 per cent or 10.2 per cent of the labour force than their more recent 5.9 per cent.

Where the professional fraction of the traditional petty bourgeoisie is concerned, taxation data shows a rise in absolute numbers, though no percentage increase from 1946 to 1972 (see Table 2.12, page 49).

It is more difficult to determine statistically just how much the new petty bourgeoisie, which groups *both* the salaried professionals and administrators has grown since the war. Taxation data tells us such things as the number of teachers and professors or the total number of government employees. It does not, however, isolate the professional from white collar or blue collar government employees or managers from the employee sub-group as a whole. Census data is more useful here, but suffers from two defects: 1) the category "professional" in the census includes architects, lawyers, doctors, dentists, etc., many of whom are self-employed; 2) there is a major change in the categories used in the 1971 Census making comparison with earlier census years impossible.

TABLE 2.10

Farmers as a Percentage of all Occupations (using tax data)

	1946 Nos.	%	1950 Nos.	%	1955 Nos.	%	1960 Nos.	%
Farmers	117,647*	3.7	197,150	5.1	205,830	4.1	209,720	3.6
Total Returns	3,162,032	100.0	3,866,160	100.0	4,923,700	100.0	5,850,611	100.0

	1965 Nos.	%	1970 Nos.	%	1972 Nos.	%
Farmers	246,977	3.1	276,686	3.0	279,714	2.7
Total Returns	7,163,160	100.0	9,183,407	100.0	10,382,005	100.0

*N.B. Incomplete Returns for 1946

Source: Same as for Table 2.9

TABLE 2.11

Agriculture in Relation to the Total Labour Force by Major Occupation Groups

	1941 Nos.	%	1951 Nos.	%	1961 Nos.	%	1972 Nos.	%
All Occupations	4,195,951	100.0	5,124,913	100.0	6,342,289	100.0	8,329,000	100.0
Agriculture	1,083,816	25.8	830,441	15.9	648,910	10.2	491,211	5.9

Sources: Noah M. Meltz, *Manpower in Canada 1931 to 1961*, Dept. of Manpower and Immigration, Ottawa, 1969, Table A1, p. 58; *Canada Year Book 1973*, Ottawa, 1973, Table 8.5, p. 356.

TABLE 2.12

Professionals* in Relation to all Occupations

	1946		1950		1955		1960	
	Nos.	%	Nos.	%	Nos.	%	Nos.	%
Professionals	23,596	0.7	31,690	0.8	40,680	0.8	48,719	0.8
All Occupations	3,162,032	100.0	3,866,160	100.0	4,923,700	100.0	5,850,611	100.0

	1965		1970		1972	
	Nos.	%	Nos.	%	Nos.	%
Professionals	56,021	0.8	67,538	0.7	73,970	0.7
All Occupations	7,163,160	100.0	9,183,407	100.0	10,382,005	100.0

*The 1972 Taxation Statistics for the first time speak of self-employed professionals, though presumably this was also the case before. The professionals in question include accountants, doctors, dentists, lawyers and notaries, engineers and architects, entertainers and artists.

Source: Same as for Table 2.9

For the 1941, 1951, and 1961 census years, there is the following breakdown of the managerial and professional categories (see Table 2.13, next page).

One must *stress* that the category managerial in the 1941, 1951, and 1961 censuses includes *owners* as well as managers, a significant number, one can be sure, of the nearly 150,000 listed in retail trade, 44,000 in wholesale trade, 36,000 in construction, 34,000 in finance, insurance and real estate, and so on in the 1961 census.[21] In short the managerial category before 1971 includes most of the small business category, not to speak of the big bourgeoisie itself.

The 1971 census, on the other hand, provides a more precise breakdown of the managerial and professional categories, highlighting the rise to prominence of such "new" tertiary sector occupations as the natural sciences, the social sciences, health and government administration. The managerial category in the 1971 census *excludes owners*, while including government officials and administrators and most business and corporate managerial positions. If all the 372,240 members of this category were classified as new petty bourgeoisie, they would total 4.3 per cent of the total labour force of 8,625,925 in the 1971 census. [22] (N.B. This 8,625,925 includes 737,270 whose occupations are not stated, so the 4.3 per cent figure and subsequent percentages relating to the 1971 census probably understate the picture.)

In fact, a certain number of the 41,000 general managers and senior officials in the 1971 managerial category might well through the stock they own and/or power they wield belong to the big bourgeoisie or alongside the business proprietors of the smaller bourgeoisie. So too might some of the 7,710 financial managers and 21,315 managers and administrators in mines, durable and non-durable goods manufacturing, construction, transportation, trade and service industries. How many exactly is impossible to determine, but if we lop off a liberal 50 per cent from the total 70,000 in these sub-categories, we are left with approximately 337,000 managerial/administrative members of the new petty bourgeoisie, or approximately 3.9 per cent of the labour force.

If all those listed in the natural sciences, social sciences, religion, teaching and related occupations, medicine and health,

TABLE 2.13

Total Labour Force, Distributed by Selected Occupation Classes

	1941		1951		1961	
	Nos.	%	Nos.	%	Nos.	%
All Occupations	4,195,951	100.0	5,214,913	100.0	6,342,289	100.0
Managerial	225,551	5.38	392,896	7.53	500,911	7.9
Professional	282,242	6.73	385,676	7.40	634,271	10.0

Source: Meltz, *Manpower in Canada 1931 to 1961*, Table B.1, p. 62.

and artistic, literary and related occupations were to be classified as members of the new petty bourgeoisie, they would total 1,013,108, or 11.7 per cent of the labour force.[23] (By comparison, the roughly analogous professional and technical categories in the 1951 and 1961 censuses constituted 7.4 per cent and 10 per cent of the total labour force in those two years, cf. Table 2.13) Not all those listed in the professional category, however, qualify as members of the new petty bourgeoisie. For example, in the 1971 census, there are some 18,000 technologists and technicians in the physical sciences and some 8,500 in the life sciences, who are probably not salaried professionals in the full sense of the word. There are some 10,000 surveyors, 27,000 draftsmen, 24,000 architectural and engineering technicians in a similar situation. It is hard to classify the majority of the 22,500 system analysts and computer programmers, 18,000 non-social workers in welfare and community services, 98,000 nursing assistants and orderlies, or 38,500 medical and dental technicians as the new petty bourgeoisie, any more than the roughly 24,000 religious ministers, monks and nuns. Moreover, most of the 16,315 lawyers and notaries, 28,580 physicians and surgeons, 6,425 dentists, 4,040 architects and 2,315 painters and sculptors to cite some other examples are presumably self-employed (however much their income ultimately derives from the state-sector).

Removing the sub-categories cited from the figure of 1,013,108 above would reduce it by some 336,000. With some further rounding downwards, to make allowance for others who may not qualify, we would arrive at a figure somewhere between 650,000 and 700,000 for salaried professionals, or between 7.5 per cent and 8 per cent of the total labour force. If we add to this the 3.9 per cent classified earlier as managerial and administrative, we arrive at a grand total of between 11.4-11.9 per cent for the *new petty bourgeoisie* which we can round out to 12 per cent.

This 12 per cent figure is not directly comparable to any figure that can be derived from the 1961 census or earlier. As the 1971 Census publication on occupation tells us:

> The classification is considerably different from those used to present census data in the past, and many areas have been treated with far greater consistency and detail than ever before. Included in this list are such traditionally amorphous

groups as managerial occupations and newer occupations such as those developing in the Social and Physical Sciences, particularly in the burgeoning scientific support fields represented by technician and technologist occupations.[24]

An acccurate statistical reconstruction of the growth of the new petty bourgeoisie as a whole since 1945 is thereby rendered impossible.

That this 12 per cent is a high and not a low-point for the post-war period is however evident from other sources. Where teachers and professors are concerned, a fairly important element in the new petty bourgeoisie, taxation statistics going back to the middle 1940s show a clear rise in both absolute and relative importance, at least until 1970 (see Table 2.14, next page).

The most rapid development of education occurred in the 1960s, with the percentage of Gross National Product allocated to it increasing from less than 5 per cent to almost 9 per cent.[25] While the number of elementary and high school teachers went from 153,000 in 1961 to 262,000 in 1971, the number of university teachers shot up more spectacularly from 8,000 to 25,000.[26] Some twenty new universities were opened in this decade, as well as scores of community colleges across the country.[27] Overall university enrolment grew by an annual average of 11 per cent in the 1960s compared to 8 per cent in the 1950s, jumping from 113,864 in 1960-1 to 356,736 a decade later;[28] enrolment at community colleges went from almost nothing in the early 1960s to 134,000 by 1971;[29] the participation rate of the age group 18-24 in post-secondary education doubled from 9.7 per cent to 18.1 per cent over the decade.[30]

This explosion of the university and student estate was a phenomenon common to most capitalist societies in the 1960s, accompanied as we know by very serious ideological conflict and revolt. What is important here is to recognize that the universities are the recruiting grounds for most of the salaried professionals, and that the growth of education, especially higher education, in the post-war period is another indication of the growing importance of the new petty bourgeoisie in Canada. Table 2.15, taken from an excellent study of the state sector in post-war Canada by Hugh Armstrong, points to the growing importance of

TABLE 2.14
Teachers and Professors in Relation to all Occupations

	1946		1950		1955		1960	
	Nos.	%	Nos.	%	Nos.	%	Nos.	%
Teachers and professors	70,840	2.2	71,320	1.8	94,440	1.9	148,105	2.5
All occupations	3,162,032	100.0	3,866,160	100.0	4,923,700	100.0	5,850,611	100.0

	1965		1970		1972	
	Nos.	%	Nos.	%	Nos.	%
Teachers and professors	230,254	3.2	347,489	3.8	314,891	3.0
All occupations	7,163,100	100.0	9,183,407	100.0	10,382,005	100.0

Source: Same as Table 2.9

54

employment in education in relationship to the work force as a whole.

It is probable that this rate of growth has now been arrested, as the dip from 1970 to 1972 in both the absolute numbers and relative percentage of the work force in teaching in Table 2.14 would indicate. So too would declining enrolments at various levels of the educational system in the early 1970s. But for the crucial decade 1961-71, when a new English Canadian nationalism began to develop, education was undergoing massive expansion. And as we shall argue later, the two phenomena were closely linked.

TABLE 2.15

Educational Workers as a Percentage of all New Workers, 1946-71

Time Span	New Educational Workers	Percentage of all New Workers
1946-51	22,723	5.3
1951-56	36,723	7.5
1956-61	48,885	10.4
1961-66	107,593	9.8
1966-71	104,196	11.2
1946-71	320,120	9.3

Source: Hugh Armstrong, *The Patron State of Canada: An Exploratory Essay on the State and Job Creation in Canada since World War Two*, M.A. Thesis, Department of Sociology and Anthropology, Carleton University, 1974, Table 5-4, p. 135.

In another area, hospitals, there was a five-fold increase in revenues and expenditures between 1961 and 1974; [31] employment shot up by a factor of almost five between 1946 and 1971, while hospital workers as a percentage of all workers went from 1.5 per cent to 3.9 per cent. [32] While only a fraction of these would have been salaried doctors, nurses, and other health professionals in the new petty bourgeoisie, their relative increase in numbers was still larger than that of the labour force as a whole.

TABLE 2.16

Absolute and Relative Increase in Number of Health Professionals, 1951 to 1971

	1951 (numbers)	1971 (numbers)	% Increase 1971 over 1951
Physicians (mostly self-employed but presumably including interns)	14,341	28,580	99.8
Nurses (including nursing supervisors for 1971)	41,088	109,345	166
Total labour force	5,214,913	8,626,925	65

Source: Urquhart, ed., *Historical Statistics of Canada*, Series B108-115, "Number of Physicians, nurses, and dentists, Canada, 1871-1960", p. 44; Canada, *1951 Census*, Labour Force, Bulletin 4-2, p. 4-1; *1971 Census of Canada*, Occupations, Vol.: III-Part:2 (Bulletin 3.2-3), pp. 2-1, 2-3.

Without a doubt a most significant area of employment for the new petty bourgeoisie was the state sector itself, which experienced very rapid growth over the period 1945-1972. Unfortunately, taxation statistics on federal, provincial and municipal employment exclude such important employers of salaried professionals as provincial utilities, e.g., various hydro corporations, and such federal crown corporations as Atomic Energy of Canada or the Canadian Broadcasting Corporation. Still, the numerical and percentage increase in public employment at all three levels between 1945 and 1972, shown in Table 2.17, embraced a significant number of university graduates.

As Hodgetts and Dwivedi argued in a 1969 article which, if anything, underestimated the development of the state sector: [33]

> ... the more highly-trained, highly educated personnel in the administrative, professional, and technical groupings of the public service are now numerically strong contenders for first place in an occupation traditionally viewed as the great repository of clerical and operational personnel. Indeed, the figures for the provinces indicate that from one-third to one-

TABLE 2.17

Federal, Provincial and Municipal Employees in Relation to all Occupations

	1946		1950		1955		1960	
	Nos.	%	Nos.	%	Nos.	%	Nos.	%
Federal, Provincial, and Municipal Employees*	278,368	8.8	328,360	8.5	437,730	8.9	576,745	9.9
All occupations	3,162,032	100.0	3,866,160	100.0	4,923,700	100.0	5,850,611	100.0

	1965		1970		1972	
	Nos.	%	Nos.	%	Nos.	%
Federal, Provincial and Municipal Employees	759,021	10.6	991,804	10.8	1,145,325	11.0
All occupations	7,163,160	100.0	9,183,407	100.0	10,382,005	100.0

*Excludes employees of crown corporations and the armed forces.

Source: Same as for Table 2.9

half of their employees now fall in this superior category of "high-level manpower."[34]

TABLE 2.18

Occupational Distribution of Government Employees at Federal and Some Provincial Jurisdictions
Percentage Distribution

Occupational Groups	Federal 1966	Ontario 1966	B.C. 1966	N.B. 1965	Quebec 1964	Sask. 1964
Administrative	8.6	6.3	1.8	5.8	17.3	14.0
Professional and scientific	6.7	28.4	18.6	18.8	14.0	20.0
Technical	11.0		36.2	22.4	8.8	19.0
Total	100.0	100.0	100.0	100.0	100.0	100.0

Source: J.E. Hodgetts and O.P. Dwivedi, "The Growth of Government Employment in Canada," *Canadian Journal of Public Administration*, 1969, pp. 224-238, Table IV, p. 233.

For our purposes, it is the first two categories, administrative and professional and scientific, that are especially important. It is interesting to note that the emergence of a new petty bourgeoisie by 1964 is particularly remarkable in Quebec following the reforms of the so-called Quiet Revolution, but that a similar growth was to be observed in social democratic Saskatchewan. The process of professionalization of the civil service, both federally and provincially, has if anything gone further in the last ten years, with the branching out of government into such areas as urban affairs and planning, environment, and science and technology.

The significance for English Canadian nationalism of the growth of the new petty bourgeoisie which we have been documenting in the post-war period and especially the 1960s will be discussed more fully in Chapters 5 and 6 below. As a preliminary hypothesis, we can draw attention to the fact that most of the salaried professionals and public administrators were in the state and para-state sector, and that many self-employed professionals, e.g., artists, writers, urban planners, and even doctors and lawyers, depended fairly directly on the public sector for their livelihood. Armstrong estimates that in 1971, fully 22.1

per cent of the labour force was working for the state or in state-financed institutions: (and this excludes the 1,739,000 welfare recipients, students, unemployed, prison inmates, etc., he calls "clients of the state"[35]).

TABLE 2.19
State Workers in Canada from 1946 to 1971

Year	Government workers	Education	Hospitals	Total state	State workers as a % of all workers
1946	278,368	70,840	68,222	417,430	8.9
1951	361,609	93,563	93,725	553,897	10.9
1956	442.402	130,286	134,320	707,008	12.6
1961	613,000	179,171	192,391	984,562	16.3
1966	814,044	286,764	266,930	1,367,738	19.1
1971	1,077,207	390,960	313,005	1,781,172	22.1

Source: Armstrong, *The Patron State of Canada*, Table 5.9, p. 149.

TABLE 2.20
Total Government Revenue as a Percentage of Gross National Product in Canada for Representative Years from 1947 to 1974

	1947	1950	1955	1960
Gross National Product at Market Prices (in million $s)	13,473	18,491	28,528	38,359
Total Government Revenue (Fed., Prov., & Municipal) (in m. $s)	3,961	4,634	7,458	10,710
Government revenue as a % of GNP	29.4	25.1	26.1	27.9

	1965	1970	1974
GNP at Market Prices in million $s	55,364	85,685	139,493
Total government revenue in m. $s	16,761	31,954	56,458
Government revenue as a % of GNP	30.3	37.3	40.5

Source: Canada, Department of Finance, *Economic Review, 1975*, Reference Table 8, "National Income and Gross National Product 1947 to 1974," p. 109; Reference Table 51, "Total Government Revenues 1947 to 1974," p. 158.

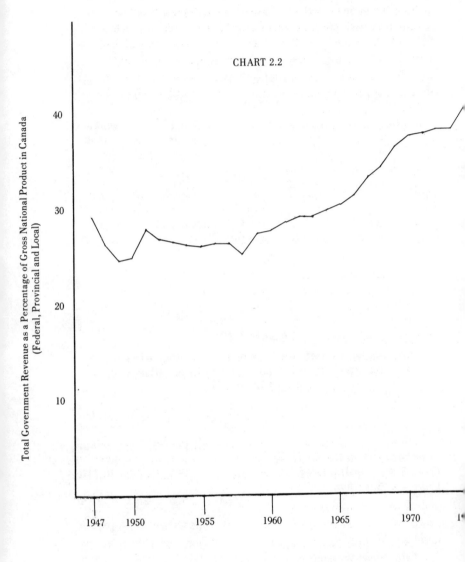

CHART 2.2

The fact that so many of the new petty bourgeoisie, and those in training for the new petty bourgeoisie, are not in the private sector, the no less decisive growth in the percentage of Gross National Product passing though the three levels of government (cf. Table 2.20 and Chart 2.2), makes a certain identification of new petty bourgeois class interest and nationalism inevitable. It is here that parallels suggest themselves between the development of a certain "middle class" nationalism in Quebec after 1960, [36] and in English-speaking Canada from the mid-1960s on.

Where the working class is concerned, there has been an important shift from the primary and secondary to the tertiary sector over the last few decades (see Table 2.21, next page).

Essentially comparable figures are available for censuses from 1941 to 1971 for such occupations as clerical work, sales, and services, and they indicate the continuous increase in absolute and relative importance of the latter (see Table 2.22, next page).

By comparison, all the sub-categories of manufacturing only totalled some 1,524,000 in 1971, construction trades 568,565, transportation 338,430, and such primary industries as forestry and logging or mining (including oil and gas exploration) a mere 67,260 and 59,160 respectively. [37]

The implications of these figures for our conception of the working class are, of course, enormous, and at a minimum entail much closer attention to the white collar component of the working class than was true of socialist and Marxist writers of an earlier period. To be sure, not all the 3,160,000 workers in the clerical, sales, or service sectors are white collar; indeed, a goodly number, especially in the service sector, are engaged in menial work of the most direct kind. (One thinks of the 13,000 chambermaids, 18,000 firefighters, 51,000 guards and watchmen, 127,000 waiters and waitresses, 169,000 janitors, charworkers and cleaners to name but some. [38]) Conversely, a certain number of those the 1971 census classifies in the tertiary sector, e.g., the 98,000 engaged as insurance, real estate, advertising, or business service salesmen, [39] are considerably closer to the traditional petty bourgeoisie in class terms than to the working class. The largest number of so-called tertiary sector workers, however, are white collar workers whose jobs are characterized

TABLE 2.21

Share of the Labour Force in the Primary, Secondary and Service Sectors

	Numbers in Thousands				%			
	1956	1961	1966	1971	1956	1961	1966	1971
All Industries	5,585	6,055	7,152	8,079	100.0	100.0	100.0	100.0
Goods	2,794	2,693	3,010	3,024	50.0	44.5	42.1	37.4
Primary	1,033	865	767	734	18.5	14.3	10.7	9.1
Secondary	1,761	1,828	2,243	2,290	31.5	30.2	31.4	28.3
Service Industries	2,793	3,362	4,143	5,055	50.0	55.5	57.9	62.6

Source: Statistics Canada, *The Labour Force*, Vol. 28, No. 1, Jan. 1972, p. 46.

TABLE 2.22

Clerical Work, Sales, and Services in Relation to the Labour Force

	1941		1951		1961		1971	
	Nos.	%	Nos.	%	Nos.	%	Nos.	%
All occupations	4,195,951	100.0	5,214,913	100.0	6,342,289	100.0	8,626,925*	100.0
Clerical	303,655	7.23	563,083	10.8	818,912	12.9	1,373,565	15.0
Sales/Commercial and Financial	247,248	5.89	348,971	6.69	492,628	7.77	815,740	9.4
Services	439,714	10.48	446,040	8.55	683,933	10.78	969,920	11.2
% of total labour force in these three sectors		23.60		26.04		31.46		35.6

*Once more I draw particular attention to the fact that 737,270, or some 8.5% of the 1971 labour force are listed as "occupations not stated," far larger than in previous censuses. The figure 35.6% must be read with this in mind.

Sources: Meltz, *Manpower in Canada 1931 to 1961*, Table B.1, pp. 62-5; 1971 Census of Canada, *Occupations*, Vol.: III, Part: 2 (Bulletin 3.2-3). pp. 2-5 to 2-9.

both by a certain drudgery and by a certain distance from the direct production of social wealth. (One thinks of the 246,000 secretaries and stenographers, 201,000 bookkeepers and accounting clerks, 113,000 tellers and cashiers, 242,000 sales clerks, etc.[40])

The transformation of the Canadian economy over the last thirty years into an increasingly service-oriented one has therefore meant an increased importance for the white collar segment of the labour force. Labour congresses such as the Canadian Labour Congress (CLC) have been aware of this, commissioning a study on *The Unionization of White Collar Workers* in the early 1960s[41] and making repeated efforts to broaden their membership from a blue collar base. While most white collar workers are in the private sector, often in fairly small businesses, and resistant to unionization, a growing minority work in the state or para-state sector, where conditions for unionization are usually more favourable (cf. Table 2.27 below).

By way of comparison, the Confederation of National Trade Unions in Quebec was probably more successful than the CLC in recruiting white collar workers, especially in the public sector, in the middle-1960s.

TABLE 2.23

Distribution of Members of the Confédération des Travailleurs Catholiques du Canada (CTCC)/ Confédération des Syndicats Nationaux (CSN)* by sector (as a % of 100)

	1940	1945	1955	1960	1966
Primary	7.92	3.79	5.31	5.19	2.4
Secondary	81.69	88.75	76.96	75.96	47.1
Tertiary	10.37	7.44	17.71	19.18	47.3

*The Canadian Confederation of Catholic Workers became the Confederation of National Trade Unions in 1960.

Source: Louis Le Borgne, *La CSN et la Question Nationale, 1960-1973*, thèse de maîtrise, Département de Science Politique, Université du Québec à Montréal, 1975, p. 50.

And it was precisely in the late 1960s that the CNTU began to adopt a more nationalist position, under pressure from its

members in the tertiary sector—both new petty bourgeois
teachers and civil servants and less professional white collar
employees. As Louis Le Borgne notes:

> If we can state fairly confidently that the majority of CNTU
> members in the public and para-public sectors and for that
> matter private tertiary sector were favourable to the Parti
> Quebecois by 1971 and that an important proportion of
> unionized workers in large primary and secondary enter-
> prises were favourable as well, one cannot say the same for
> the workers in smaller enterprises throughout the province,
> still quite numerous in the CNTU. The anti-PQ position of the
> central council of Saguenay-Lac St. Jean is an excellent
> example of this . . . [42]

The figures on unionization for Canada as a whole illustrate the
changing fortunes of large industrial and craft unions,
headquartered in the United States, through the thirty-year
period.

TABLE 2.24
Trade Union Membership in Canada, Selected Years, 1945-1972

	Total Union Membership (in thousands)	Membership in Unions with International Affiliations (in thousands)	Membership in Internationals as a % of total union membership
1945	711.1	471.1	66.2
1951	1028.5	725.6	70.6
1955	1268.2	893.8	70.5
1960	1459.2	1052.0	72.1
1962	1514.9	1011.6	66.8
1968	2146.4	1353.2	63.0
1972	2377.2	1442.7	60.7

Sources: Urquhart, *Historical Statistics of Canada*, Series D412-413, "Union membership in Canada, 1911 to 1960," p. 105; Department of Industry, Trade and Commerce, Corporations and Labour Unions Returns Act (CALURA), *Report for 1968, Part 2*, Table 3, p. 25, *Report for 1972, Part 2*, Table 3, p. 20.

The rise in the percentage of all unionized workers in so-called international unions between 1945-1960 parallels the take-off of American investment in mining, petroleum and manufacturing during the rising phase of the American empire (cf. Chart 1 and Statement 1 above). No less significant, however, are the figures from 1960 on, indicating a steady drop in the percentage of Canadian unionists in international unions to some 60 per cent today.

The period 1960-72, as we have seen, coincides with the take-off of the state and para-state sector in Canada and with growing unionization therein. The unions in this field such as the Canadian Union of Public Employees (CUPE), the Public Service Alliance of Canada (PSAC) and various provincial civil service associations are, of course, Canadian-based; their increased importance within the Canadian Labour Congress becomes evident by the early 1970s. Not only has a union such as CUPE replaced the Steel workers as the largest trade union in Canada by 1974,[43] but the public sector unions were to provide a good deal of the impetus for greater nationalism within the CLC. At the same time, the weakening of American imperialism was to make American internationals less attractive homes for a growing number of Canadian workers in primary and secondary industries and greatly increase the drive to autonomy by Canadian sections of international unions (see Chart 2.3, next page).

To be sure, the figures in Table 2.24 are for Canada as a whole. More refined figures are fortunately available for English Canada without Quebec. Naturally, international unions are more strongly represented in English Canada without Quebec than in Canada as a whole, while national unions, which for Canada as a whole include the Confederation of National Trade Unions and other Quebec-based unions, are less strongly represented in English Canada alone (see Table 2.25, page 67).

In English Canada, international unions accounted for 1,122,372 of total membership of 1,701,830, or 66 per cent, in 1972. This is considerably larger than the 60 per cent figure cited for Canada as a whole in Table 2.24. On the other hand, when the figure for Canada as a whole was 66 per cent, as it was in 1963, fully 71.8 per cent of English Canadian workers were in international unions.[44] Though less advanced on the road to national unionism

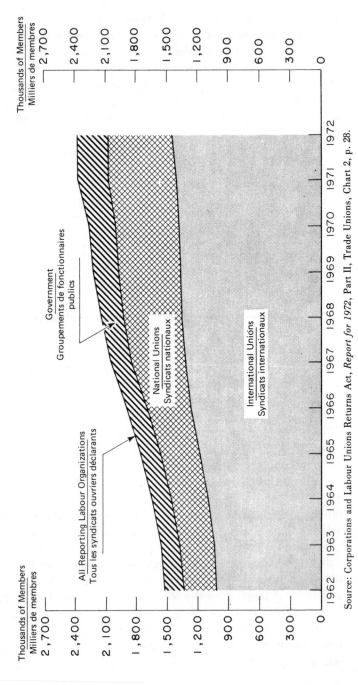

CHART 2.3

Growth in Canadian Membership of Reporting Labour Organizations, 1962-1972

Accroissement des effectifs Canadiens des syndicats ouvriers déclarants, 1962-1972

Thousands of Members
Milliers de membres

Government
Groupements de fonctionnaires publics

National Unions
Syndicats nationaux

All Reporting Labour Organizations
Tous les syndicats ouvriers déclarants

International Unions
Syndicats internationaux

Thousands of Members
Milliers de membres

Source: Corporations and Labour Unions Returns Act, *Report for 1972*, Part II, Trade Unions, Chart 2, p. 28.

TABLE 2.25

The Comparative Importance of International and National Unions in English Canada and in Quebec in 1972

	Members of all reporting unions		Members of internationals		Members of national unions	
	Nos.	%	Nos.	%	Nos.	%
Quebec	635,371	28.4	320,338	22.2	335,033	38.0
English Canada	1,701,830	71.6	1,122,372	77.8	579,458	62.0
Total	2,377,201	100.0	1,442,710	100.0	934,491	100.0

Source: CALURA *Report for 1972, Part II*, Tables 14A, 15A, 15B, pp. 40, 43.

TABLE 2.26

Membership in International and National Unions in Different Sectors of the Economy, 1972

	Total Member-	%	In International Unions	%	In National Unions	%
Mining	43,192	100.0	40,008	92.6	3,148	7.4
Manufacturing	778,556	100.0	697,557	89.6	80,999	10.4
Construction	261,008	100.0	242.080	92.7	18,928	7.3
Transportation	357,845	100.0	191,960	53.6	165,885	46.4
Service Industries	429,822	100.0	116,709	27.1	313,113	72.7
Public Administration	337,160	100.0	21,481	6.4	315,679	93.6

Source: CALURA *Report for 1972, Part II*, Tables 27A, 27B, 27C, pp. 67-9.

than Quebec, English Canada had begun to travel the same route in the 1960s.

The figures on unionism by industry group flesh out the significance of this trend, though unfortunately they do not allow for the same delineation between English Canada and Quebec. For Canada as a whole in 1972, Table 2.26 shows union membership in certain important sectors, and the numbers and percentages in each which were in international or national unions.

Bearing in mind that the figures for English Canada without Quebec might show a stronger weighting towards international unions, certain conclusions are nonetheless possible. International unions tend to dominate in mining, manufacturing and construction. The first two of these, as shown in Table 2.8, are the sectors with the highest degree of foreign domination. Transportation, a Canadian-dominated sector, is more evenly divided, while service industries and public administration, both in the tertiary sector and Canadian-controlled, see predominantly Canadian unions. The political economy of national/international unionism is a microcosm of the Canadian political economy as a whole.

To be sure, union members made up but 32.2 per cent of all paid workers in 1972.[45] Moreover, not all members of the trade union movement are, strictly speaking, members of the working class, e.g., some of the new petty bourgeoisie we have spent so much time examining in this chapter, while conversely, the majority of the working class are not unionized.

TABLE 2.27

Percentage of Workers Unionized in Different Industries, 1972

Industry group	Percent of workers unionized
Fishing and trapping	93.1
Construction	65.8
Public administration	61.2
Transportation, communication & other utilities	51.1
Manufacturing	43.5
Mines, quarries and oil wells	37.6
Forestry	36.6
Service industries	21.3
Trade	7.3
Finance	1.2
Agriculture	0.3

Source   CALURA *Report for 1972, Part II*, p. 73.

Some of the most important categories in the tertiary sector—trade, finance, service industries—have the lowest rates of unionization of all non-agricultural groups, while the primary and secondary sectors tend to be over-represented in the ranks of organized labour. For purposes of this study it is not possible, alas, to explore further the parameters of working class consciousness *per se*, particularly where non-unionized workers are concerned. It is, however, possible to pay special attention to the division between tertiary and primary/secondary sector unions, and come to at least some conclusions on how different sections of the organized working class relate to nationalism.

This chapter has sketched some of the more important developments in both Canadian and international political economy between 1945-75. The data is by no means exhaustive, but it provides a material base on which to build the historical chapters that follow.

Before doing this, however, let us briefly address an important theoretical question posed towards the end of Chapter 1, namely, whether English Canadian nationalism is that of an oppressed or colonized nation in the age of American imperialism. The data in this chapter would seem to point to an advanced capitalist economy, in no way analogous to the resource-intensive, agriculturally-based economies of most third world countries. To compare Canada's hinterland position within the American empire with that of more classically exploited areas of the third world[46] is no more acceptable, accordingly, (at least not without *very important* qualifications) than the specious claims advanced for Quebec's "third world" status by certain theoreticians of separatism in the early 1960s.[47]

Does it follow, however, that English Canada's is a typically national capitalism like that of Sweden or Holland, or further, that Canada is an imperialist power in its own right vis-a-vis certain areas of the third world?[48] The figures on Canadian investment abroad indicate a total of $5,040 million of direct investment in 1969, or $10,356 million for all Canadian long-term investment abroad in that year.[49] These figures, however, include the equity of non-residents—a not-insignificant $1,918 million in the case of direct investment abroad and an undetermined figure in the case of other investment. While some of this Canadian investment is in the West Indies, Brazil and southern Africa, while there is every reason to speak of the economic imperialism practiced by such corporations as Alcan, Falconbridge, Brascan or the principal Canadian banks,[50] that is only part of the picture. The other part lies in the relative weakness of specifically Canadian interests in third world countries and the fact that Canadian capital (when the corporations in question are, in fact, Canadian-controlled) relies on the umbrella provided by the United States or other capitalist powers. Canada's role in the West Indies, Brazil or southern Africa is very much a junior one, and if one is to speak of imperialism, it is the mini-imperialism of a *not entirely* autonomous capitalism.

One should not overstate the case. Canadian multinationals are hardly innocents abroad, and Canada benefits from the unequal exchange which characterizes relations between developed and underdeveloped countries.[51] It does not follow, however, that Canada's own relations with the United States are not characterized by an element of colonialism, even as Quebec's relations are with English Canada. There is a dialectic between nationalism and imperialism in the contemporary period which does not end where first and third worlds meet. Analyses such as that of Steve Moore and Debbi Wells err, when they argue:

> Left-nationalist anti-imperialism conceals an underlying national chauvinism, a complete disregard for the victims of Canadian-owned multinationals in the Third World . . . this national chauvinism is the product of a failure to recognize that Canada is a secondary imperialist power . . . Nationalism in an imperialist country, like Canada, is the root cause of reformism.[52]

Dependency is, in fact, possible in relations between a weaker capitalist power and a stronger, and such was the fate of English Canada, and Canada as a whole, in its relations with the United States in the post-war period. To call English Canada an "oppressed" nation, however, in the Marxist sense of the term, would be going too far. Oppression connotes political, military and economic domination by a large power against the wishes of a smaller—hardly the case for Canada after 1945. The reality which nationalists, including nationalists of the left, must face is that English Canada *was not a victim*, but a *willing participant* in the process of continentalization. Or put another way, the vast majority of English Canadians, at least during the decades of Cold War, could conceive of no other position for Canada save as a staunch ally or junior partner of the United States.

Analogies to nineteenth century Ireland or Poland oppressed by England or Russia have little application, any more than do analogies with China experiencing Japanese invasion in the 1930s, or Vietnam combating French and American imperialism after 1945. If English Canada was and is a kind of colony of the United States, it was and is an extremely privileged one by world standards, as the figures cited in this chapter or in United Nations Statistical Yearbooks would indicate. In examining English Canadian nationalism then, it is doubly important to examine the class forces which have supported it over the last thirty years, with neither illusions nor facile simplifications of a fairly complex picture.

Chapter Three
THE POLITICS OF DEPENDENCY
1945-55

The Second World War heralded a major realignment in international politics, with the emergence of the United States after 1945 as the dominant power in the non-Communist world. Where Britain and Germany had been the main contenders in the European theatre of the 1930s, where Japan had been the rising power in Asia, Britain was now prostrate after six years of war, and Germany and Japan lay defeated. Even the Soviet Union, militarily strong in eastern Europe, was economically exhausted and it would take twenty years of effort for it to reach some kind of rough equality both in political and military influence with the United States. The immediate post-war period, therefore, was marked by American supremacy in the political, economic and military fields, with direct consequences for the politics of a host of associated and client states.

Where Canada was concerned, the symbolic changeover from the British to the American sphere had occurred as early as 1940. To be sure, in the economic area American capital had already replaced British as the most important source of foreign investment by the 1920s.[1] But it was not until 1940, with the Ogdensburg Agreement between Roosevelt and King establishing a Permanent Joint Board of Defence Canada-United States,[2] that military and political reality began to follow economic ties. As a number of observers noted at the time, Ogdensburg heralded "a profound change in the balance of power across the Atlantic and across the Pacific" and a new regional focus for Canada's security.[3] It was followed in 1941 by the Hyde Park Declaration of April 20, which provided for integration of defence production between the two countries, or, in the words of Mackenzie King

> an acceptance of the economic inter-dependence of Canada and the United States as the foundation of the programme of war production in both countries.[4]

This economic inter-dependence, more properly Canadian dependency on the U.S. across the board, was to be enormously strengthened in the post-war period.

What is striking in re-examining the decade 1945-55 is the realization of how strongly most Canadians supported the ascendancy of the United States. In the late 1940s, some 20 per cent of Canadians actually favoured political union with the United States, and though this figure had declined to a mere 9 per cent by the early 1950s, it was one indication of the limiting factors for any Canadian nationalism.[5] More significant were the 60 per cent of Canadians who in 1950 wished to encourage further American capital inflow,[6] or the 63 per cent who in 1956 felt that U.S. influence on Canada was not excessive.[7] (If one looks at English Canada alone, the percentage of those who in 1956 felt that the Canadian way of life was *not* being too influenced by the United States was higher than the 63 per cent average everywhere save in British Columbia, i.e., 67 per cent for the Maritime provinces, 67.7 per cent for Ontario, 68.7 per cent Manitoba, 75 per cent Saskatchewan, 72.3 per cent Alberta, and 60.1 per cent B.C.[8])

Yet the preceding decade had seen the largest relative increases in American direct investment in years,[9] the forging of a peacetime military alliance involving the stationing of some American personnel on Canadian soil,[10] cultural penetration through various media, and political penetration which had led the Canadian Secretary of State for External Affairs to proudly declare:

> We are the junior partner of a North American partnership
> which will not be dissolved by communist blandishment or
> isolationist timidity.[11]

How did the different classes in Canadian society perceive the
process of Americanization, what forms did English Canadian
nationalism take, and what role did Canada come to play within
the American empire?

The big bourgeoisie is in many ways the most important actor
in this period, setting the tone for policies of continentalism that
were to shape Canadian policy, especially in the economic field,
for most of the post-war era. As early as October 1945, a
representative sample of Canadian businessmen could answer
positively a questionnaire in the *Financial Post*, "Does Canada
Need Foreign Capital?"

> A substantial amount of venture capital, both Canadian and
> foreign, is absolutely essential for full development . . .[12]

> I don't know of any logical reason why Canada should
> exclude foreign capital . . . I believe the encouragement of
> free trade in all commodities including capital investment is
> Canada's greatest hope for the future.[13]

> Our natural resources must be developed more quickly than
> the financial resources of twelve million people can
> accomplish.[14]

The President of the Royal Bank of Canada, in early 1946, could
reiterate the neo-colonial position Canadian financial capital had
always taken[15] and would be taking through most of the post-war
period on the issue of foreign ownership:

> . . . the more any one studies Canada's position the more he
> realizes that we of all nations can least afford to paddle our
> own canoe. Our geographical position makes us the link
> connecting two great industrialized powers, Great Britain
> and the United States.[16]

And an article in the *Financial Post* in the autumn of 1946, significantly titled "Marked for Soviet Conquest?," could place the Canadian bourgeoisie's support for an American orientation in the larger context of Cold War politics:

> Russia is on the move. The overthrow of capitalism is her declared objective. Canada stands between Russia and the last great citadel of capitalism. Canada is economically very vulnerable. Canada stands in great need of becoming alert to the dangers which lie in her path. [17]

There was one important fraction,* however, in the ranks of the big bourgeoisie, which for all its anti-Communism could not look with unrestricted favour at American political and economic domination in the years to come. This was the pro-British element, essentially Tory in its politics, and unhappy with the displacement of Great Britain by the United States. In England, Empire-oriented Conservatives had denounced "the robust buccaneering spirit of modern American economic imperialism" at the time of the British post-war loan in 1945 pointing out that "The British Empire is the oyster which this loan is to prise open." [18]

In Canada, similar elements were to speak out against the Abbott Plan, introduced as an emergency measure by the Liberal government in late 1947 to deal with the shortfall of American dollars, or against the too close alignment of Canadian foreign policy on American in the early 1950s. [19] Such sentiments were to be further reflected from time to time in the pages of business-oriented publications such as the *Financial Post* and *Saturday Night*, with their frequent articles on Britain and the desirability of closer Canadian-British trade and ties.

But the sand was running out on the British Empire, and the North Atlantic triangle was irretrievably broken. Whatever the sentimental importance of Tory-style nationalism in the period of

---

*The author is using the term fraction in a loose way to refer to sub-groupings of a class, in this case the big bourgeoisie. As was made clear in Chapter Two, he rejects the view that there is some *permanent* division between foreign-owned and indigenously-owned capital, pro-American and pro-British, etc. He does not, however, rule out differences on specific questions that allow us to speak of "fractions" of the Canadian bourgeoisie in an informal and *ad hoc* way.

Liberal domination, in the Diefenbaker years, or since, it was
never based on a viable economic strategy. If a fraction of the big
bourgeoisie was sentimentally unhappy with aspects of
American domination, the political economy of the post-war
world (cf. Table 2.1) with its clear alignment of countries such as
Canada with the United States in the developing Cold War,
brought most of them into line. Still, there are nuances in the
attitudes of the Canadian bourgeoisie towards American policy
which a careful analysis must bring out.

The Abbott Plan of November 1947, named after the Liberal
Minister of Finance, Douglas Abbott, was as important a
turning-point in post-war Canadian-American economic relations
as the U.S.-Canadian defence agreement for collaboration in the
north, announced by Mackenzie King on February 12, 1947, had
represented in the military field. In a nutshell, the Abbott Plan
curbed Canadian imports of American automobiles, food, and
consumer goods as well as travel expenditures in the U.S. to deal
with the drop in Canada's dollar reserves from $1,250,000,000 at
the end of 1946 to $500,000,000 some ten months later.[20] Canada
obtained a $300 million credit from the United States and the
possibility of private dollar loans on the New York market. More
to the point, Canada would in future seek to balance its trade with
the United States by encouraging greater exports of Canadian
natural resources and of manufactures by American subsidiaries.

Canada was in fact seeking a complementary, though
subordinate, position, within a continental economy. Implicit in
the Abbott Plan, as in speeches by the minister and prominent
Canadian capitalists, was the need to maintain an open door for
American investment in the country, and

> not lose sight of the inevitable connection between Canada
> and the United States, in trade as well as in defence and in
> culture.[21]

The subsequent American announcement in February 1948 of the
continuation of the close working partnership on economic
problems originally established by the Hyde Park Declaration of
1941 confirmed the course on which Canada was now set.[22] As
Kenneth Wilson of the *Financial Post* observed,

> Let's recognize as clearly as we can that something big,
> something unique, something very important has happened
> by the stated and implicit assumption that Hyde Park
> "principles" are here to stay, and can be made to work in
> peace as well as in war.[23]

The debate in Parliament following the introduction of Bill 3,
i.e., the Abbott measures, on December 11, 1947, was unique in
crystallizing for a moment the balance of forces for and against
unabashed continentalism. The Liberal government, and behind
it much of big business, defended the Abbott Plan as essential to
Canadian recovery, pooh-poohing charges the measures had
been dictated in Washington.[24] The Conservatives, the CCF, and
Social Credit attacked the government's measures, charging that
they would discriminate against British exports no less sharply
than against American, further driving Canada into the arms of
the United States. The Conservative criticisms are of particular
interest in reflecting the nationalism of elements of the big, small
and petty bourgeoisie.

> There was none of this kowtowing and cringing to another
> country (in 1932). Canada took her place at the conference
> table with the other nations of the Commonwealth beside her
> and debated trade questions man-to-man fashion. There was
> none of this business of Canada fawning on the United
> States.[25]

> We are being drawn into the United States orbit year by year
> ... the situation is developing to the point where we are not
> going to be a partner of the United States but a poor
> relative.[26]

> ... the government are with Washington first, last and all
> the time and have surrendered too much economic, social,
> financial and military initiative to Washington all along as in
> this bill.[27]

In the end the government measure carried, by the narrow
margin of 102-92.

To get a clearer idea of the contending views within the business community, we can look at a debate, taking place at almost the same time, over that hardy perennial, free trade between Canada and the United States. There is evidence that behind the scenes negotiations were taking place in the early months of 1948 between Canadian and American officials regarding a customs union;[28] indeed, magazines such as *Life* sounded the call publicly.[29] In both business and other circles there was considerable reluctance to carry things that far. A former president of the St. John, New Brunswick, Board of Trade, for example, feared that political union would inevitably follow on economic;[30] a Brantford industrialist argued that it would disrupt the established east-west orientation of the Canadian economy, preferring instead expanded Canadian trade with the sterling bloc;[31] while the general manager of Goodyear Tire of Canada argued that customs union with the United States was neither desirable nor profitable, and cooperation with U.S. was possible without it.[32] On the other hand, the heads of several prominent American branch plants in Canada, e.g., Philco Corp. and International Harvester, favoured just such a scheme, and there was no absence of editorial support, particularly in Western Canada.[33]

To speak of a polarization between Canadian-controlled and American-controlled capital would be an exaggeration. But there did seem to be somewhat greater support for free trade on the part of certain American branch plants than Canadian corporations, and in Western rather than Eastern Canada. (A quarter of a century later it would be the Economic Council of Canada which would be beating the drums of free trade most loudly.)[34]

The Canadian bourgeoisie as a whole *tended* to support American direct investment in Canada and broader aspects of American economic, political, and military policy in the 1945-55 period.

> Occasionally some one gets up on a platform and argues that the development of Canadian resources should be reserved for Canadian capital only. Fortunately these people are few . . .[35]

Thus argued the *Financial Post* in 1950. An article on oil the following year stated:

> The Yanks know what to do, when to do it and how to do it
> fast . . . By and large, Canadians are glad that the U.S.
> oilman is on the job.[36]

The President of the Canadian Manufacturers Association, in a
1953 speech, affirmed:

> With an enormous area still of almost virgin country to be
> opened, Canadians need and welcome foreign investments
> and with their own healthy stake in the national development
> they have no fears of any domination.[37]

All seemed quiet on the northern front.

In the resource field, the *Financial Post* welcomed Eisenhower's turning down of prohibitive tariffs on Canadian lead,
zinc, and aluminum exports in 1954, hinting at a continental
resource deal.[38] The President of Trans-Canada Pipe Lines
urged "a free exchange of gas and petroleum" between the two
countries,[39] while a further *Post* article stressed the strategic
importance of Canadian oil reserves to the United States in any
future crisis.[40]

Where military alliances were concerned, be it NATO or
specific Canadian-American arrangements in the far north, the
thinking of the big bourgeoisie paralleled that of the Canadian
government.[41]

> The establishment of the Atlantic Pact was a necessary
> result of the failure of the UN to do certain things.[42]

> The democratic nations . . . believe that there is a more
> dreadful calamity than war. Slavery is worse.[43]

> However late—we must apply ourselves diligently, coura-
> geously and—above all—with unanimity—to the task of
> rearming.[44]

> To adopt a narrow national defence would be to return to
> 1914 and 1939.[45]

Yet not all was sweetness and light. From time to time important spokesmen for the Canadian bourgeoisie would differ from American perceptions and policies, underlining in the process the existence of particularly Canadian interests. One good example was the presidential address by Hugh Crombie, Vice-President and Treasurer of Dominion Engineering, to the annual meeting of the Canadian Manufacturers Association in 1952:

> Charity is a wonderful thing but charity should begin at home. It appears to me that Canada has given a lot in some regards, and got little back in return, particularly vis-a-vis the United States.

To be sure, Crombie went on, Canada had vast natural resources, but it must remain wary of American intentions. The Americans would relegate Canada to the role of hewer of wood and drawer of water, unless Canadians insisted on processing their raw materials at home to the fullest extent possible. The less Canadians had to rely on American capital to achieve these ends the better, however helpful the Americans had been hitherto.[46]

The least one can say is that this spoke to a certain economic nationalism. More to the point, it articulated the interests of Canadian industrial capitalists in the maintenance of a high level of manufacturing activity in Canada, despite the boom in demand for Canadian resources. As American control over the Canadian economy intensified in the 1950s, the Canadian Manufacturers Association became increasingly an apologist for American investment (see Chapters Four and Five). But it is interesting to see a President of the Association rejecting the logic of the Paley Commission and of a certain economic continentalism in the early 1950s.

There was a certain flexibility where other issues were concerned. *The Canadian Banker,* for example, rejected the simplifications of American China policy as early as the winter of 1950, arguing that if all Western countries, including the United States, recognized China, the latter's independence from Moscow would be encouraged:

Of the Communist satellites only China and Jugoslavia do not owe their "liberation" to Russian armies.[47]

The Financial Post, for its part, was far from enthusiastic about McCarthyism south of the border[48] (one knew how to defuse communism so much more deftly at home). It backed up C.D. Howe's threat to build a purely Canadian seaway, in the absence of Congressional approval for a joint venture[49] (but then even the American administration was not unfriendly to the seaway venture[50]). It too criticized American China policy,[51] and most interestingly of all, began in late 1954 to call for a National Energy Policy,[52] strongly opposing the export of Canadian power to the United States, as Kaiser was proposing to do on the Columbia. Canadian policy, it argued, should not be one of "giving away power resources to run competitive industries in another country."[53]

The Federal Minister of Northern Affairs and Natural Resources, Jean Lesage, future premier of a nationalist-oriented government in Quebec, shared these sentiments in a hard-hitting speech in Vancouver in May, 1955:

> If Canada does not want to see the economic future of its west coast area jeopardized, it cannot allow the sale in the United States of on-site or down-stream power from British Columbia at a price corresponding to the average price of power presently available in that market . . . Is Canada reasonably expected to encourage new industries to locate on the other side of the boundary where they will have immediate access to the U.S. markets, where they will enjoy tariff protection and get cheap power as well . . . Canada might find itself without cheap power to process its own raw materials and forced to export these as well . . .[54]

The ultimate fate of the Columbia River was a repudiation of every word in this statement, and proof of the long-term ability of foreign capital to play off federal and provincial governments against each other. But in the 1955 context, the Lesage statement spoke to a form of bourgeois nationalism . . . within the empire.

In simple fact, the Canadian bourgeoisie, short of committing suicide, was forced to articulate minimum national interests even in a period of professed junior partnership. It could not accept outright political or economic union with the United States; it would from time to time seek to improve the terms of Canada's subordinate relationship to the United States. But very seldom, either in the period under consideration or after, would members of the Canadian bourgeoisie aspire to full-fledged independence or to a thorough break with American influence. As Louis St. Laurent expressed it in the early 1950s:

> *While we sometimes differ about tactics*, the rest of the free nations cannot quarrel with the strategy of American leadership.[55] (Our emphasis)

Perhaps the best illustration in the 1945-55 period of latent nationalism on the part of the big bourgeoisie, the government, or for that matter, sectors of the petty bourgeoisie, was in an area where it would cost least, namely culture. The Royal Commission headed by that eminent scion of established Canadian wealth, Vincent Massey, addressed the question which the traditional petty bourgeoisie in Quebec has stressed ever since the Conquest, namely *la survivance*.[56] For the Commission, Canada's cultural problems stemmed from the "stern realities of our geography and economics."[57] The size and proximity of the United States, a common language, accounted for influences "pervasive and friendly," but not without danger to Canada's cultural life.[58] Canadian graduate students trained in the United States, because of inadequate funding of Canadian universities, would inevitably be imbued with American values. A disproportionate amount of books, periodicals, films and broadcasts "coming from a single alien source" would stifle creative effort by Canadians themselves.[59]

Where nationalism was concerned, the Commission's philosophy adumbrated that of the Canadian federal state and bourgeoisie for decades to come—the search for a mythical Canadian unity:

> We thought it deeply significant to hear repeatedly from representatives of the two Canadian cultures expressions of hope and confidence that in our common cultivation of the things of the mind, Canadians—French and English-

speaking—can find true "Canadianism." Through this
shared confidence we can nurture what we have in common
and resist those influences which could impair, and even
destroy, our integrity. In our search we have thus been
made aware of what can serve our country in a double sense:
what can make it great, and what can make it one.[60]

In line with the historically defensive role of the state in
Canadian economic development,[61] and the new importance of
the state in post-war capitalism, the Commission argued for an
increased role of government in the arts.[62] Massey and his more
academic colleagues[63] had little hesitation in recommending
increased federal grants to education and the establishment of
what was to become the Canada Council.[64] They further upheld
the dominant position of the Canadian Broadcasting Corporation
in Canadian Broadcasting, including television,[65] and the
importance of the National Film Board.[66]

On the whole, the Commission's recommendations met with
favourable reception in the press and public opinion.[67] Where
there was criticism it was with respect to the CBC monopoly over
the licensing of broadcasting; Arthur Surveyer, the other
business representative on the Commission, and a number of
Canadian newspapers and Members of Parliament, objected to
this particular recommendation.[68] The *Financial Post*, however,
articulated the larger interests of the Canadian bourgeoisie in
supporting the Massey Report. The long-term future of Canadian
business, it argued, depended on future generations continuing
to think of themselves as Canadians, rather than as "second-
carbon copies of Uncle Sam."[69] Or as Vincent Massey told his
fellow members of the bourgeoisie in an address to the Canadian
Club of Montreal, shortly after the report came down:

> I know that for a generation it has been fashionable to decry
> "nationalism." I am, however, not convinced that in doing
> what we can to strengthen and to enrich our own national life
> we are doing any disservice to the international cause. On
> the contrary it seems to me that for many a year, and even
> for many a generation to come, we can do our best service to
> the world at large by "rightly ordering our own
> household."[70]

The limits of the Massey Report and of bourgeois nationalism are no less evident. Reference has already been made to the Report's denial of the separate national character of Quebec. More important still were the implicit Cold War assumptions that underlay its work. In the Introduction to its recommendations, the Commission quotes a passage from the special study prepared for it by that future ideologue of Tory nationalism, George Grant:

> Unfortunately, just as in the Western world, we are beginning to understand how deeply our spiritual traditions need guarding, just as we are ready to divert some of our energy from technology for that purpose, our society is being challenged to defend itself against a barbaric empire that pits its faith in salvation by the machine.[71]

The unity of the Western world against the Soviet empire was underlined while the Commission went on to stress the "present crisis," i.e., the Korean War, which formed the backdrop to its Report:

> Our military defences must be made secure; but our cultural defences equally demand national attention; the two cannot be separated.[72]

Having opted for American as against Soviet imperialism, the Commission's ability to combat American influence was open to question, as Canada's most distinguished scholar recognized shortly before his death.[73]

> Good relations with the United States are so natural and essential to Canadian external policy as to need little comment,[74]

the "nationalist" Massey had written, even before the Commission had been established. The Canadian bourgeoisie might espouse a certain minimum Canadian sovereignty in the political, economic, or cultural spheres, without putting into question Canada's subordination to the United States in the larger scheme of things. This is our reading of bourgeois nationalism during this rising phase of the American Empire.

Turning to other social classes, the smaller bourgeoisie and the traditional petty bourgeoisie of self-employed businessmen, farmers and professionals tended to follow the lead of the big bourgeoisie where relations with the United States were concerned. The occasional small businessman might speak out against American capital, suggesting that Canadians had had no difficulty in financing war-time victory loans and should look to their own resources, if necessary even to government, to finance post-war development.[75] The overwhelming majority thought otherwise:

> Our industrial and natural resources should be planned on a North American basis, not Canadian.[76]

An editorial in the *Canadian Chartered Accountant* of November 1951, several years into the Cold War, illustrates the realism with which self-employed professionals interpreted the new world order:

> Since the war there has been a subtle change in the texture of the Commonwealth which is under the King's suzerainty. The growth in the population and industrial power of the United States and the U.S.S.R. since the first great war has had its effect on the position of Great Britain and the British Empire.[77]

That same issue also included an address by Carl O. Nickle, publisher of the Calgary-based *Daily Oil Bulletin* and future Tory MP, to the annual meeting of the Canadian Insitute of Chartered Accountants of 1951, calling for common efforts by free enterprise in the United States and Canada in developing Canada's oil and gas reserves. It further underlined their strategic importance "in the defence of our democratic ideals against the evil forces lurking behind the Iron Curtain."[78] The accountants apparently agreed.

Two years later the President of the Canadian Institute of Chartered Accountants told his American homologues:

> Our two countries are bulwarks of free democracy, free

enterprise, free people . . . Aside from tariffs there are other issues of magnitude where we must stand integrated. [79]

A common commitment to capitalism led most members of the smaller bourgeoisie and traditional petty bourgeoisie to support American leadership in the post-war world.

True, the odd criticism might be voiced in the early 1950s, like the speech by the President of the Canadian Construction Association in 1952, arguing that Canadian construction firms were as competent to carry out the work for American companies coming into this country as the American firms with which American headquarters normally dealt. [80] Canadian small business wanted its share of the crumbs.

More atypical was actual concern over Canada's lopsided trade relationship with the United States:

> Our present pattern is one in which two-thirds of our foreign trade is transacted with one country whose reliability as a stable market is far from assured. [81]

But that was about the extent of any opposition.

Farmers, a significant component of the traditional petty bourgeoisie, were still 15.9 per cent of the labour force in 1951 (cf. Table 2.11). It is therefore striking to observe how enthusiastically farmer magazines, both in Ontario and Western Canada, embraced the cause of Cold War, and by implication, Canada's close alliance with the United States.

> . . . it is becoming manifest, more and more, that what the Soviet Union wants least is world peace, harmony amongst nations, reconstruction, world trade and prosperity. Communism does not thrive in that kind of a seedbed [82]

wrote *The Farmer's Advocate and Home Magazine* of London, Ontario, October 1947.

Two months later, after the Abbott Plan had been announced, the same paper observed:

> The indications are that ours will be a dollar economy and that prices will be allowed to snap up to the United States

level.[83]

Its Western counterpart, *The Country Guide* of Winnipeg, saw little merit in the Conservative criticisms of the Abbott Plan.[84]

Both papers welcomed the formation of NATO,[85] and both argued for Canadian participation in the Korean War and re-armament in subsequent years:

> Diplomacy cannot outrun military power, and if Canada is determined to uphold the viewpoint of united democracy as it has repeatedly professed to do, it cannot escape its obligations to contribute its share of military effectives.[86]

> We are simply being asked to exchange our way of life for bondage and worse . . . It would be peace with slavery.[87]

> Other nations, including Britain, have surrendered a measure of sovereignty for purposes of defence and it is quite probable that Canada would find it expedient to do likewise and to a greater extent than now obtains.[88]

There is no evidence of opposition to American investment from these sources in the early 1950s, and only occasional opposition to specific American policies, e.g., beef exports to Canada, or obstruction of the Seaway. The closest either magazine comes to nationalism is a 1953 editorial affirming a certain Canadian pride and confidence in oneself:

> The United States of America is indeed a good neighbour. By the same token Canada is a good neighbour to the United States. Without arrogance or wicked pride Canadians can well straighten their shoulders and hold their heads erect. From here on that is just what we ought to do.[89]

Farmers, too, no doubt, subscribed to a certain minimum of Canadian sovereignty. But their free enterprise ideology made most of them objective supporters of the American alliance in this period.

The new petty bourgeoisie, especially civil servants and academics/intellectuals, are a somewhat different kettle of fish.

While numerically these were less important in the late 1940s and early 1950s than two decades later (cf. Tables 2.13-2.15, 2.17-2.19), many of these were in fact highly important exponents of Canadian junior partnership, helping to formulate post-war liberal "internationalism":

> Our belief is that freedom is valuable and precious in itself, and that the loss of freedom anywhere in the world means an impairment and indeed endangering of our own freedom.[90]

As Marx has once defined such thinkers, they were the

> active, conceptive ideologists, who make the perfecting of the illusion of the class about itself their chief source of livelihood.[91]

By and large, the idea of "nationalism" had little appeal in these quarters. A CBC program director, Harry Boyle, could preface his remarks about the need for greater Canadian content in education with the phrase "Nationalism is an ugly word."[92] A Canadian historian could argue that

> in the present age that is making nations obsolete, an ardent effort to shape a strong Canadian nationalism may at least be open to query.[93]

Still another could claim that "nationalism is more often that not negative rather than positive," an emotional force whose increase would threaten our very civilization.[94]

On the larger question of Canadian relations with the United States there was no lack of strong American supporters. Fred Soward, who elsewhere termed himself a "nationalist,"[95] reacted to critics of Canada's over-dependence on the United States with the remark:

> over-emphasis on American domination of Canada only affords ammunition to the Soviet press for its barrage of propaganda to its own people and to the world.[96]

Frank Underhill, on the road from Fabianism to Cold War

liberalism, lashed out against the Massey Report:

> This use of the word "alien" seems to me to reveal a fallacy
> that runs through much of Canadian nationalistic discussion.
> . . . These so-called "alien" American influences are not
> alien at all; they are just the natural forces that operate in the
> conditions of twentieth-century civilization.[97]

The editor of a Canadian chemistry magazine could praise North
American joint efforts in defence and industrial mobilization in
the early 1950s or the pursuit of a continental petroleum policy.[98]

Two social scientists in their study for the Massey Commission
pointed to the financial lure which American universities held for
Canadian scholars.[99] In a more intellectual vein, it can be argued
that the very size and scale of American disciplines in both the
natural and social sciences gave them an overwhelming
advantage in the international marketplace of ideas, especially in
the immediate post-war period.[100] Canadian university faculties
were small, Europe was experiencing major problems of
reconstruction, the main source of intellectual production would
naturally enough be the dominant capitalist power, the United
States.

There are additional elements in explaining the Canadian
intelligentsia's relative anti-nationalism in this period. In
economics, Keynesian thought was dominant, and the evils of the
1930s were laid at the door of a narrow nationalism. In philosophy
and political theory, the battles of the Cold War placed most
Canadian intellectuals firmly on the side of the angels against
Lucifer. A George Grant could even permit himself the lampoon:

> Society suffers the tragedy of their youth finding faith in
> such childish hopes as Marxism, in such unbalanced cults as
> the Jehovah's Witnesses.[101]

In the larger picture, the branch plant character of the Canadian
economy vis-a-vis first Britain, then the United States, the
relative backwardness and underdevelopment of Canadian
intellectual life, meant an absence of indigenous traditions and
schools of thought.[102]

Yet just as the big bourgeoisie could not reject all forms of

nationalism, so *a fortiori* could salaried professionals, intellec-
tuals, and civil servants ill afford to do so. The Massey
Commission spoke to the concerns of many that at a minimum
Canadian culture be preserved. As Henry Angus put it:

> There are many reasons why the Government of Canada
> should be particularly active at the present time. The most
> important is the danger of cultural absorption by the United
> States, an absorption that would be fatal to visions of a
> Canadian nation. [103]

For writers like Hugh McLennan this was the *sine qua non* of
their existence; for musicians like Ernest Macmillan, hardly less
important. [104] By extension, a scientist like J.W.T. Spinks could
point to the deleterious effects which a branch plant economy was
having on indigenous research and development. [105] And in
another area, an ex-civil servant like Wynne Plumptre, no enemy
of continental arrangements, could take pen in hand to warn of
the dangers of annexation inherent in any special trade deal with
the United States. [106]

What was lacking in most quarters, however, was a clear
perception of American imperialism as a system. A.R.M. Lower
occasionally came close to this in his critique of Canada's defence
alliance in the late 1940s [107] and of a larger Canadian
subservience:

> Canada in fact could hardly be more completely subject to
> American industrial imperialism than she is at the moment.
> Her business world accepts the maximum of American
> leadership and shows no originality of conception: it is
> completely imbued with the branch plant, colonial mentality.
> As a result, Canada does not enjoy all her own wealth. She is
> an exploited area in a more intense sense than India ever
> was. [108]

Yet in other writings of the early 1950s he completely
contradicted himself. [109]

Kenneth McNaught came equally close in a piece in 1950:

> Today Canada's relationship to the United States appears to

be as much one of colonial dependence as was our relationship to Britain during most of the years after 1867.[110]

Most interesting of all were the critiques of American influence by Harold Innis in such essays as "Great Britain, the United States, and Canada" and "The Strategy of Culture." Already, in articles he had written shortly after his visit to Russia in May-June 1945, Innis had commented on the difficulty which Canada, with its counter-revolutionary traditions, would have in understanding a country with revolutionary traditions such as Russia.[111] In one of his 1947 lectures in England he went on to document the encroachment of American imperialism on Canada in the twentieth century, speaking in a famous passage of Canada moving "from colony to nation to colony."[112] In discussions in the 1940s he spoke caustically of "Pearson . . . as active as possible in selling us down the river to the United States," and of the need for Canada to seek to encourage Europe to develop a third bloc able to withstand the pressure of the United States and Russia.[113] In his final essay he stated boldly:

> Not to be British or American but Canadian is not necessarily to be parochial. We must rely on our own efforts and we must remember that cultural strength comes from Europe.[114]

And as a parting valedictory to Canada:

> We can only survive by taking persistent action at strategic points against American imperialism in all its attractive guises.[115]

Less dramatically, but in a not dissimilar vein, Innis' future biographer, Donald Creighton, in a 1954 talk denounced America's fostering of its brand of packaged Cold War onto Canada, stressing the need for Canada "to remember that she is a separate and autonomous nation in North America."[116]

But that was about it. A few voices on the centre, the right, or the left advocating a measure of Canadian independence. A larger community of academics and civil servants opposed, no doubt, to formal political or economic union with the United

States or cultural eclipse, but not otherwise concerned about
Canada's place in the American scheme of things. Petty
bourgeois nationalism was as yet a dormant force.

What of the working class and the mainstream trade union
movement? Unlike the Canadian experience after World War
I,[117] the militancy of labour in the immediate post-World War II
period did not translate automatically into a political challenge to
the capitalist system. The reforms of the Liberal government in
the social security field were probably one contributing reason for
this.[118] More significant was the much stronger position in
which both the Canadian bourgeoisie and its American
counterpart found themselves in 1945. North America alone had
escaped the war economically unscathed, and in the new world
situation, the economies of both the United States and Canada
would enjoy great advantages. A triumphant bourgeoisie is not
easily dislodged from power.

The policies of the Trades and Labour Congress (TLC) and of
the Congress of Canadian Labour (CCL) were never that radical,
even in war-time. Despite the presence of strong supporters of
the CCF and of the Communist Party in leadership positions in
both federations, and more especially the CCL, [119] one can ask of
the 1940s just how radical the trade union rank and file were.
Membership in the trade union movement had almost doubled
during the war,[120] but the political consciousness of the new
members was not necessarily on the left (cf. the federal election
of 1945).[121]

More immediately, in the period 1945-48, the developing Cold
War thoroughly poisoned relations between communist and
social democratic supporters in the trade union movement, thus
making any cooperation against American military, political and
economic encroachment on Canada impossible. That the Cold
War was used as a device by governments and anti-communist
labour leaders in both Canada and the United States to rid the
trade union movement of Communist influence is clear
enough.[122] On the other side, the Canadian Communist Party,
with its slavishly pro-Soviet and Stalinist stance, did little to
enhance its position among rank and file workers at the very
moment when vigorous left-wing leadership was most called
for.[123]

The history of the routing of communist influence in the trade union movement in the late 1940s has been told elsewhere [124] and need not detain us here. What is worth stressing, however, is the attempt which the Communist Party made in the late 1940s and early 1950s to pose as the party of Canadian nationalism.

> The Abbott Plan . . . indicates the way in which the King Government proposes to subordinate (sic) Canadian economy to monopolistic U.S. finance capital.[125]

> The point we want to make perfectly clear is that *the St. Laurent government and the Canadian big businessmen it represents is selling our independence to Wall St. and Washington, willingly, knowingly, and with malice aforethought.* [126]

> The force that can—nay, which will—stop the Yankee domination of Canada and establish a Canadian national policy of full self-development for our country, is the force of patriotism; that is to say, true love of Canada, headed by the united and militant working class.[127]

The analysis was cogent up to a point, though the crude appeal to patriotism smacked more of Stalin's World War II "mother Russia" line than of orthodox Marxism. More significantly, it failed as practical politics. Where criticism of the Abbott Plan was concerned, the CP had no monopoly. Where the wholesale condemnation of American investment and control was involved, there was relatively little concern in Canadian public opinion in the early 1950s, as was pointed out earlier in this chapter. As a Canadian economist had argued in 1948, a majority of Canadians might well believe that Canada should develop as an independent country without agreeing on constructive economic policies "to keep more than a formal independence."[128]

In any case, it would have required a political coup of the first order for the Communist Party, never very devoted to nationalism in the trade union movement in the 1930s or war years, in a country where even social democracy was a minority tradition, to successfully channel nationalist sentiment in the Cold War period. Whether justly or unjustly, the party was seen as totally devoted to the Soviet cause; except for Tito, hardly a favourite of the Canadian CP, there was little evidence of distinctively national roads to socialism in the countries of Eastern Europe .

The failure of social democracy and of the leadership of the Canadian labour federations to evolve an independent position in the Cold War was more ominous. Theoretically at least, this is where the main support for what Innis called a third position between the Soviet Union and the United States should have come from. It is true that at the time of the February 12, 1947 defence agreement, M.J. Coldwell had warned:

> I do not want to see Washington substituted for Downing street. Let us see that we do not have United States control of our country.[129]

The Canadian Congress of Labour at its October 1947 Convention had passed a resolution pointing towards an independent position, but it was the last such resolution to be passed:

> Congress is of the opinion that fears of people of the world are brought about by a rampant and militant Russian communistic imperialism . . . and on the other hand by monopoly capitalistic imperialism. The peoples of the world are caught between these two predatory forces.
> **BE IT THEREFORE RESOLVED** that this Convention of the Canadian Congress Labour demands, in the interest of world peace, a cessation of the activities of Communistic and capitalistic imperialism, and goes on record as demanding the enforcement of freedom for all peoples, whether in Greece, Indonesia, or in other countries now under some form of military domination, whether by Soviet Russia, the United States, or other countries.[130]

By 1948 the CCF had rallied to the support of NATO;[131] and the CCL, having purged the Communists, followed no less enthusiastically.[132] In 1950, the Congress was arguing the need for a firm stand by Western nations against the further extension of "Russian imperialism" in Korea,[133] and A.R. Mosher, in his Labour Day message as President of the CCL, could declare:

> It is no longer possible to have any doubt regarding the
> menace of Communism to our civilization . . . The
> democratic countries have been far too complacent in
> permitting the development of Communist groups, as well as
> the spread of Communist philosophy throughout the
> world. [134]

The same stance was echoed by TLC leaders in the early
1950s. [135]

Among the reasons for this Cold War position one can cite the
following:

1) Externally, most social democratic parties of Europe had
opted for the American camp in fear of repetition of what had
occurred in Czechoslovakia or East Germany: this had its
influence on the CCF and CCL. [136]

2) Social democracy has always refused to envisage more than
a general reform of capitalist society, rather than its revolutionary
transformation. For both social democrats and the trade unionists
whom they influenced, liberalism was ideologically far more
attractive than Marxism or revolutionary socialism. [137]

3) *Most importantly*, the Canadian trade union movement was
not structurally independent from that of the United States. As
was indicated in Table 2.24, so-called international unions accounted for 66.2 per cent of all Canadian unionists in 1945 and
70.5 per cent by the early 1950s. Many of these union members
were in manufacturing, mining or petroleum where the new
American capital inflow was taking place, and the very presence
of American corporations could be used as a justification for
American-based unions, even as it had been used in earlier
periods of Canadian labour history. [138]   Ideologically, the
anti-communism practiced by Walter Reuther and others in their
struggle for control of large unions such as the United
Automobile Workers set the tone for their counterparts in both
the TLC and CCL. [139]   Admittedly even a 100 per cent
Canadian-controlled trade union movement might have been
anti-communist at this stage of the Cold War. But with the Soviet
Union defined as the principal enemy, opposition to American
imperialism, including American domination of the Canadian
trade union movement, found little support.

Where the Canadian Congress of Labour would occasionally

oppose American influence after 1948 was in those same areas where elements of the big or petty bourgeoisie might also take their stand. The congress suggested that the American dollar shortage of late 1947 provided an occasion "for building up our own industries so as to reduce our dependence on the United States."[140] It welcomed the Massey Commission, arguing in its brief that "constant vigilance" was the price of Canada's cultural existence, and that Canadians should be eager to develop their own culture.[141]

But for the most part it placed cooperation with its fellow American unionists in the war against communism first. The CCL applauded the Secretary-Treasurer of the Congress of Industrial Organizations (CIO) when he declared:

> You know that the workers of the United States and the workers of Canada have almost the same interests.[142]

Similarly, *The Canadian Unionist* seconded the comments of George Humphrey, U.S. Secretary of the Treasurer and former President of Iron Ore of Canada, when he officiated at the opening of the Ungava iron mines:

> Here you see a great development of a necessary raw material that is required *for the preservation of the security of both our countries.*[143] (Our emphasis)

There was little working-class based nationalism in this decade of Cold War and bourgeois hegemony.

The Canada we have been discussing is one where the United States was acquiring majority ownership or control in manufacturing, petroleum and natural gas, and mining and smelting (cf. Chapter Two, Statement 1 and Table 2.8); whose trade was being overwhelmingly reoriented from Britain and other countries to the U.S.[144] It was a country whose leaders, after November 1947, were determined to increase Canadian exports of resources to the United States at almost any cost, and for whom differences between domestic and foreign capital were unimportant.[145]

In the larger framework of the Cold War, it was a country which took its place enthusiastically alongside the United States, seldom bothering to ask itself whether its long-term interests were compatible with so unequal an alliance. But could it really exercize free choice?

"Canada, the Business-man's Country," *Fortune* magazine had titled its special issue on Canada in August 1952, going on to note:

> Canadian nationalism, whatever its origin, can exist because U.S. policy today is non-aggression personified . . . Where in the Soviet orbit is there anything remotely like it?[146]

Is there not a clue here as to why Canadian nationalism was so timid a force—it seemed to exist but by American sufferance.

Only a few hardened intellectuals, Communists, the occasional CCFer or Tory, the still more occasional capitalist or small businessman, could see that Canada had become a neo-colony. The rest were blinded by the glitter which the Paley Commission held out for loyal subordinates—"The future belongs to nations with an abundance of raw materials."[147]

More accurately, "the future of nations with raw materials belonged, for the time being, to the United States." And that future, as the Kolkos have observed in their study of post-war American policy, ruled out any radical or strongly nationalist politics:

> Essentially, the United States' aim was to restructure the world so that American business could trade, operate, and profit without restrictions everywhere . . . American business could only operate in a world composed of politically reliable and stable capitalist nations, and with free access to essential raw materials. Such a universal order precluded the Left from power and necessitated conservative, and ultimately subservient, political control throughout the globe.[148]

Such was the fate of English Canadian nationalism in the period 1945-55.

THEORETICAL CONCLUSIONS

As was argued at the beginning of Chapter 2, the main independent variable for our study is the rise and fall of the American empire. It is quite natural then that the 1945-55 period, given American hegemony over the non-Communist world, should have seen little overt support for nationalism by members of all Canadian classes. Canada's military and political orientation were determined by what transpired in the United States, capital and jobs seemed to depend on an expanding American economic presence, intellectual currents derived from those in the centre of post-war capitalism, the United States.

The colonialism of the Canadian bourgeoisie towards imperial centres through most of Canadian history, the staple-derived resource orientation of large parts of the Canadian economy, made this class particularly open to outside penetration. The big bourgeoisie, e.g., the Canadian Manufacturers Association, was becoming increasingly Americanized during this first post-war decade. It was not in its class interest to oppose the most dynamic capitalist power head-on, especially in what was then a bi-polar world. Though there was some resistance in its ranks to features of American domination, (e.g., cultural) and a minimum commitment to the maintenance of formal Canadian sovereignty—the Canadian state in a fundamental sense was *its* state—the big bourgeoisie could hardly indulge in systematic anti-Americanism. The logic of such a position would have been a weakening of its economic position deriving from close links to imperialism and a potential radicalization of class consciousness on the part of the Canadian working class, the big bourgeoisie's mortal enemy, in an anti-imperialist struggle.

The smaller bourgeoisie and the traditional petty bourgeoisie for their part lacked any firm class interest in challenging the big bourgeoisie or its ally, American imperialism. The prosperity of the post-war years coupled with the discovery of oil in Western Canada undercut the historical basis of agrarian populism, while small businessmen and self-employed professionals, no less than farmers, derived benefits from the resource-fueled expansion. Ideologically, anti-communism was all-pervasive, cementing the class alliance between these groups and the big bourgeoisie.

The new petty bourgeoisie was not yet the numerical force it was to become in the Canada of the 1970s; the state was but a fraction of its future size. Given the close alliance between Canadian and American capitalism in this phase of the American empire, it would have been suicidal for those working for the capitalist state, e.g., the federal civil service, to assert a strong independentist ideology. State interest and imperial interest seemed to coincide, a bond which would begin to come apart only when imperialism itself had weakened, two decades later.

The intelligentsia, e.g., the academic estate, much smaller in numbers than it was later to become, was in important respects a sheltered colonial-minded intelligentsia. It took no great persuasion for its members to transfer their loyalties from a declining England to a rising United States (the process had already begun before World War II), all the more when the overwhelming majority of scholars, as the Massey Report had noted, were receiving their advanced training in the United States. To be critical of American imperialism would have required some sense of an alternative, a project which that phase of Canadian capitalism rendered impossible. And lacking, as Innis had noted, the revolutionary tradition which in Europe, by comparison, was to turn much of the intelligentsia leftwards from the 1930s on, Canadian intellectuals came to identify with the successful custodian of counter-revolution in the post-war years, the United States. Their faith would only alter as the American star began to decline.

The working class, finally, might have been anti-imperialist *if it had been more class conscious.* There is a direct correlation between the fundamental acceptance of capitalism that characterized the Trades and Labour Congress, the Canadian Congress of Labour or the ranks of unorganized labour and the inability of the Canadian working class to oppose American imperialism. The very domination of the AFL and CIO over the Canadian trade union movement now made working class radicalism more difficult to achieve. Yet more significant was the hegemony which capitalism and the big bourgeoisie, American and Canadian, held over the working class of North America in the post-war years. Prosperity worked miracles, while the Cold War made the task of bourgeois domination a good deal easier on both sides of the border. For its part, the anti-communist leadership of the Canadian trade union movement, like that of the

United States to which it was allied, facilitated the wholesale integration of the working class into an American-dominated capitalism. Imperialism helped mould and destroy working class consciousness in Canada.

Chapter Four

THE REJECTION OF NATIONALISM
1955-65

The growth of nationalism in a dependent political state is as natural as in another context the rebellion of a working class or peasantry long-oppressed. Elements of the bourgeoisie and petty bourgeoisie may prefer collaboration to revolt, the working class itself may pay little attention to external controls, but the process can only go so far. Inevitably, the hold of the dominant country will weaken, a few intellectuals here, a few political leaders there, will draw attention to the distortions in economic, political, or cultural development of the weaker country, and the underbrush will be set afire. So, at least, the scenario for many nationalist movements in the twentieth century might suggest.

Canada in the immediate post-war period was, as we have seen, in a peculiar position. Nationalism was seen as a disease by spokesmen for all social classes, while the very development of the country seemed to hinge on the closest possible relations—political, no less than economic—with the United States. To be sure, the existence of a separate Canadian state was not seriously challenged by the U.S., nor need it have been. For aside from culture, there was little questioning, save for isolated elements on the right or left, of Canada's position as a junior partner to the United States.

The second decade of the Cold War saw some changes in this picture, with the first stirrings of a new economic nationalism and the first hints that the American empire might really have feet of clay. Yet the decade closed on an anti-nationalist note almost as strident as that which had marked the period 1945-55; only French Canada seemingly heeded the prophets of nationalist revolt.

What this chapter will trace is the global rejection of nationalism between 1955-65 (despite a false start towards nationalism in the period 1955-57) by broad sections of business, the civil service, the intelligentsia and the trade union movement in English Canada. At the same time, we shall examine more limited forms of nationalism that did make their appearance, and English Canadian attitudes both to the changing imperial fortunes of the United States and to the new Quebec.

The prevailing philosophy of the Liberal government towards foreign investment had been amply stated by C.D. Howe, Minister of Trade and Commerce, in the Commons Debate on natural resources and development of July 1956.

> The free and unhampered flow of foreign investment into Canada has brought so many benefits to this country that it certainly is entitled to a fair and unbiased hearing from the Canadian people.
>
> . . . if one allows for Canadian investment abroad and the use of foreign resources as a percentage of net capital formation, it turns out that not more than 6 per cent of Canadian investment in the post-war world depended on foreign resources.
>
> . . . Canada's economy has been growing at such a rapid rate that the role of foreign investment in relation to our productive capacity has diminished and will continue to do so.[1]

Yet in the previous year and a half, opposition to different aspects of American investment had been gathering, reflected in the statements of bank presidents and statisticians, journalists and Conservative and CCF spokesmen. The Pipeline Debate of

May 1956 marked a turning point in the hitherto positive attitude to American capital inflow, and the defeat of the Liberals a year later, and still more the Conservative landslide of 1958, could be interpreted by some as a signal victory for Canadian nationalism.[2] Just how significant was the debate between 1955-57, and what are some of the lessons of this first foray into economic nationalism?

As early as December 1954, the President of the Bank of Toronto, B.S. Vanstone, had urged capital self-sufficiency as a new goal for Canadians.[3] In the spring of 1955, the Liberal government, despite C.D. Howe's reluctance,[4] established a Royal Commission on Canada's Economic Propects which among other things would delve into "prospective requirements for industrial and social capital."[5] In May 1955, the new President of the Bank of Canada, James Coyne, weighed in with the first of what was later to become a succession of speeches, in this instance predicting

> a greater measure of autonomy and independence on the part of Canadian management, . . . growing national strength.[6]

Several months later Coyne returned to the charge in a more dramatic vein:

> Modern history is filled with sad examples of foreign corporations operating in a country with almost complete disregard for their inherent obligations to the people of the country in which they operate.

> Why then cannot more of the foreign corporations doing business in Canada . . . recognize that the Canadian people not only desire to be, but are becoming determined to be, active partners in Canadian enterprises?[7]

Bourgeois nationalism had found an important spokesman in the state-owned pinnacle of finance capital.[8]

Coyne's, moreover, was *not* a solitary voice. The President of Ford of Canada, Rhys Sale, could disparage Canadian willingness "to see such a large share of Canadian enterprise slip across the border.''[9]

T.F. Moore, formerly a Canadian investment dealer, now Vice-President of another major United States subsidiary, Imperial Oil, could be more explicit:

> If the spread of the American way of living is to be conducted on the basis of absentee ownership, then Americans must reconcile themselves to the hostility that has frequently been the lot of the absentee owner in all parts of the world. A good deal of this sort of hostility can be avoided by sound and well conceived policies. I would suggest that decentralization— including local shareholder representation where feasible— should be a cornerstone of such policies.[10]

In the interest of the American empire itself, American branch-plant presidents and indigenous bourgeois spokesmen articulated exactly the same demand—greater Canadian equity and managerial participation in American-controlled enterprises.

In early 1956 the debate took a sharper tone. Michael Barkway, in a series of articles in *The Financial Post,* highlighted Canada's growing dependence on U.S. investment.[11] *The Financial Post,* citing a recent Dominion Bureau of Statistics study on the scale of American investment, argued that Canadians had never been less enthusiastic about the idea of being taken over by the United States.[12] And the Leader of the Progressive Conservative Party, George Drew, declared in Hamilton, Ontario that ''Canadians should declare their economic independence of the United States.''[13]

Frustration with continental economic arrangements was to reach a crescendo in the combined Conservative and CCF opposition to Howe's proposal for an $80 million loan to the America-controlled Trans-Canada Pipeline to complete its gas pipeline from Alberta to the east. Speaking for a fraction, at least, of the Canadian big bourgeoisie, Drew could call for ''an all-Canadian pipeline under Canadian control.''[14] Another Conservative member, Margaret Aitken, summed up Liberal policy on the pipeline in five words, ''United States first, Canada second.''[15] And the future Conservative Minister of Finance once again spoke of asserting ''Canada's independence of United States economic domination.''[16]

The main grievances of the Tory nationalists were outlined in the debate which the Conservatives sparked on July 8-9, 1956, on natural resources. They mentioned a heavy outflow of interests and dividends to the United States; foreign interests controlling the pricing policies of subsidiaries; senior positions in subsidiaries not being held by Canadians; a lack of information about the affairs of the subsidiary; exports and industrial research by subsidiaries being held back; and the application of American anti-trust laws in Canada.[17] Their motion called for a national development policy, greater processing of natural resources in the country, and wider financial participation by Canadians.[18]

Significantly, George Drew prefaced his critical remarks about United States investment with genuflections at the altar of the Cold War:

> Behind every consideration of the future must be a recognition of the reality of the Soviet empire.[19]

And Donald Fleming added:

> The United States is a good neighbour. Let no one misunderstand anything we have to say concerning our trade with the United States. We recognize the burden of leadership that the United States is bearing in the world today. We recognize the burden that she is carrying for the benefit of all the western world.[20]

Anti-imperialism, at least opposition to American imperialism, mixed very uneasily with Conservative ideology.

Nonetheless, from mid-1956 on, a limited form of bourgeois nationalism had come home. Michael Barkway, in an October 1956 article, could correct C.D. Howe's jaundiced view of a mere 6 per cent Canadian dependence on foreign capital for new investment, estimating it at one-third.[21] The Dominion Bureau of Statistics, noting that no other highly industrialized country has such a large proportion of industry controlled by non-resident companies, soon updated the figure to 40 per cent.[22] Bank presidents weighed in, underlining Canadian concern about "extremely small Canadian participation" in "important sectors of their economy"[23] and suggesting that "a somewhat smaller flow" of American capital "might be healthier for us."[24] Even C.D. Howe, stalwart defender of post-war continentalism, found it prudent in two October 1956 speeches in Milwaukee and Chicago to warn American investors to

> reckon with the pride of Canadians . . . with the normal feeling of nationalism which is present in Canada, just as in the United States.[25]

More specifically Americans should: a) admit equity participation for Canadians, b) make use of Canadians in top management, c) publish the financial results of Canadian companies, and d) allow branch-plants to engage in export trade.

The *Preliminary Report* of the Royal Commission on Canada's Economic Prospects (the Gordon Commission) in 1956 and the *Final Report* a year later sounded a stronger warning. They spoke of traditional Canadian insecurity *vis-a-vis* the United States reinforced by American domination in the resource and manufacturing sectors. This in turn sparked fear of full-scale economic and political integration with the United States and was affecting the political climate in Canada.[26] The Commission documented the growing rate of American direct investment in the post-World War II period,[27] suggesting that "legitimate Canadian interests" might be "overlooked or disregarded."[28]

Yet the tone of the *Reports* was "moderate," to quote the commissioners themselves, and their specific recommendations regarding Canadians in senior management, Canadian equity participation, and full disclosure of the financial operations of Canadian subsidiaries[29] recalled C.D. Howe and others.

Repeatedly the Commissioners stressed that foreign capital brought great advantages—from a high rate of economic growth and standard of living to access to technology and research[30]—while their final exhortation betrayed ultimate agreement with the larger purpose of junior partnership within the American empire:

> . . . to do nothing would be to acquiesce in seeing an increasing measure of control of the Canadian economy pass into the hands of non-residents and to *run the risk that at*

some time in the future a disregard for Canadian aspirations will create demands for actions of an extreme nature. After considering the problem long and carefully we have come to the conclusion that the best course for both Canada and for foreign investors with capital in this country would be for us to take action along the *very moderate* lines we have suggested. We do not believe such action would result in any appreciable slowing down in the rate at which foreign capital will continue to flow into this country. We do believe, however, that any harmful effects and implications of non-resident control would be reduced substantially if the proposals we have made are implemented.[31] (Our emphasis)

"Then know that I, one Snug the Joiner, am . . . no lion's dam," the successors to that earlier enterprise in bourgeois nationalism, the Massey Commission, seemed to be saying.

The proof of the essential vacuousness of the economic nationalism of the 1955-7 period was swift in coming. The election of the Diefenbaker government in June 1957 theoretically gave the Conservatives the power to enact the very measures they had lambasted the Liberals for ignoring a year before. Upon entering office the new Prime Minister judiciously declared that while not against American investment in Canada, he felt Canadians were presently discriminated against.[32] Several months later, in his first speech in the United States, at Dartmouth, New Hampshire, he sounded a moderately nationalist tone:

There is an intangible sense of disquiet in Canada over the political implications of large-scale and continuing external ownership and control of Canadian industries . . . Canadians ask that United States companies investing in Canada should not regard Canada as an extension of the United States market, that they should be incorporated as Canadian companies making available equity stocks to Canada . . .[33]

Yet little concrete followed.

Trade talks between Canadian and British Ministers at Mont Tremblant, Quebec in October 1957 came to naught, to no small extent due to Canadian failure to seriously envisage a major shift from the United States to Britain.[34]

A Royal Commission on Energy was established, ultimately leading to the establishment of the National Energy Board. But in the real world of energy negotiations of the 1960s, e.g., Canadian oil and gas exports to the United States, the National Energy Board was to prove worthless.[35]

Ford Motor Company prevented its Canadian subsidiary from exporting trucks to China in early 1958, but no legislation resulted.[36]

The Financial Post documented the continuing takeover of Canadian corporations and assets through 1958, but might as well have been talking to itself.[37]

There was little to justify John Diefenbaker's boasting to the Pilgrim Society in New York in October 1958:

> Tonight I feel reassured that beneficial changes have taken place in Canadian-American relations since I spoke at Dartmouth fourteen months ago.[38]

Diefenbaker's Minister of Trade and Commerce, Gordon Churchill, betrayed the shallowness of Tory convictions in his declaration to a Chicago conference around the same time:

> There is no real alarm of fear in Canada. There is no real anti-Americanism.[39]

Despite an undoubted element of nationalism that had surfaced in English Canada in the middle 1950s, in the Pipeline Debate, in General McNaughton's defence of Canadian interests on the Columbia River,[40] or in the outcry that had followed Herbert Norman's suicide in Cairo following repeated hounding by Congressional Committees,[41] there was little willingness to challenge the American empire head on. In the defence and foreign policy fields, Canada remained in the American hip pocket, as even the rare critic could note at the time:

> The tragedy of Canada in world affairs is that its ambition has been much greater than its situation could support. We would be much more secure in our aspiration to contribute to

world causes if we paid more attention to our own national identity.[42]

In the economic field, even those who questioned features of American investment or influence in Canada rarely challenged American leadership in the larger world. The free nations of the West must stick together, argued Walter Gordon in a January 1958 speech. U.S. leadership was moral as well as economic and political. Allied countries should make constructive suggestions and criticize policies, but this should not be done too often or too vehemently.[43]

The President of the Canadian Manufacturing Association for 1958, H.V. Lush, one who welcomed the Conservative triumph that year as an assertion of the "innate Canadian spirit of independence" and of Canada's unwillingness to become a 49th state, went on to argue that the election had not been the outcome of hatred for the United States. Americans should recognize "the difference between a willing partner and an unwilling satellite."[44] *Willing partnership* with the United States certainly was to be provided on most questions by the Diefenbaker government—like Liberal governments before and after.

American power in the late 1950s and to a lesser extent early 1960s, as our discussion in Chapter Two would suggest (cf. Table 2.4), was still sufficiently hegemonic to dampen moves to nationalism in allied and associated states. Britain and France had been forced, under American pressure, to bite the dust at Suez, and it was only with the termination of the Algerian War in 1962 and against the backdrop of the growing economic power of the Common Market that de Gaulle, and de Gaulle *alone* among European leaders, could give freer reign to his nationalism. The Cold War was far from over in the 1955-65 years, despite the beginnings of Soviet-American rapprochement in the Khrushchev years. Whatever the rhetoric of Canadian nationalism might have been between 1955-57, the reality of subsequent years pointed to the rejection of nationalism.

The Diefenbaker government entered into a new defence alliance with the United States, NORAD, soon supplemented by the Defence Sharing Agreement; the Pearson government in 1963 accepted the nuclear weapons that capped the arrange-

ment.[45] The Columbia negotiations ultimately ended in the
export of Canadian power and the alienation of downstream
benefits.[46] The Autopact of 1964 opened the door to even closer
integration of the Canadian automobile industry with that of the
United States, while repeated Canadian appeals for exemption
from American tax equalization legislation and capital export
controls underlined the vulnerability of a branch-plant economy.
In 1964, *Time* and *Reader's Digest* were exempted from
legislation taxing Canadian advertisements in foreign periodicals;[47] in 1965 the Merchant-Heeney Report elevated the concept
of quiet diplomacy, i.e., Canadian subservience to American
foreign policy, to official doctrine. In Vietnam, all the while,
despite occasional dissent, Canada toed the American line on the
International Control Commission, even while increasing its arms
sales to the United States under the Defence Sharing
Agreement:[48]

> . . . the intervention of the United States in Vietnam was at
> the request of the Government of the country. It was an
> honourable intervention, we should remember this, not
> inspired by any mean or nationalistic motive or
> imperialistic motive.[49]

To be sure, in a minimum way Canadian nationalism, by which
we mean the sense of Canada as a distinct country, continued to
exist through the second decade of the Cold War. A Conservative
Minister such as Davie Fulton might attack American anti-trust
legislation, threatening Canadian legislative retaliation for any
encroachment on Canada;[50] his colleague the Postmaster
General attacked American magazine split runs, arguing that
Canada had to have an economic and cultural pattern of its
own.[51]

The Conservative Minister of Finance, Donald Fleming,
imposed a 15 per cent withholding tax on interest and dividend
payments to non-residents in December 1960;[52] his Liberal
successor, Walter Gordon, sought to up the *ante* in his ill-fated
budget of 1963. In foreign policy, Canada did *not* break
diplomatic relations with Cuba following the Revolution (though
not unrelatedly, Canadian banks, unlike American banks, *were*
compensated, following nationalization in 1960[53]). Diefenbaker

and Green tried to avoid arming the Bomarc with nuclear weapons and paid the price in April 1963.[54] Even Pearson, a committed continentalist, permitted himself an occasional difference with American policy, as in his Temple University speech of April 1965 calling for a temporary American suspension of the bombing of North Vietnam;[55] while on the home front, his government could indulge in symbolic gestures, such as the maple leaf flag of that same year.

Overall, nationalism was not a dominant concern of government or of any social class in English Canada. Here and there, however, spokesmen and theorists of nationalism made their appearance. As often as not they came from the ranks of the big bourgeoisie, less often from the smaller bourgeoisie or the petty bourgeoisie, old and new, almost never from the working class. The result was that nationalism in this period took a decidedly bourgeois form, though the big bourgeoisie *as a whole* was overwhelmingly opposed to any but the most cosmetic form of it. By comparison, nationalism in Quebec in the early 1960s tended to be more of a new middle class or new petty bourgeois phenomenon, something it was to become in English Canada as well between 1965-75.

Why it should have been the Walter Gordons or James Coynes or in a related field financial journalists such as Michael Barkway and James B. McGeachie, who articulated a limited form of English Canadian nationalism, particularly economic nationalism, is an interesting question. At the least it suggests that a fraction of the Canadian bourgeoisie (and its ideologists) had the same perception of nationalism and its uses as the bourgeoisies of long-established countries such as Britain, France and the United States had always had, or that from time to time had motivated the Canadian bourgeoisie itself (e.g., the National Policy, the building of the CPR, the rejection of Reciprocity in 1911). It is after all natural that a big bourgeoisie that indentifies its own interests with a nation espouse a form of nationalism:

> Founded in this very city within five years of Confederation, the Canadian Manufacturers Association has survived and gone from strength to strength through good times and bad—as Canada, the nation, has done.[56]

What is therefore interesting is not that *some* bourgeois spokesmen supported nationalism but rather *how few* comparatively these were. *In the heyday of American imperialism, the major portion of the bourgeoisie of a dependent country such as Canada came to see its class interest as lying in the closest possible interaction, short of outright absorption, with the bourgeoisie of the imperial power, represented in the Canadian economy through the branch-plants.*

What after all were the grievances of the bank and branch-plant presidents between 1955-57, if not those of loyal collaborators wanting a better deal? Robert Fowler, President of the Canadian Pulp and Paper Association, stated the precise maximum that most Canadian capitalists wanted from the American corporations in the 1955-65 period:

> The first essential is decentralized, autonomous Canadian management in the subsidiary . . . An American company operating in Canada must go to some lengths to discover what are the broad objectives of Canadian policies and what are the basic aspirations of the Canadian people, and seek not only to identify with them but to work towards furthering them.[57]

Fowler in his speech ruled out any legislative coercion against American companies, even while underlining the basic compatibility of the branch-plant system and Canadian development.

A similar statement of corporate philosophy lay in the brief of the Canadian Manufacturers Association to the Gordon Commission. It argued many of the same points regarding Canadian managers and equity participation which the Commission was itself to make. But the Association opposed "legislative compulsion to achieve these ends,"[58] while its President for 1957 advocated "the continuation of a business climate which will attract and welcome outside capital."[59]

A still better indication of the way the wind was blowing came with the formation of the Canadian-American Committee in 1957, eventually grouping some 60 prominent Canadian and American leaders from business, the professions, and labour. (See Appendix 1 for a list of Committee members in 1958 and 1964.) The *raison d'etre* of this Committee, as its Canadian

Co-chairman, Robert Fowler, outlined it at its opening session lay in

> the growing interdependence of the United States and Canadian economies stemming from their rapid growth; the imperative for seeking out and eliminating basic causes of friction in United States-Canadian relations; and the particular opportunities available to a group of private citizens from both countries to marshal facts and reach well-reasoned and practical solutions for United States-Canadian problems.[60]

While there was nothing in this statement incompatible with demands for more Canadian directors, equity, etc., of the type we have been outlining, (and men like C.D. Howe, Walter Gordon, [61] and several branch-plant presidents were members of this Committee in its early years), it did not presage a critical, let alone a strongly nationalistic approach to Canadian-American relations. Interdependence was taken for granted, not least of all by the Carnegie Foundation that paid the initial tab.[62] The Committee remained carefully attuned to "increased sensitivities in Canadian-American Relations" in the early 1960s, [63] becoming a proponent of "a North American common market in capital,"[64] free trade between Canada and the United States, [65] and much besides.

What was true for the Canadian-American Committee was no less true for many members of the Canadian big bourgeoisie. The President of the CPR, N.R. Crump, in a 1957 New York address, repudiated "any sentiments of narrow nationalism" in Canadian attitudes towards the United States. Stressing a common tradition of democracy and freedom, he argued the positive effects of American investment for Canada's growth and trade balance.[66] The spokesman for the main 19th century beneficiary of protectionism in the era of British imperialism, now peddled a tune more in keeping with the big bourgeoisie's American alliance.

And as James Coyne began his series of speeches on foreign investment in 1960-61 that were to culminate in his removal from office, the opposition of bankers, insurance company presidents and industrialists to any interference with the inflow underlined how superficial earlier criticisms of American practices (between 1955-57) had been. One spokesman dismissed the whole debate on foreign capital as "twaddle talk,"[67] a second underlined the stake Canadians had in the position of the United States at the head of the Western Alliance,[68] while still a third stressed the contribution American investment had made to the Canadian standard of living, while decrying anti-Americanism.[69]

Yet there was a minority sentiment in the ranks of the big bourgeoisie critical of American investment, and indeed, of other features of American domination. We have already made reference to James Coyne, and a few representative quotations from his 1960-61 speeches will bring home the thrust of his concern:

> No other country in the world with something like our relative state of development has ever had such a degree of foreign domination, or even one half or one quarter the degree of foreign domination. Canada is being pushed down the road that leads to loss of any effective power to be masters in our own household and ultimate absorption in and by another.[70]

(The foreshadowing of the Quebec Liberal slogan in the 1962 provincial elections, *"Maitres chez nous,"* in this October, 1960 speech of Coyne points to a certain parallel between the concerns of English Canadian and French Canadian nationalism.)

> Unless the inflow of capital is reduced, all attempts to rectify the deficits in our balance of payments must be self-defeating . . . In the end we can buy Canada back. But first we must stop selling Canada out.[71]

In a similar vein, Walter Gordon began his crusade for a Canadian capitalism in a Vancouver speech of August 1960, arguing that Canada had been losing a good deal of her political and economic independence and was in danger of becoming "a more or less helpless satellite of the United States."[72]

In his 1963 budget address, shortly after assuming the Finance portfolio, Gordon attempted to act on his moderately nationalist beliefs. While defending the contribution that foreign direct investment had made to Canada, he proposed tax write-offs for firms with at least 25 per cent beneficial Canadian ownership as a means of increasing both Canadian equity and directors in foreign-owned subsidiaries.[73] He also proposed a 30 per cent sales tax on the sale of listed Canadian corporations to non-residents, arguing that such sales "rarely conferred any benefit on the Canadian economy."[74]

The sequel is well known. Not only did Gordon's budget proposals go up in flames under the attacks of Eric Kierans and others, but within days, officials from the Department of Finance were in Washington pleading for exemption from American tax equalization legislation.[75] A year later, Gordon had another bitter pill to swallow, defending the exemption of *Time* and *Reader's Digest* from increased Canadian taxation on advertising in foreign periodicals as the *quid pro quo* for the Canada-United States Autopact.[76]

Still, in his years as a Liberal Cabinet Minister, Gordon was to champion the Canadian Development Corporation, stringent restrictions on the Mercantile Bank and other foreign incursions into Canadian finance,[77] and as his last gesture, back the Report of the Task Force on the Structure of Canadian Industry (the Watkins Report). In the short-term, however, both Gordon's and Coyne's careers were to end in ruin. The hour for bourgeois nationalism was yet to strike, and as Gordon himself noted in *A Choice for Canada*:

> During the two-and-one half years I held that office (Minister of Finance), the influence that financial and business interests in the United States had on Canadian policy was continually brought home to me. On occasion, this influence was reinforced by representations from the State Department and the American Administration as a whole. It was pressed by those who direct American businesses in Canada, by their professional advisers, by Canadian financiers whose interests were identified directly or indirectly with American investment in Canada, by influential members of the Canadian civil service, by some representatives of the university community, and by some sections of the press.[78]

There were a few other voices of muffled nationalism in the

ranks of the Canadian bourgeoisie in this period. The editorial columns and pages of *The Financial Post* are of particular interest in underlining the schizophrenic quality of whatever bourgeois nationalism did in fact exist.

Its editorials in the 1955-57 period generally welcomed American capital, providing Canadian interests were met:

> The foreign investor must be warned that his success in Canada will depend, in the long run, on his adapting his enterprises to Canadian needs and susceptibilities. He must realize that this country is still fiercely independent, and that our superficial resemblance to the United States conceals a distinctive character which he will have to learn. If our silence leads American investors to suppose that they can treat Canada as a mere annex of the United States, it can only lead to future trouble.[79]

As though to stress the difference between responsible and extreme nationalism, however, a January 1957 editorial chided Nasser's failure to respect contracts (i.e., the nationalization of the Suez Canal), comparing this negatively with the guarantees Canadian governments had historically offered foreign investors. "What Laurier Had Over Nasser" was the extraordinary title. [80]

In the spring of 1957 the paper was up in arms over the suicide of Canada's Ambassador to Cairo, Herbert Norman, arguing that the honeymoon in Canadian-American relations was over;[81] six months later, it was arguing the irrelevance of sovereignty to Canada's defence needs.[82]

In mid-1958 it criticized Diefenbaker for softness towards the Americans, suggesting his government was lapsing into "the childish habit of pretending all is well" in Canadian-American relations.[83] In late 1958 it strongly praised the proposed National Energy Board, hoping it would result in a good deal more processing being done in Canada.[84] It carried through with an attack on the extra-territoriality of American laws,[85] and by August 1959 was asking "Can We Survive U.S. Investment?"[86]

In early 1960, the paper praised both Walter Gordon and James Coyne for posing the question of Canadian political and economic independence from the United States, and through the fall of 1960 and spring of 1961, it gave much publicity and a fair measure of support to Coyne's position.[87]

The paper welcomed the O'Leary Report with its recommendations for an end to tax privileges for American periodicals.[88] As
its regular columnist, James B. McGeachie, argued:

> Communications of a nation are vital to its life and its
> defences . . . The right of Canadians to their own media of
> communication (must be protected.)[89]

In the summer of 1962, the paper denounced the takeover of
Canadian Oil by Shell, urging Canadian capitalists to step into
the breach. When the takeover went through, it lamented:

> Have we already passed the point of no return? Do we stop
> trying to be an independent country?[90]

By February 1963, in somersault fashion, *The Financial Post*
was back to strongly pushing continentalism in the defence
field.[91]

In the early summer of 1963, it criticized Gordon for not having
done his homework in preparing his budget,[92] and went on once
again to distinguish between reasonable and extreme forms of
nationalism:

> . . . there is no suggestion or possibility that Canada will try
> Mexico's old remedy. Canada does not drink tequila, stage
> revolutions or import its economic policies from the Latin
> republics.[93]

Within weeks, the paper was at it again, noting Canada's
humiliation in having to beg exemption from the U.S.
equalization tax and berating Canada's reliance "for too long on
unlimited quantities of U.S. capital to finance Canadian
growth."[94]

The Financial Post opposed any large-scale incursion by the
First National City Bank into Canada,[95] but supported the
Automobile Free Trade Agreement the following year, arguing it
made "Continental Common Sense."[96] It also did a complete
about-face on its mid-1950s stand on the Columbia River,
supporting the export of power to the United States under the

revised Treaty.[97]

To complete this survey in schizophrenia, one can point to *The Financial Post*'s strong editorial support for Walter Gordon during most of the 1963-64 period when he was Minister of Finance,[98] and to its equally strong opposition to the Canadian Development Corporation, one of Gordon's main proposals for repatriating the economy.[99] In a more nationalist vein, in 1965 the paper strongly seconded General McNaughton's opposition to the proposed North American Water and Power Authority (NAWAPA), [100] and pointed to the tightening American embrace posed by some $25 billion in long-term investment in Canada. [101] Yet in an astonishing review of George Grant's *Lament for a Nation*, the paper observed:

> If any political party has sold Canada down the river to "continentalism," or is likely to do so, it can't possibly be the party of which Walter Gordon is the designated spokesman on economic and financial questions. [102]

Within days, Gordon had resigned from the government.

If we have dwelt at some length on the editorial policies of *The Financial Post* over this decade, it is because its contradictions reflect those of the Canadian bourgeoisie as a whole. There is an element of nationalism in the discussion of foreign investment, but it is tempered by remarkable concessions to continentalism in the economic field (the Autopact, the Columbia River Treaty), and by wholesale continentalism in the defence field. There is a fear of vigorous government intervention to check American investment, coupled with Oblomov-like longing for an independent Canadian capitalism never-to-be. Day dreams and reality, nationalism and continentalism, seem hopelessly intertwined.

What these contradictions reflect is the impossibility of a thorough-going bourgeois nationalism. As Chart 1 and Table 2.8 in Chapter Two, and other studies, show,[103] a majority of Canadian manufacturing, mining and petroleum was controlled from abroad, principally from the United States, from the 1950s and on. As the Parks showed in their pioneering study of the early 1960s, Canadian banks played a linchpin role in mediating between foreign-controlled and Canadian-controlled capital. [104] There was no way the Canadian-controlled segment of the big bourgeoisie would challenge the very existence of American-controlled capital, no matter how much individual Canadian capitalists might want to see the Canadian-owned share of primary or secondary industry increase. [105]

Far more typical were the views of "some leading Toronto industrialists," cited in a London *Times* article of early 1960:

> Their general answer was that complete economic integration with the United States was inevitable and that Canadians were not prepared to give up their standards of living just to stop this insidious process . . . [106]

. . . Or the views of Graham Towers, former Governor of the Bank of Canada and now President of the Canada Life Assurance Company, suggesting Canada's managerial and financial resources were not unlimited. [107] Or those of Canadian Manufacturers Association Presidents defending the noteworthy contribution Canadian-based subsidiaries were making in various fields. [108]

Equally interesting were the views of Roy A. Matthews of the Private Planning Association of Canada who in a 1965 article let the cat out of the bag by talking about "Canada, 'The International Nation'." In the name of reducing Canadian dependence on the United States he talked of internationalizing capital flows into the country and of adopting free trade. [109] Canada's mission lay in some kind of virtuous internationalism, a view echoed by the practitioners of Canadian foreign, no less than economic, policy.

The one area of strong Canadian nationalism on the part of the English Canadian big bourgeoisie lay in its reaction to the aspirations of Quebec and its more nationalist petty bourgeoisie. As the so-called Quiet Revolution unfolded and Quebec began to challenge Ottawa's jurisdiction in the social security, taxation and other fields, the Canadian bourgeoisie began to feel "its" nation under attack, in a way that American domination had seldom alarmed it. Initial sympathy for the Lesage government gave way to scepticism, as separatism made its appearance, and bilingualism and biculturalism no longer seemed to suffice. By the middle and late 1960s, the Canadian bourgeoisie had begun to tighten the screws on new investment in the province, and through the Canada Committee[110] and other such groups made clear its opposition to any form of separatism.

An editorial in *The Financial Post* as early as July 1961 dismissed the nascent separatist movement with a few paragraphs. Separatist movements, it argued, were neither new nor deeply disturbing. How did the separatists propose to get Quebec out of a federal union without the consent of the other provinces? And what would be the life expectancy of "Laurentia" on its own?[111]

Over the next few years, *The Financial Post* welcomed many of the concrete reforms of the Lesage government, convincing itself of its long-term contribution to Canadian unity.[112]

The 1962 President of the CMA chimed in with his own optimistic interpretation, stating that he supported increased French Canadian influence in national affairs, the better to preserve and develop the "Canadian identity."[113]

Yet there was opposition to such concrete moves as Quebec's adoption of French as the official language of government communications[114] (a foreshadowing of the later Bill 22), to Daniel Johnson's proposals for a constituent assembly to rewrite the BNA Act,[115] to any suggestion of turning Canada into two "associate states."[116] Bilingualism and biculturalism marked the limits acceptable to the Canadian bourgeoisie, no less than to the Canadian state.[117]

To be sure, most French Canadian capitalists were no less committed to the cause of a united Canada than their English Canadian counterparts, underlining "the inevitable economic losses that a separation would bring about."[118] But there was a more menacing quality to the speeches of English Canadian capitalists, particularly as the 1960s wore on:

> All who would hold this country together have a right to expect that the manufacturing industry will throw its full weight into the scales on the side of Canada.

> More than any other it has made Canada one of the great and rising nations of the world . . . more than any other it has most to lose from any tearing asunder of the hundred-year old fabric of Confederation.

We must spare no effort then to hurl back the challenge of the would-be splitters and range ourselves, our companies, our Association and our industry by word and deed four-square with those who are determined that Canada should not break up. [119]

As far as the big bourgeoisie was concerned, *they* had built Canada, it was *their* country, and they would be damned if French Canadian separatists tried to take Quebec down another road.

Another potential target was the organized trade union movement. An interesting company ad appeared in *The Financial Post* in 1957, during the famous strike by the Steelworkers against Gaspe Copper Mines (controlled by Noranda Mines) at Murdochville, Quebec:

The Truth about Murdochvile

The strike was part of the strategy of the Union leaders and their Pittsburgh, USA headquarters to obtain a stranglehold on the Canadian mining industry. The hardships and misery which accompany a strike mean nothing to them. They are not concerned with the effects on employees and their families. These are the same Union Leaders who followed instructions from the United States to amalgamate the Congress of Canadian Labour with the Trades and Labour Congress into one labour congress which would force its will upon all of Canada. The situation at Murdochville is an example of this policy and its attempted enforcement by violence and lawlessness. [120]

The least one can say is that it was not patriotism that motivated Noranda Mines' opposition to the Steelworkers, but anti-unionism pure and simple. Yet nationalism was a convenient weapon in its hands (and in that of Negro King regimes such as Duplessis') in their struggle against workers. The socialist suspicion of bourgeois forms of nationalism is not without foundation.

Turning to the smaller bourgeoisie and traditional petty bourgeoisie in the period 1955-65, one finds a certain diversity in the views of nationalism held by small businessmen, farmers and self-employed professionals. While there was no organization grouping small businessmen in the way the Canadian Manufacturers Association grouped the largest Canadian-controlled and American-controlled firms, there are occasional indications of small business sentiment.

Thus a Vancouver exporter, William Comer, is quoted as being "damned aggravated" by the refusal of Alcan and other producers to sell $1 million of aluminum to China in 1959. [121]

The General Manager of the Graphics Arts Industries Association, David McLellan, in reacting to the O'Leary Commission of 1961, argued the case for original Canadian writing and thinking:

> Let us have more and better Canadian publications. Let us also buy them, subscribe to them, and advertise in them . . . We cannot merely allow ourselves to be brainwashed by the outpourings of other people. [122]

The President of the Investment Dealers Association of Canada, D.S. Beatty, (much like the President of the Canadian Construction Association whom we quoted from in the previous chapter), criticized the use by American subsidiaries of insurance, advertising, etc. from outside the country, in a 1962 speech. [123]

More interestingly an attempt was made in the summer of 1962 by Edward Speers, a scientist and president of a small firm, Nuclear Enterprises Ltd., to found an Organization of Canadian Manufacturers as a counterweight to the Canadian Manufacturers Association and the Canadian Chamber of Commerce. [124] This new organization would be limited to companies 100 per cent Canadian-owned and managed, in contradistinction to groups like the CMA. (Parenthetically, one might point to the numerous pictures in publications of the CMA showing American branch-plant presidents interacting with politicians and representatives of Canadian-owned capital.) [125] Though this new organization denied that it was anti-American, one of its main purposes was to analyze whether Canadian policies were designed to help or hinder the growth of Canadian-owned firms. The organization proved still-born, but was in a way the forerunner to the more successful Canadian Federation of Independent Business organized in the 1970s, and to which we will be making reference in the next chapter.

On the other side of the fence were the views of one of the most successful small businessmen in the country, hardware salesman turned Premier, W.A.C. Bennett:

> "Texas is a small place compared with British Columbia . . . and no place in the free world is expanding like our province." . . . Bennett again defended the investment of American funds in B.C. industry and declared, "If our exports to the United States were stopped for one month there would be unemployed walking the street."[126]

Another example from a small-town western newspaper similarly reflects the views of small businessmen as well as certain farmers. The occasion was the Pipeline Debate of 1956 and the Vernon *News* observed:

> The Conservatives know as well as anybody that if the flow of United States capital to their country were turned off suddenly, our vaunted prosperity would vanish overnight.

> Hating the United States is a luxury far too rich for the Canadian diet.[127]

And from the other end of the country, H.J. Flemming, former Premier of New Brunswick and Minister in the Diefenbaker government, noted in the debate on Walter Gordon's 1963 budget that all his life he had been associated with businesses financed by American capital, when Canadian money had not been forthcoming.

> Do you wonder, Mr. Speaker, that I cannot get very excited or exercized unduly when I hear about our friends in the United States buying Canadian businesses . . . The business employs Canadians. The business pays them well. The business operation is subject to Canadian laws.[128]

By and large, then, small business was scarcely more nationalistic than big in the period under consideration.

Farmers were a declining but still important force in the Canada of the late 1950s and early 1960s (cf. Table 2.11). Indeed, they provided a good deal of support for Diefenbaker and the Conservatives in their victories of 1957 and 1958. It is therefore interesting to observe a strain of nationalism in some of the farm journals, coupled with inconsistencies which recall the contradictions of *The Financial Post*.

During the Pipeline Debate, for example, *The Farmer's Advocate* strongly supported the proposition that any gas pipeline linking Alberta with the east be Canadian-controlled, whether privately or publicly owned:

> Canadians would feel much happier about the transcontinental natural gas pipeline from Alberta to Central Canada if control and operation were retained, like the line itself, wholly within this country. There is growing realization that the United States investments, while needed and welcome for development purposes, are nevertheless depriving Canadians of the jurisdiction they should excercize over the affairs of this nation.[129]

Yet a year later, in rebutting the proposals for nationalization of the CPR that had been passed by the Inter-Provincial Farm Union Council, *The Farmer's Advocate* took a diametrically different position on the question of foreign ownership:

> Any policy or programme that can be interpreted as a challenge to free enterprise will seriously block the flow of investment capital into the development of the nation's resources and do Canada irreparable harm.[130]

In 1960, however, as Coyne began his speeches on the theme of Canadian self-sufficiency, he found a ready echo in the pages of *The Farmer's Advocate*:

> Farm folk have always been thrifty and independent. They owe it to the nation to add their voice to the protest against

overexpansion and overdependence on foreign capital.[131]

The Western-based *Country Guide* also gave limited support to Coyne's drive, suggesting greater Canadian capital self-sufficiency might reduce the extent of imports and conversely increase Canada's ability to compete in export markets.[132]

It is significant, however, that the position of farmers as reflected in these papers was more reactive than active. The major positions were taken by people like George Drew or James Coyne, and there is no evidence of a specifically farmer-based nationalism, let alone of an ideologically original formulation. The agricultural, and more especially wheat, economy which had given rise to the Farmer-Labour Coalition, Progressives, the CCF and Social Credit[133] was dead and gone, and in the advanced capitalist economy of the 1960s other social forces would influence the politics of the country.

Where self-employed professionals are concerned, anti-nationalism seemed to dominate. Richard Rohmer, Q.C., future author of second-rate nationalist thrillers like *Exxoneration* and *Ultimatum* had the following comments about NDP proposals coming out of the founding convention in 1961:

> The scheme of taxation and nationalization proposed by the New Party would put an immediate and permanent stop to the investment of foreign capital in Canada. It would direct investment capital of Canadians to other countries.[134]

The President of the Canadian Institute of Chartered Accountants, a bastion of self-employed professionals, advised his colleagues in 1961 to help foreign businesses in Canada get started on the right foot, by informing them of legitimate methods of reducing their heavy tax burdens. Their failure to succeed in Canada would "reflect against our country and slow down the international flow of business."[135]

And a different type of traditional petty bourgeois professional, the clerical, seemed little addicted to nationalism, if an editorial in *The United Church Observer* in early 1963, deriding anti-American policies as made in Moscow, can be taken as representative:

The United States is a good friend with whom we must share the common defence of North America. [136]

To be fair, one might point to a John Diefenbaker or Howard Green, both lawyers, and suggest that their policy on nuclear weapons in the 1962-63 period reflected a traditional petty bourgeois nationalism. [137] To the extent that this may be true, theirs was however a minority class position. Moreover, Diefenbaker's visceral anti-communism substantially limited his ability to pursue independent policies *vis-a-vis* the United States, especially in the defence and foreign policy fields. [138]

The class we referred to in Chapter Two as the new petty bourgeoisie, i.e., salaried professionals such as civil servants, academics, scientists, journalists, and many of the managers, was by and large opposed to nationalism in the 1955-65 period, with some notable exceptions. The take-off of employment in education and the public sector in this decade (cf. Tables 2.13-2.19) seems to have had no immediate effect on attitudes towards nationalism. It would take the serious weakening of the American empire, as the Vietnam war unravelled, to make this new petty bourgeoisie (at least in the state sector) a greater force for nationalism in the late 1960s and early 1970s.

To be sure even between 1955-65 there is evidence of some support for nationalism by members of the new petty bourgeoisie. Thus during the controversy about Canadian equity and managerial participation in American subsidiaries there were a number of statisticians and journalists who took moderately nationalist positions.

The two DBS statisticians responsible for analyzing investment flows into Canada pinpointed the scale of American investment in a paper in 1956. This was no mere throw-back to an earlier era of Canadian growth, Blyth and Carty suggest, but rather represented a potentially permanent equity stake in the growth sectors of the Canadian economy. [139] Moreover U.S. investment was concentrated in larger firms which were more productive and capital intensive than Canadian firms in the same sectors. [140] Without disputing the benefits to Canada's industrial development derived from U.S. investment, the two statisticians concluded:

The fact that over one-half of the corporate income of the larger companies in Canadian industry is already under non-resident control gives us a rough gauge of the possible strength of the factors which are likely to be at work in maintaining and perpetuating the non-resident ownership and control of Canadian industry . . . We leave it to an articulate audience like this to estimate the cost in economic, social, and political terms. [141]

The veteran Montreal journalist, G.V. Ferguson, spoke to the Canadian Political Science Association in 1956:

For the first time in Canada's history, we are faced with the full, naked force of American influence without the modifying influence of any counter-pressure. [142]

He pointed to the pressures for a continental energy policy emanating from the prairie oil lobby and from the supporters of the Columbia treaty, side by side with various aspects of joint defence, as an indication of the real decline of Canadian sovereignty. [143] And he went on to predict that "Canadian national sentiment and commonly held nationalist ambitions" were at odds with inexorably growing continental pressures. The stage was set for a first class domestic political conflict, "for Canadian nationalism, in its more extreme forms, will not go down without fighting." [144] This prophecy was to begin to be fulfilled—a decade and a half later.

Another journalist of nationalist persuasion was Michael Barkway, long-time Ottawa correspondent for *The Financial Post* and later publisher of *The Financial Times*. A 1960 piece epitomizes his criticisms:

It was no accident that the most rapid and widespread growth of American control over the Canadian economy, which took place during the 1950s, coincided with a period of boastful and arrogant self-assertiveness which was fundamentally alien to the Canadian character. In our illusions of grandeur we imagined ourselves marching down the path of history in American footsteps. . . . The Canadian problem is not to find ways of asserting independence: it is to find the will. [145]

In 1960, the CBC's Washington correspondent, James M. Minifie, entered the lists with his book *Peacemaker or Powder-Monkey*, arguing the case for Canadian neutralism in the Cold War. [146] The book got a friendly reception from James B. McGeachy, [147] whose weekly pieces in *The Financial Post* were among the few journalistic criticisms of the prevailing pro-Americanism in Canadian policy. Thus in a 1962 piece, McGeachy strongly attacked John Holmes' criticism of the "Europe Firsters" (i.e., de Gaulle) for resenting American leadership, noting that any deviation from a two-power world was regarded as abnormal. [148]

Commenting on a U.S.-Canadian conference that same year attended by the likes of A.R.M. Lower, Harry Johnson, and John Holmes, McGeachy observed:

> I can only say from long experience of such affairs . . . that the Canadians are always scrupulously careful to say that the Americans are the best neighbour any country could have, that their foreign policy is wise and that of course Canada accepts their leadership. [149]

By 1965 he was openly praising de Gaulle's refusal of a two-camp world arguing:

> De Gaulle's policies are made in Paris; can we say ours are made in Ottawa? [150]

And in October of that year he had only praise for the Vietnam Teach-In held at the University of Toronto which had expressed scepticism of the U.S. role in that country and American claims to be defending the Western world against calamity. [151]

There are a number of other examples of petty bourgeois nationalism one can cite in the early 1960s. A research physicist, Roger Hutchins, argued Canada could never develop its own national character or identity if it simply copied the United States. Echoing the case that had been made by J.W.T. Spinks in his study for the Massey Commission, [152] Hutchins argued that American branch-plants entailed research and development outside the country and the emigration of skilled Canadians. Yet his specific recommendations—education of U.S. corporate leaders to Canada's special requirements, a buy-Canadian policy by American branch-plants, and tax concessions to write off research costs—might have been the program of the Canadian big bourgeoisie. In particular, Hutchins aped the CMA and other such bodies with his denunciation of overdependence on government as a solution to the foreign investment problem, arguing that this would destroy the qualities that had built Canada.[153]

A 1961 editorial in the Toronto-based publication, *Canadian Chemical Processing*, destined for executives and managers in the chemical industry, was entitled "Subsidiaries: autonomy is not enough."[154] All it did, however, was to quote R.M. Fowler, President of the Canadian Pulp and Paper Association and Co-Chairman of the Canadian-American Committee, on the need for American companies in Canada to go to some lengths to discover and identify with the broad objectives of Canadian policy. The alignment of managerial with corporate views is fairly evident.

The civil service was characterized by at best a very limited nationalism in the early 1960s. The Deputy Minister of Trade and Commerce echoed the two DBS statisticians when he spoke in 1960 of "alarming proportions of our manufacturing and natural resource industries" owned and controlled from abroad.[155] The federal superintendant of insurance noted matter of factly in 1962:

> It is doubtful whether there is any major country in the world, other than Canada, where such a large proportion of the fire and casualty business is transacted by companies from alien countries.[156]

As for academics, students and writers, there was relatively little nationalism before 1965. Kenneth McNaught might continue to address the theme of an independent Canadian foreign policy in his contribution to the new manifesto of social democracy, *Social Purpose for Canada*,[157] but there was as yet little echo in the universities. Hugh MacLennan could restate his concern for the survival of Canadian culture and media of

communications while suggesting "that we accept the fact that
the American economic tide is probably here to stay."[158] And
George Grant could pen his pessimistic tract of 1965 on Canada's
long-term survivability, combining prescient analysis of branch-
plant Canadian society with hopeless nostalgia for a conservative
past never to be again.[159]

On the left, the first currents of opposition to American
imperialism were stirring in the protests of the Voice of
Women,[160] in the nascent student movement (the Student Union
for Peace Action, the 1965 Toronto Teach-In on Vietnam), or in
the pages of a magazine like *Canadian Dimension*. Interestingly,
this new left-wing and petty bourgeois English Canadian
nationalism could adopt a sympathetic attitude to the nationalist
aspirations of the Quebec petty bourgeoisie, which were a mirror
image of its own:

> We know that French Canada is a nation, and that English
> Canada *can* be a nation if it overcomes its own internal
> regional and ethnic fragmentation. . . . A loosening of the
> French-English tie may be the prerequisite for a strengthen-
> ing of the intra-English ties.[161]

Turning to the other side of the equation, Gad Horowitz argued
the need to oppose the Americanization of Canada, without
chauvinism, but without "a fake, self-effacing, embarrased
cosmopolitanism":

> [W]e want Canada to be something other than a collection of
> disintegrated particularisms sinking into the American
> Mind.[162]

Overwhelmingly, however, the ideology of the new petty
bourgeoisie in the 1955-65 period was anti-nationalist. Economists led the parade, followed by civil servants and diplomats,
salaried professionals and other academics. A 1955 article by the
Dean of the School of Business Administration at Western
University in London, Ontario sets the tone for what is to follow:

> The movement of United States capital into Canada is
> making a valuable contribution to the continued growth of

Canadian commerce and industry.[163]

The 1956 Presidential Address of J. Douglas Gibson to the
Canadian Political Science (and Economics) Association bristled
with anti-nationalism:

> Nationalism is rampant throughout the world today and acts
> of stupidity and worse are being committed almost
> continuously in its name. There is a certain amount of latent
> anti-American feeling in Canada, which is quite easily
> aroused, and this feeling combined with the pressures of
> sectional interests and prejudices could lead to actions which
> are not really in our national interests.[164]

The research director for the Gordon Commission of 1955-57,
Douglas LePan, long-time diplomat and future Principal of
University College, Toronto, stated his own philosophy on
Canadian-American relations some years after the tabling of the
Final Report, opposing any limitations on foreign investment in
Canada as "self-defeating" and arguing that nationalism could
impede "the technical and economic causes making for greater
scale production."[165]

Key academicians like Norman A.M. MacKenzie, President of
U.B.C., and W.A. Mackintosh, Vice-Chancellor and Principal of
Queen's University were founding members of the Canadian-
American Committee in 1957 (soon to be joined by Andrew
Stewart, President of the University of Alberta), and as such were
vitally concerned with defusing possible tensions flowing out of
the continental relationship. As MacKenzie observed in a letter
to Robert Fowler in March, 1961:

> . . . I share your feelings and those of Mr. Stuart [American
> Co-Chairman of the Committee and a former American
> ambassador to Canada] about the value and importance of
> continued activities of the Committee. As far as I can judge,
> the matters of greatest public concern in Canada are
> defence and the nature and condition of our economy.[166]

The then Senator MacKenzie observed years later:

The fact is that we are forever tied to the United States by reason of geography, history and circumstances, so let's not whine about but rather make the most and the best of it in intelligent and practical ways.[167]

The same strand of pragmatic continentalism characterized the pronouncements of historicans like A.R.M. Lower or Frank Underhill, the former arguing the case for Canada's acceptance of nuclear weapons in the earlier 1960s,[168] the latter arguing the virtues of American leadership in the Cold War:

> . . . this (North Atlantic) enterprise—alliance or community—can be carried out only under the leadership of the United States; . . . it behooves the rest of us, therefore, to avoid the temptation to indulge in continuous bellyaching about American leadership . . .[169]

Underhill was also one of a number of English Canadian academics to criticize the new Quebec nationalism of the early 1960s, declaring that the Lesage government was ignoring federal spheres of jurisdiction under the BNA Act and leading to the fragmentation of the country.[170]

More menacing was the tone of W.L. Morton, the Tory historian, himself a nationalist of sorts where Canada as a whole was concerned:[171]

> I deny that any province has the right to secede. I think that any such attempt should be resisted by every means, including force if necessary . . .[172]

More sophisticated, but no less anti-nationalist, were the views of Ramsay Cook, that future champion of Pierre Elliott Trudeau in English Canada:

> Today, French and English Canadians are moving towards an impasse because each is swayed by outdated concepts of nationalism, Canadian and French-Canadian . . . nationalism is an emotion which hides real problems behind an abstraction.[173]

Or, as the *Preliminary Report* of the Royal Commission on Bilingualism and Biculturalism[174] put it officiously in 1965:

> ... English Canadians as a whole must come to recognize the existence of a vigorous French-speaking society within Canada ... They must come to understand what it means to be a member of a minority.
>
> On the same evidence, it seems to us that French-speaking Canadians ... would need to beware of the kind of thinking that puts "la nation" above all considerations and values ... They, as well as the English-speaking, must remember that, if a partnership works, each party must give as well as get.[175]

To return to English Canadian attitudes towards the United States, the position of civil servants was generally favourable to American investment, though occasionally stressing the desirability of Canadian equity and managerial participation.[176]

On the larger subject of Canadian-American relations the basically continentalist position of senior civil servants in Ottawa is well reflected in the views of a man like A.D.P. Heeney, two-time Canadian ambassador to the United States and co-author of the 1965 report, *Canada and the United States: Principles for Partnership*.

> I regarded the Canada-United States alliance as our most precious international asset, the loss or erosion of which would be tragic for Canada,[177]

Heeney wrote of an awkward moment in Canadian-American relations during the Diefenbaker years.

> I asked (Howard) Green whether it would not be politically possible to launch a spirited political defence of United States policies, at least in terms of general objectives.[178]

One begins to wonder whose country Heeney was representing. With respect to the 1965 report which sparked a fair amount of

controversy in both Canada and the United States for its implicit
suggestion that Canadian public criticism of the United States be
muzzled, Heeney unrepentedly argued:

> I continue to believe that it is possible to reconcile a
> Canadian position of influence and authority in Washington
> well beyond that of Canada's deployable resources with a
> consistent and self-respecting nationalism . . . I believe we
> have no self-respecting option but to seek the expression of
> our Canadianism in the kind of limited partnership which
> Merchant and I describe in our report.[179]

The prevailing "internationalist" mentality in the federal civil
service is further reflected in the views of men like A.F.W.
Plumptre, long-time official in the Department of Finance, and
subsequently Principal of Scarborough College, Toronto:

> We live in a world that is increasingly complex and
> interrelated. It is not clear that national self-preservation is
> best attained by a process of attempted withdrawal and
> isolation.[180]

As the author of a study on the top decision-makers in Finance
and the Bank of Canada, from which this quotation is taken,
observed:

> Senior members of the Canadian public service financial
> elite do not consider themselves to be "pro-Canada" in any
> nationalistic sense and they were not of sympathy with the
> economic nationalism espoused by Walter Gordon.[181]

It is the academic economists, however, who provided the most
vivid evidence of endemic anti-nationalism in the early 1960s.
One important example was the campaign launched by H.
Scott Gordon, then of Carleton, and fellow members of the
economic guild against James Coyne in 1960, culminating in their
demand that the Governor of the Bank of Canada be removed
from office:[182]

> . . . *ownership* and *operation* are two different things. The

important thing, from the economic standpoint, is not who owns an industry but what policies it follows in its actual operation. . . . The emphasis in the speeches of Mr. Coyne, and of others, on the question of foreign ownership has drawn attention away from . . . important issues. Mr. Coyne speaks on this question in emotion-charged terms and in the process has given voice to one of the least rational elements in Canadian politics at the present time.[183]

Another example were the arguments of men like Harry Johnson, rejecting "the small-town pettiness" implicit in Canadian nationalism and its diverting the country "into a narrow and garbage-cluttered *cul-de-sac*."[184]

Still other examples were the pro-free trade/pro-free capital movement position of economists like Arthur J.R. Smith (future Chairman of The Economic Council of Canada) in his background studies for The Canadian-American Committee,[185] on whose staff he served from 1957 through to the middle 1960s. Or the generally pro-continentalist position of A.E. Safarian and the Wonnacott brothers in their respective studies of *The Performance of Foreign-Owned Firms in Canada* and of *United States-Canada Free Trade: The Potential Impact on the Canadian Economy* for the same Canadian-American Committee.[186] It is unfashionable, after all, to bite the hand that feeds you.

Even Melville Watkins, future Chairman of The Task Force on the Structure of Canadian Industry and *guru* of the Waffle movement had some fairly anti-nationalist things to say as late as 1966 in a review article entitled "Economic Nationalism":

The major burden of economic nationalism is perhaps not the extent to which it lowers the standard of living—real though that is—but the extent to which, by monopolizing politics, it narrows vision and lowers the quality of national life.[187]

The moral of the story is clear. The new petty bourgeoisie of English Canada—from government through the universities—largely rejected nationalism in the 1955-65 period, both for themselves and for Quebec.

Turning to the organized working class, we find only limited support for nationalism by the newly-formed Canadian Labour

Congress (CLC) after 1956, coupled with a strong affirmation of internationalism, especially international unionism. As Table 2.24 shows, the overwhelming majority of Congress members were in so-called international unions during the period, with inevitable consequences for policy. It is also highly significant that key CLC officials like George Burt (UAW), Claude Jodoin (CLC President), Donald Macdonald (CLC Secretary-Treasurer and later President), William Mahoney (Steelworkers) and Joe Morris (IWA and later CLC President) became members of the Canadian-American Committee (cf. Appendix 1), as though to underline their continentalist convictions. Still, on certain issues, the Congress did not hesitate to take positions critical of the United States.

In a joint brief by the old TLC and CCL to the Gordon Commission just prior to their merger into the CLC, "preservation of a free, independent Canadian nation, even at some economic cost" was placed as a high priority, second only to the maintenance of a high standard of living.[188]

> We are not isolationist . . . We are not anti-American, we recognize and accept the uniquely intimate relationship of the Canadian and American economies, and the best proof that we do is that most of our members belong to international unions. But we also believe that within the limits set by the nature of the world we live in, Canada—its Government, its industry and its unions—should control its own destiny . . .[189]

The two Congresses urged the fullest possible processing of raw materials in Canada, and strongly supported public ownership of the Trans-Canada Pipeline as the only alternative to "a gigantic giveaway of a priceless and irreplaceable natural resource" and to what would otherwise be "a deadly threat to the future economic development of Canada."[190]

They pointed to certain dangers in American control of the economy, including patent restrictions, automation affecting Canadian jobs first, and the absence of financial statements by wholly owned subsidiaries.[191] But they vehemently denied any American control over Canadian unions, arguing:

1) American unions cannot order Canadian workers out on strike to serve American ends.
2) American unions were not pushing members to demand guaranteed annual wages.
3) American unions were not hampering Canadian development by demanding American wages for their members in Canadian plants.
4) American unions were not taking large sums out of the country. Indeed, they were probably making larger payments for strike relief in Canada than what dues flowed to the United States. [192]

In July 1956, an editorial in *Canadian Labour*, the CLC's monthly publication, returned to the subject of U.S. investment in Canada, citing new DBS figures showing significant American stakes in manufacturing and mining. While reiterating the benefits American capital had brought to Canada ("Nobody except the Communists is really opposed to American investment"), the editorial went on to make a number of recommendations to remedy the situation: It spoke of pressing American firms to give top managerial jobs to Canadians, of expanding scientific training in Canadian universities, compelling publication of financial records, revising patent laws, and encouraging Canadian investment. And in a more radical vein, not to be repeated:

> If necessary, we can nationalize the industries, and operate them in the interests of the people of Canada rather than for the profit of American investors. [193]

In a September 1956 speech to the AFL-CIO in San Francisco, however, Claude Jodoin revealed the other face of CLC bravado:

> Co-operation between the AFL-CIO is natural, because both are national, autonomous labour centres and will never be satisfied until free trade unions are established all over the world. Co-operation between the two centres is an example, in my opinion, for all free trade unions in the world, too. The co-operation between our two countries on this North

American continent is also an example to the world.[194]

Figures on CLC finances in this period further underline the contradictions:

TABLE 4.1

Contributions to the Canadian Labour Congress 1957

International unions	$ 673,444
National unions	103,243
Locally chartered unions	334.877
Total	$1,111,564

Source: *Canadian Labour*, May, 1958, Appendices.

It was infinitely easier to attack American capital than American labour domination.

That there were political side effects to international unionism is obvious, even from scanning the pages of *Canadian Labour*. The February 1959 issue describes a visit by Richard Wigglesworth, U.S. Ambassador to Ottawa, accompanied by his labour attache, to CLC Headquarters. Among the items discussed were Canadian participation in the International Conference of Free Trade Unions, the International Labour Organization, etc.[195] At the CLC Congress in Montreal in April 1960, delegates sang O Canada!, God Save the Queen!, and The Star-Spangled Banner![196] A picture in *Canadian Labour* in April 1961, shows a beaming Claude Jodoin and other CLC officials escorting Livingston Merchant, U.S. Ambassador to Canada, and his labour attache around CLC headquarters.[197] One sees no evidence of CLC brass fraternizing with the ambassadors of other countries, or of delegates to CLC conventions singing the *International*, a far more working class and internationalist song than *The Star Spangled Banner*.

To be sure, Canadian labour did not simply follow American labour down the line. The CLC showed a greater openness on foreign policy questions such as recognition of China or maintenance of relations with Cuba. Unlike the AFL-CIO, the CLC became involved in direct political action, with the formation of the New Democratic Party in 1961. Unions affiliated to or outside the AFL-CIO in the U.S. were not automatically in the same position *vis-a-vis* the CLC (e.g., the SIU, the UAW).

Yet to speak of a trade union-based nationalism when CLC leaders vigorously defended so-called international unionism would be absurd.

> The outlook of the Canadian labour movement has never been a narrowly nationalistic one. [198]

> We have taken the position of defending and promoting international unionism because we believe it is a correct position in a continent with the complementary economies and institutions found in North America. [199]

A phoney version of "international unionism" was not the only feature of the CLC leadership's pro-American stance. There was no support for neutralism in Canadian foreign and defence policy:

> The Congress does not believe that Canada can make a contribution by unilateral disarmament or by pursuing a policy of armed or disarmed neutrality. [200]

> Canada cannot afford the luxury of neutrality or neutralism. Heavy cost (and Canada's) geographical position (rules it out) . . . Canada's policy must be advanced in the councils of her friends and allies. Otherwise she would lose the opportunity to pursue a policy of peace and disarmament. [201]

But there was support for Canadian membership in the Organization of American States, with the specious argument that CLC experience with the (CIA-financed)[202] Regional Organization of the Americas of the International Confederation of Free Trade Unions had been positive.[203]

On other issues in the early 1960s, the CLC did take mildly nationalist positions. For example, in its brief to The Royal Commission on Publications (the O'Leary Commission), it called for protection for Canadian periodicals.[204]

It opposed the placing of nuclear weapons on Canadian soil, [205] and expressed cautious reservations about the Columbia River Treaty and Protocol of 1964:

> (There is) uncertainty about the outcome of these

negotiations. Does Canada retain the right to control, including diversion? No. The United States may have gained immeasurably at Canada's expense, with the potential loss of jobs (to come).[206]

Finally, while suggesting there were many sensible things in the Merchant-Heeney Report of 1965, the CLC argued:

> To make a vow of public silence on (critical) issues would suggest that Canada was an uncritical satellite of the United States.[207]

Overall, however, the record of the CLC in this period was scarcely more favourable to nationalism than that of the big or petty bourgeoisie. (The NDP, with which the CLC was aligned, did however pass a number of resolutions opposing increased foreign ownership of the Canadian economy and the American role in Vietnam at its 1965 Convention.[208] Potentially, then, nationalism had some appeal to trade union cadres and middle class professionals, the two main groups in the NDP, though an unequal appeal, as subsequent developments were to show.)

To close this discussion of English Canadian nationalism in the decade 1955-65, let us make reference to global public opinion on two crucial questions.

Where Canadian-American relations were concerned, public opinion polls show majority support for U.S. investment in Canada through the decade, though some decline from a highpoint of 68 per cent approval in 1956 to 55 per cent in 1963.[209] On a regional basis, 70 per cent of respondents in the Maritimes favoured U.S. investment in Canada in 1957, 64 per cent in Ontario, 59 per cent on the Prairies and 73 per cent in British Columbia. In 1963, 59 per cent of respondents in Ontario held that U.S.-financial development had been good for Canada, while 54 per cent concurred in the four western provinces.[210]

Paradoxically, that same year a majority of respondents in Ontario and Western Canada held that Canada's dependence on the United States was not a good thing, indicating that a limited form of nationalism *vis-a-vis* the United States did enjoy support in much of English Canada:

TABLE 4.2

Do You Think Dependence on the United States is a Good Thing for Canada or Not a Good Thing?

	A Good Thing	Not a Good Thing	Qualified	Can't Say
National	48	44	2	6
Maritimes	57	34	1	8
Quebec	65	27	1	7
Ontario	42	50	3	5
West	39	53	3	5

Source: Canadian Institute of Public Opinion, July 6, 1963.

Yet the next year a *Maclean*'s survey found fully 65 per cent of respondents in a Canada-wide survey favouring economic union with the United States with the following regional breakdown:

TABLE 4.3

Regional Support for Economic Union with the United States (percentage favouring economic union)

Canada as a whole	65
Maritimes	75
Quebec	78
Ontario	57
Western Provinces	57

Source: *Maclean's*, June 6, 1964, "The U.S. and Us," pp. 14-15.

Where politics was concerned, a not insignificant 29 per cent of all respondents favoured political union with the United States:

TABLE 4.4

Regional Support for Political Union with the United States (percentage favouring political union)

Canada as a whole	29
Maritimes	39
Quebec	33
Ontario	24
Western provinces	29

Source: *Maclean's*, June 6, 1964, "The U.S. and Us," p. 12.

To be sure, an even larger 62 per cent opposed political union, and as the survey suggested:

> The small towns of Ontario whose citizens are of predominantly British stock and have incomes of under nine thousand dollars a year provide the stoutest opposition to American annexation.[211]

Yet the substance of any Canadian nationalism was open to question.

The same *Maclean*'s survey found that only 9 per cent of Canadians believed that Americans had a markedly different way of life, while 53 per cent of Canadians (and a still larger, though unspecified, percentage of English Canadians) supported military arrangements with the United States involving the stationing of American weapons on Canadian soil.[212]

No wonder a journalist like James B. McGeachie could lament:

> It is distressing to me that some of us think the country's history up to now was all a mistake and are prepared to become Americans from sheer inertia.[213]

The legacy of two decades of Cold War and continental alliance was coming home to roost.

Where French Canada was concerned, almost all English Canadians appearing before The Royal Commission on Bilingualism and Biculturalism articulated the concept of nation in pan-Canadian terms:

> When English-speaking Canadians talked of "the nation" they usually meant all the people living in Canada.[214]

Though a minority might support the principles of bilingualism and biculturalism, all tended to reject anything that smacked of special status for Quebec:

> If Quebec thinks for one moment that we—the rest of Canada, possibly 12 or 13 million—are going to let the Province of Quebec set up a state within a state, take away a third of our population and a quarter of our national wealth,

they've got another think coming to them. [215]

I represent an organization that states quite bluntly and simply that any more concessions other than (those) in the law today . . . given to French Canada, and we . . . will have no alternative than to organize the working people . . . to take us into the country to the south. [216]

For myself, I think I am a moderate man on most civic and national issues, but on the issue of national unity I am not moderate at all. For me the preservation and strengthening of a national unity must come first if Canada as a nation, and a bicultural nation, must endure and grow. [217]

The concept of a specifically English Canada lay dormant, while confrontation with Quebec nationalism loomed as a real possibility in the years ahead. The last cannon shot of a Canadian nationalism might be aimed, not against the United States, but against Quebec.

THEORETICAL CONCLUSIONS

Much as in the 1945-55 period, American imperialism continued to be the dominant influence on the Canadian political economy between 1955-65. Though American hegemony was beginning to be challenged both within the Western alliance and without, all Canadian classes continued to identify with American leadership in the political, economic and cultural fields.

Yet this identification was not total, and there are interesting examples of opposition by members of the big bourgeoisie and other classes to American domination.

Where the big bourgeoisie is concerned, its class interests dictated some measure of autonomy from the American bourgeoisie, *if only to justify its privileged position in the expropriation of surplus value from the wage earners of the country*. Calls for participation in the equity and ownership of American firms in Canada reflected this concern, coupled with less frequent criticism of the scope and scale of American capital inflow. Nonetheless, the mainstream of the Canadian big bourgeoisie had made its peace with imperialism, provided it retained significant economic and political power alongside American capital in this country.

The smaller and traditional petty bourgeoisie, while occasionally disturbed by aspects of American domination, were no more prepared in this decade to oppose American imperialism or its allies in the Canadian big bourgeoisie. Ideologically committed to "free enterprise" despite latent anti-monopoly sentiment, neither small businessmen nor self-employed farmers and professionals had a sufficiently cohesive sense of class interest to oppose the neo-colonial conception of nation articulated by the big bourgeoisie.

The English Canadian new petty bourgeoisie, unlike its counterparts among the petty bourgeoisie in Quebec, did not yet see nationalism as in its class interests. There were not the same ethnic factors to turn it against the Canadian big bourgeoisie or its American allies, while its ideologues came directly under the influence of their American counterparts. Two decades of continentalism had so weakened the Canadian state that its civil servants had real difficulty in distinguishing Canadian from American interests. The take-off of the state and para-state sector may have begun by the early 1960s; the implications for petty bourgeois nationalism were only to hit fully home from the late 1960s on, with the American empire in increasing difficulty.

The trade union movement continued to be dominated by international unions, usually based in precisely those sectors of the economy where American capital dominated. There was no more fundamental criticism of American imperialism than there had been a decade earlier, though here and there the policies of the CLC might differ from those of the AFL-CIO. What is crucial is that the trade union movement and the working class as a whole still lacked any consciousness of itself as a class-for-itself, as a class holding a socialist counter-vision of both society and the nation. A class conscious working class could not but have challenged the alliance between the Canadian and American bourgeoisies, even while opposing capitalism itself. Or put another way, anti-capitalism in Canada could not be separated from anti-imperialism. In this period one saw precious little of either in the ranks of the working class.

Chapter Five
THE ERUPTION OF NATIONALISM
1965-75

A minor power militarily, an appendage of the United States economically and of limited interest culturally, [Canada] was one nation that seemed destined to live out its days in boring tranquility. [1]

The decade 1965-75 was to witness a spectacular take-off of nationalist sentiment in English Canada. This nationalism would embrace economic, political and cultural questions, and would have as its primary objective the loosening of American domination over Canada. Secondarily, it would aim at some type of *modus vivendi* with Quebec, preferably through a refurbished Confederation, though not necessarily nor at any cost.

What is crucial to any understanding of the politics of this decade is the weakening of the American position internationally. 1965 began with the United States escalating its commitment in Vietnam; 1975 heralded the final defeat of American imperialism and its client regimes in Indo-China. In 1965 the American economy still accounted for approximately 50 per cent of all goods and services produced in the non-communist industrialized countries (cf. Table 2.4), while the United States dollar was the reserve currency of the West. A decade later the American position had slipped to 40 per cent or less of the goods and services produced in capitalist countries (cf. Table 2.6), and the U.S. dollar had been devalued and dislodged from its hegemonial position. In the late 1960s American-based multinational corporations were the new Leviathans threatening to sweep the nation state before them;[2] by the mid-1970s, the energy crisis symbolized a remarkable reversal of relations between resource-exporting countries and industrialized powers and a new nationalism that threatened the very foundations of American economic imperialism.[3] The shifting political balance was further reflected in the emergence of China into the ranks of the great powers following its twenty-year American imposed isolation, the stand-off between the United States and the Soviet Union in the Cold War evidenced by the policy of detente, and the passing of control of the General Assembly of the United Nations from the western countries led by the United States, to a third world bloc.

Internal politics in the United States were a mirror image of this external decline. The Vietnam War spelled an end to the consensus which underlay American foreign policy in the Cold War years. Massive student opposition at home coupled with military reversals abroad sparked the disillusionment of broad sections of public opinion and of Congress with the war, leading to the forced withdrawal of one President (Johnson) and a severe weakening of the ability of others to conduct foreign policy with impunity.[4] The 10 per cent surcharge on imports into the United States announced by Nixon in August 1971 coupled with the abandonment of the gold standard marked an attempt by the United States to pass the costs of the war—inflation, balance of payments deficits, declining productivity (cf. Tables 2.5-6 and the paragraph following)—onto allied states, a complete reversal of policy from the years of the Marshall Plan, i.e., the late 1940s and early 1950s. Watergate, meanwhile, took on dimensions far beyond a political scandal, pointing to a crisis of legitimacy which decades of imperialism abroad had wrought in the institutions of the republic. The decline and fall of the American empire (accelerated by subsequent revelations about the role of the Central Intelligence Agency) had begun.

THE NEW NATIONALISM

In English Canada, changes in public opinion and governmental policy were slow and gradual, yet unmistakably in a nationalist direction. Where economic nationalism was concerned, the evolution was from the rejection of Walter Gordon's position at the Liberal Policy Convention in the autumn of 1965[5] to the tabling of the Watkins Report in early 1968[6]; from government intervention to head off the sale of Denison Mines to foreign interests in 1970[7] to the establishment of the Canadian Development Corporation in 1971.[8] The following year the Report on Foreign Direct Investment (the Gray Report) was tabled, while 1973 saw the passage of Bill C-132, the Foreign Investment Review Act, by a parliament in which the Liberals depended on NDP support. Under the terms of this bill, the proposed takeover by or establishment of foreign-controlled businesses in Canada could be refused by a Foreign Investment Review Agency, "if it did not provide significant benefit to Canada."[9]

The debate on foreign ownership embraced the major political parties in Canada, and had seen the emergence of two nationalist movements, the Waffle within the NDP, and the Committee for an Independent Canada, grouping well-known personalities of diverse political allegiance. As Pierre Elliott Trudeau, no great admirer of nationalism himself, recognized by the end of 1970:

> I think the times have changed a bit and that in four years Canadians have become a lot more nationalist economically than they were before. [10]

Public opinion polls reflected this change. In 1967, a clear majority of Canadians, with Ontario in the lead felt that American investment had been beneficial to the country (Table 5.1).

Seven years later, a large majority had come to favour restrictions on foreign investment (Table 5.2).

That same year a cross-Canada sample of 5,000 showed the following breakdown regarding proposed options for Canada in industrial strategy (Table 5.3).

At the provincial level as well, several governments, e.g., Ontario and Prince Edward Island, had taken action to deal with

TABLE 5.1

Do You Think U.S. Financing of Canadian Development Has Been a Good Thing for Canada or Not? (Percentages)

	Total East (Including Quebec)	Ontario	West	Total Canada
Good thing	54	63	54	57
Not good thing	29	23	33	28
Qualified	2	4	4	3
No opinion	15	10	9	12

Source: Canadian Institute of Public Opinion, July 15, 1967.

TABLE 5.2

Would you Favour or Oppose Legislation Which Would Significantly Restrict and Control Further Foreign Investment in Canada? (Percentages)

	Favour	Oppose	Undecided
Canada as a whole	69	18	13
Atlantic provinces	69	20	11
Quebec	59	21	20
Ontario	72	17	11
Prairies	71	19	10
British Columbia	77	16	7

Source: Canadian Institute of Public Opinion, March 2, 1974.

foreign ownership of land, though there was significant resistance to economic nationalism by provincial governments both in the Maritimes and in the West. [11]

The decisive turning point in Canadian-American relations, however, was August 15, 1971, the date Richard Nixon announced a 10 per cent import surcharge as a temporary measure to improve the U.S. balance of payments. True, there had been some cautious moves to greater independence in Canadian policy, e.g., the White Paper on Defence with its emphasis on protecting Canadian sovereignty,[12] or recognition of the People's Republic of China in early 1971; still, it was American action that signalled the end of a thirty year "special relationship."

TABLE 5.3

Options as to the Best Industrial Strategy for Canada by Region

	Total Canada	Maritimes	Quebec	Ontario	Prairies	B.C.
Stay as we are	42.3%	48.9%	44.2%	41.4%	41.2%	36.4%
Closer to the U.S.	18.0	21.3	25.5	13.7	15.9	13.6
Closer to Europe/Asia	29.7	18.9	22.3	33.7	32.2	41.4
No opinion	9.9	10.9	8.1	11.2	10.7	8.6
Total number of respondents	4,980	444	1,411	1,812	799	514

Source: Survey by Elliott Research Corporation, Toronto, cited in J. Alex Murray & Laurence LeDuc, "Public Opinion and Current Foreign Policy Options in Canada," unpublished paper, University of Windsor, 1974 (?), p. 8.

Initial Canadian reaction to the American action had been horror, coupled with pleading for special treatment:

> I hate to think that the United States is now turning its back on a partnership in the development of North America that has served both our societies well for centuries.[13]

It took Nixon, at meetings with Trudeau in December 1971 and again in Ottawa in April 1972 to formalize the American Declaration of Canadian Independence from the Empire:

> It is time for Canadians and Americans to move beyond the sentimental rhetoric of the past. It is time for us to recognize that we have very separate identies; that we have significant differences, and that nobody's interests are furthered when these realities are obscured.[14]

From that point on, one saw some new departures. Mitchell Sharp unveiled his so-called three options for Canadian foreign policy in the autumn of 1972, making clear his preference for the third:

1) Canada can seek to maintain more or less its present relationship with the United States with a minimum of policy adjustments.
2) Canada can move deliberately toward closer integration with the United States.
3) Canada can pursue a comprehensive long-term strategy to develop and strengthen the Canadian economy and other aspects of its national life and in the process to reduce its present vulnerability.[15]

Suddenly, Canadian policy would be concerned with lessening "the impact of the United States."[16]

In the fields of oil and gas exports, environment, and the law of the sea, Canada would begin to show more "clear-eyed appreciation of the nationalist interest," though continuing to regard the United States as "the first among all our partners."[17] If there was a new nationalism in official Canadian policy in the early 1970s, it was because in the eyes of the Canadian establishment the United States itself had become "a good deal more nationalist in the Nixon era."[18]

Cultural policy also saw greater nationalism, e.g., tougher directives by the Canadian Radio and Television Commision regarding Canadian content in broadcasting, and the ending of tax privileges for *Time* magazine. The Ontario government, for its part, appointed a Royal Commision on Book Publishing in December 1970, following the ruckus over the sale of Ryerson Press to McGraw-Hill,[19] and came to the rescue of McClelland and Stewart with a $1,000,000 interest-free loan.

Finally, where Quebec was concerned, English Canada rallied to Trudeau's conception of national unity in 1968 and again during the October Crisis.[20] If only a small minority held Quebec's separation to be likely,[21] a significant minority in the early 1970s supported Quebec's right to peaceful separation, should its people so decide:

Table 5.4

Has Quebec the Right to Quit Canada if a Majority of its People Want to, or Should it be Held in Confederation by Force, if Necessary?
(Percentages)

	Should have right	Should not	Undecided
All of Canada	40%	46%	14%
Maritimes	41	42	17
Quebec	30	50	20
Ontario	41	46	13
The West	49	44	7

Source: Canadian Institute of Public Opinion, April 7, 1971.

What this suggests is that English Canadians were not likely to fight a civil war to keep Quebec inside Confederation against her will. Furthermore, it would appear that English Canada's own sense of identity was by the early 1970s less dependent on the French fact or on the maintenance of a united Canada from sea to sea. What may have been emerging, at last, was a specifically English Canadian nationalism, not simply the pan-Canadian nationalism of yore.

Let us now examine how the different classes in English
Canada responded to the decline in American power, to the lure
of nationalism, and to the new Quebec.

THE BIG BOURGEOISIE

The big bourgeoisie, overall, was hostile to anything that
smacked of nationalism, though for reasons slightly different
from those that may have motivated them between 1945-65. The
important new feature of Canadian capitalism in the period under
consideration was the emergence of a number of Canadian-based
multinational corporations and banks, alongside their American,
European, and Japanese counterparts, onto the centre stage of
the world economy. In Chapter Two, reference was made to
Canadian-based corporations figuring in *Fortune* magazine lists of
the 300 largest industrial corporations and 50 largest banks
outside the United States. Table 5.5 lists these corporations, their
relative rank, and presumed ownership and control.

Inevitably, the corporate view of these organizations would be
opposed to interference with the free movement of capital into or
out of Canada or any other area of investment. "The world is my
oyster" view is clearly reflected in the comments of men like
Robert Bonner, President of MacMillan-Bloedel in the early
1970s. Attacking "the dilettantes who espouse the narrow
nationalisms of the separatists and the neurotic left," he argued
that cutting Canada off from the "free flow of capital" would
guarantee Canada nothing but high unemployment. Rather
Canadian corporations should proceed "to the next logical phase
of their evolution, that is to the multinational stage."[22]

Similarly, the Presidents of the principal Canadian chartered
banks addressing a New York investor conference in March 1971
appealed to U.S. financiers to step up investments in Canada.
The bankers indicated their opposition to any government
restrictions on foreign capital:

> Profits paid to foreigners are a measure of the service
> Canadians have received from foreigners. The greater the
> profits, the greater the services and the Canadian tax
> revenues.

TABLE 5.5

Canadian-based Industrial Corporations and Banks Figuring in *Fortune* Listing of 300 Largest Industrial Corporations and 50 Largest Banks Outside the United States

Name of Corporation	Rank on Fortune list	Majority Ownership
Ford Motor of Canada	35	87.8% U.S.
Imperial Oil	47	69.4% U.S.
Alcan Aluminum	79	44.1% U.S. 10.5% other
Massey-Ferguson	111	Canadian
International Nickel	115	35% U.S. 15% other
Gulf Oil Canada	132	68.3% U.S.
Canada Packers	134	Canadian
MacMillan Bloedel	138	Canadian
Noranda Mines	167	Canadian
Steel Co. of Canada (Stelco)	170	Canadian
Moore Corp.	189	Canadian
Northern Electric	198	Canadian
Domtar	220	Canadian
Seagrams	225	Canadian
Cominco	244	Canadian
Texaco Canada	254	68.2% U.S.
Canadian General Electric	264	91.9% U.S.
Consolidated-Bathurst	268	Canadian
Dominion Foundries and Steel	270	Canadian
Genstar	286	Europe 50% U.S. 10%

Name of Bank	Rank on Fortune list	Majority Ownership
Royal Bank	19	Canadian
Canadian Imperial/Commerce	26	Canadian
Bank of Montreal	28	Canadian
Bank of Nova Scotia	42	Canadian

Sources: *Fortune* Magazine, August 1975, pp. 155-65; *The Financial Post*, July 26, 1975, p. 13.

W. Earle McLaughlin, President of the Royal Bank, went on to oppose the federal legislation limiting foreign participation in Canadian banking to 25 per cent, underlining that Canadian banks operated abroad and preached reciprocity in return. His colleague, G. Arnold Hart, Chairman of the Bank of Montreal, took dead aim at the Canadian Development Corporation for

"scaring the daylights out of the business community in
Canada," while deploring "the narrow attitude" of those who
resented foreign competition.[23]

Successive spokesmen for the Canadian Manufacturers
Association, for their part, defended "the help of foreign capital
in developing both our resources and our industries";[24]
castigated "those who seek to make bad blood or even loosen ties
between Canada and the United States in the name of misguided
and shortsighted nationalism";[25] while defending the multinational corporation as a phenomenon here to stay, adding:

> It isn't all that important that multinational corporations
> control large industrial, commercial and financial holdings in
> Canada. What *is* important is that we constitute in Canada
> strong industrial formations capable of competing not only in
> the local market but also in the world market.[26]

Not surprisingly, then, the Canadian Manufacturers Association and its sister organization, the Canadian Chamber of
Commerce, were in the forefront of opposition to federal
legislation restricting foreign investment. They argued, for
example, that significant detriment rather than significant
benefit be the determining factor in blocking any proposed
transaction (placing the onus on government, rather than the
corporation, to prove its case),[27] and that

> Foreign ownership policy should not militate against an
> adequate supply of investment capital to provide continued
> economic growth and improving standards of living.[28]

As the Gray Report had suggested, organizations like the CMA
spoke in good part for American capital in Canada,[29] or as this
study would argue, for large foreign-controlled *and* Canadian-
controlled corporations, many with multinational aspirations. The
CMA's opposition to economic nationalism was perfectly logical
and can be symbolized in a picture which it proudly published in
a resume of its 100th annual meeting in 1971. The caption read:

> When the President of the United States, Richard M. Nixon,
> came to New York City in December 1970 to speak to the

National Association of Manufacturers, CMA President
A.G.W. Sinclair was seated fifth on the President's right. [30]

Such was the place the Canadian big bourgeoisie, indigenous and
branch-plant, saw itself occupying in the international capitalist
economy.

A minority of large capitalists did, however, support a form of
bourgeois nationalism, and a very few even lent their names to
the Committee for an Independent Canada when the latter was
organized in September 1970. (See Appendix 2 for a list of some
of the members of the original steering committee.) The most
prominent, of course, was Walter Gordon, first Honourary
Chairman of the CIC, who continued to plead the cause of a
Canadian capitalism through the early 1970s. In a January 1971
speech, for example, he outlined the main planks of the CIC as
follows:

1) Policies to increase the proportion of Canadian ownership;
2) A federal agency . . . to supervise the conduct of foreign-
controlled operations;
3) Establishment of the CDC;
4) A well thought-out policy *re* energy sources;
5) Greater allocation of resources to less-developed regions;
6) Autonomy for Canadian trade unions;
7) Protection of Canadian jurisdiction in the Arctic;
8) Reasonable Canadian content and number of nationals in
universities and colleges;
9) A foreign policy to serve Canadian independence.[31]

Though some of these points, e.g., numbers 8 and 9, reflected
the concerns of the new petty bourgeoisie most especially, the
first few points spoke directly to a bourgeois, as well as petty
bourgeois, nationalism. Gordon stressed his own preference for
joint government-private ventures and for a federal review
agency, and had he had a comparative perspective, might well
have invoked such successful ventures as British Petroleum to
buttress his case.

In a 1974 *Financial Post* article he reformulated his concern,
outlining a nine-year program to buy back, in two stages,
foreign-owned firms in the resource sector with assets in excess

of $500 million; and a twelve-year program to buy back
foreign-owned manufacturing corporations with assets exceeding
$250 million.[32] Rejecting "nationalization or any other form of
arbitrary expropriation" as "distasteful in principle to many
Canadians," Gordon stressed his commitment to market
mechanisms and the responsible and practicable character of his
proposal. As a financial journalist, Alexander Ross, had argued
in 1970, Gordon was very much the patrician, preaching to the
Canadian corporate elite. Ross lamented:

> Yet few Canadian businessmen besides him seem to give a
> damn whether or not Canada survives as an independent
> nation.[33]

One that purported to care was William Turner, President of
Power Corporation in the late 1960s. He had little hesitation in
wrapping his conglomerate's ambitions inside the Canadian flag:

> If as a country we do not have more such funds (as Power), it
> seems to me we are going to continue to lose control of more
> and more companies . . . If as part of the national strategy
> they (governments) feel that government-influenced com-
> panies like the CDC would fit in, there's a lot of room for
> them.[34]

A corporate president whose nationalism was equally suspect
was J.H. Moore of Brascan, whose track record in Brazil was
substantially worse than that of most multinationals in Canada.[35]
Yet Moore, as a founding member of the CIC, had no hesitation
in calling for "clearly defined regulations" dealing with
non-resident ownership in Canada, further arguing that
"unrestricticted internationalism" must not be allowed to
override Canada's "national aspirations."[36] He no doubt knew
first hand of what he spoke.

Nor was David Kinnear, chairman of the T. Eaton Company,
above supporting a *moderate* form of economic nationalism in a
1972 speech, suggesting that reasonable guidelines on foreign
ownership were justified and would not impede thoughtful
investors.[37]

What the more perceptive Canadian capitalists of the early

1970s could realize, especially after the Nixon economic measures of August 1971, was that a form of Canadian nationalism was here to stay, and that a certain accomodation on their part was in order. Perhaps the best example of this thinking can be found in a 1973 address by Duff Roblin, President of CP Investments and former Conservative Premier of Manitoba:

> I share the strong and rising faith of present day Canadians that their country yet may live and in that life, contribute to mankind. In this faith there should be no wish to cut Canada off from her great American neighbour or from the wide world.[38]

Roblin suggested a judicious arrangement of incentives and penalties in setting the terms of operation for foreign-controlled enterprises, singling out natural resources as an area of high priority for Canadian control, and truncation as the single greatest evil of foreign intervention. In reacting to the Connallys and Kissingers who were now making American policy, there was need for "united single-mindedness" regarding Canadian interests.[39]

N.R. Crump, shortly before retiring as President of the CPR, revised his anti-nationalist tone of the 1950s slightly, arguing:

> We need more "nationalism"—not the strident, abrasive, jingoistic kind, but a nationalism that builds upon what we are and what we have to offer. A "constructive nationalism"—a philosophy which does not seek empires abroad and does not denigrate others.[40]

And there are a number of other examples of the same pragmatic "nationalism" from other bourgeois spokesmen in the early 1970s.[41]

Overall, however, any bourgeois flirtation with nationalism was kept within very careful limits. *The Financial Post*, whose schizophrenia on the subject was discussed in Chapter Four, continued to equivocate in the late 1960s, increasingly taking an anti-nationalist line. It criticized the Watkins Report, pointing out that "tens of thousands of Canadians, including many of the most articulate and best educated," worked for foreign-controlled subsidiaries;[42] in 1970, it attacked the Report of the Commons Committee on Foreign Investment (the Wahn Report) for being too "toughly nationalistic."[43] It criticized J.J. Greene, Canada's erstwhile Minister of Energy, for "taking pot shots at a deeply troubled ally and friend,"[44] in a speech he had made in Denver, Colorado repudiating a continental energy policy. On balance, it concluded that American investment represented no threat to Canadian sovereignty, true nationhood lying "not in the bank balance" but "in the heart and mind."[45]

The paper's underlying rationale was that which had led many Canadian capitalists to plump for the multinational corporation—the hope of emulating these themselves.[46] In a decade showing increasing internationalization of capital, the house organ of the Canadian bourgeoisie found a purely home-grown capitalism less and less appealing. To support a strategy of fostering Canadian corporations of world magnitude meant to soft-pedal nationalism.

THE SMALLER BOURGEOISIE
AND THE TRADITIONAL PETTY BOURGEOISIE

If the big bourgeoisie was predominantly anti-nationalist, the same was no longer true for the smaller bourgeoisie or traditional petty bourgeoisie in the decade 1965-75.

Comprising some 7.8 per cent of all occupations in 1965 and some 8.2 per cent in 1972 (cf. Table 2.9), the smaller bourgeoisie and self-employed business sector were still of considerable importance to the politics of the country. It is therefore striking to find a number of small businessmen on the list of steering committee members published by the CIC shortly after its inception (cf. Appendix 2). These included for English Canada:

John Carter	President	Mt. Scio Farms Ltd.
		St. John's, Newfoundland
W.J. Duthie		Duthie Books
		Vancouver, B.C.
G.F. Francolini	President	Livingston Industries Ltd.,
		Tilsonburg
Malim Harding	Chairman	Harding Carpets Ltd.,
		Brantford, Ontario

Mel Hurtig	President	M.G. Hurtig Ltd., Edmonton, Alberta
Jack McClelland	President	McClelland & Stewart, Toronto, Ontario
J.W. Ritchie		Scotia Bond Co. Ltd., Halifax, N.S.
Lloyd Shaw	President	L.E. Shaw Ltd. Halifax, N.S.
Arthur R. Smith	President	Cantrans Services (1965) Ltd., Calgary, Alberta

While one would not want to read too much into these names, it is interesting to see the broad regional character represented, and the conspicuous role of two publishers, Jack McClelland and Mel Hurtig, who were to serve as future Chairmen of the CIC. The self-serving connection between the publishing of Canadiana and the espousal of Canadian nationalism need come as no surprise, or put another way, Canadian nationalism could also mean good business. This is not to suggest that Hurtig, McClelland or the members of the Independent Publishers Association formed in April 1971 did not have a genuine commitment to English Canada's cultural identity above and beyond any mercenary motives. *Tout au contraire*. But let's not fool ourselves—class interest played its role. As Paul Audley describes the activities of the Independent Publishers Association:

> (It) lobbied vigorously for government intervention to prevent further sales of Canadian firms and to provide much needed capital in the form of low-interest loans to support the Canadian segment of the industry.[47]

What about the much larger number of small businessmen, the 377,736 business proprietors or 479,191 investors and property-owners listed in Table 2.9 for 1972? Were they in any sense supporters of nationalism? We are in a somewhat better position to answer this question than for previous decades due to the formation in August 1971 of a Canada-wide association of small business, the Canadian Federation of Independent Business, headquartered in Toronto. This body claims "to represent the interests of small and medium-sized Canadian business" and to speak "to federal and provincial government officials on a regular and continuing basis."[48] As of May 1975, it had some 26,000 independent business members, and claimed it was growing at the rate of 1,000 businesses a month.[49]

An interesting feature of the federation was its Mandate program, whereby members were asked to respond to questionnaires regarding upcoming legislation and matters of public concern. These responses were collated and used as the basis for lobbying with government.

One of these membership surveys in November 1974 bears directly on the question of nationalism. Members were asked their opinion on Walter Gordon's 1974 proposal (see above) to invest some $10-$15 billion over a twelve-year period to purchase the largest foreign-owned corporations in Canada. The result of this questionnaire is as follows:

TABLE. 5.6

Are You For or Against a Proposal to Buy Back a Major Sector of the Canadian Economy from Foreign Control? (Percentages)

For	Against	No opinion
54.4%	38.6%	7.0%

Source: Canadian Federation of Independent Business, *Mandate* No. 28, December, 1974, p. 2.

Another illustration of economic nationalism is in a federation brief submitted to Parliament in early 1975 on the subject of the Combines Investigation Act revisions. This brief, not surprisingly, stresses the importance of independent business vs. big business "in a healthy, free market economy and in preserving competitive markets," and goes on to note that "U.S. multinationals bargaining with European, Asian and South American exporters" use the Canadian market as an annex to the American, cutting out individual Canadian distributors in the process. Canadian independents pay higher interest rates at the bank, and lacking the marketing, technical and management services of a parent company, pay higher operating costs.[50]

A 1975 address by John F. Bulloch, President of the Federation was still more critical of Canada's economic position *vis-a-vis* the United States, arguing we had become an "industrial abattoir." (cf. the Waffle's de-industrialization thesis and critiques of it.)[51] The Autopact, Bulloch argued, was a disaster area, and the energy story equally depressing. We had "given away our oil and gas at bargain basement prices," and "a ten to twenty-year program to build a viable Canadian-owned secondary industry" was necessary.[52] Government must provide tax incentives to encourage more medium-sized business, while itself reducing spending at the rate of 1 per cent of GNP per year for five years and bringing down the size of the civil service.[53] His final barb, however, was saved for the multinationals:

> The concept that a foreign-owned branch-plant can be a good corporate citizen is a myth . . . Branch-plants are good corporate guests—they can never do what a Canadian-owned company is capable of doing.[54]

If this can be taken as representative of small business views, it is significant for two reasons: 1) overt articulation of a small business class interest as against the big bourgeoisie and the multinational corporations; 2) criticism of the increasing size and role of the state, and by analogy, of the chief beneficiaries of this process, the new petty bourgeoisie. If small business will support a form of economic nationalism, it is one which will further its own class interest, e.g., tax incentives in its favour, rather than more statist varieties.

As James R. Conrad, Director of Policy and Research for the Canadian Federation of Independent Business and himself a former chairman of the Toronto branch of the CIC, put it in a personal communication to the author on the subject of nationalism:

> I have an intense dislike for the word "nationalism." It is frequently used as a put-down to the natural concerns of people anywhere who wish to have a greater say in the decisions that affect their lives. (For example, Trudeau's, Sharp's, Ramsay Cook's book etc.)

It is a fact that excesses of nationalism (Hitler, Mussolini, etc.) have been very harmful and destructive to civilization, being often a root cause of war and strife.

It is imperative, in my opinion, to avoid at all costs using the word "nationalism" in discussing the issues in economic, political, and cultural sovereignty and independence. The word detracts from a rational consideration of the issues. I myself deny being a "nationalist." Newspapers, like the *Toronto Star*, who frequently use the term "nationalist" do great and irreparable harm to any efforts at achieving a responsible, domestic consensus on these issues. In fact, the *Toronto Star* is a major factor in the relatively slow progress to date.

On the other hand, the Canadian Federation of Independent Business has had a rapid growth due to its responsible, moderate and credible approach to the problems of the independent businessman. We represent owner-managers in their ongoing battle to survive in a frequently hostile environment, in which government itself it is often the principal culprit.[55]

The moral is clear—the term "nationalism" is not particularly attractive to small businessmen and property owners. But certain aspects of political or economic independence are (cf. Table 5.6), provided government is not the principal beneficiary.

Turning to farmers, one notes a decline to a mere 5.9 per cent of the total labour force by 1972 (cf. Table 2.11). While not without importance in both provincial and federal politics, their historic kingmaker function was at an end. Yet as the 1964 *Maclean's* poll from which we quoted at the end of the previous chapter had suggested, small town Ontario, including presumably many farmers, was a strong reservoir of opposition to American annexation.

There is some evidence that farmers continued to provide support for nationalism in the 1965-75 decade, though it is difficult to generalize. The most interesting examples occur in some of the letters which the CIC received in the years following its formation:

From Macklin, Sask.: I have read of the difficulty our people have finding a Canadian beach that is not owned by Americans, all fenced and picketed. Land is cheap in this country, yes, but should not be just for the benefit of land greedy foreigners. When fat-purse foreigners flock in hoping to get a good bargain at our expense something must be done to put a stop to it, or we will end very shortly being no better off than the darky slaves to a bunch of arrogrant money grabbers. (N.B. the racist term used.)

From a man in Stoney Creek, Ont., whose family has lived on the same farm for five generations: We of the Old UEL stock have taken on all comers in the past, including the U.S.A. armies of 1812. Hoping to hear more from your work.

From an Alberta couple: We are farmers in the Peace River district where we see the wholesale takeover actually in action. Gas, oil, coal and timber are being gobbled up and great waterfalls are becoming in danger of being in the centre of slash. The large park in northern Alberta is being attacked by the local chambers of commerce. Our people are becoming serfs for jerry-built houses, cars and beer. They are really our most important resource but they are going down the drain with the rest.[56]

Another example of farmer support for nationalism is provided in the profile of Waffle members published in *Canadian Dimension* in 1971 (see Appendix 3), which showed that 10 per cent of these were farmers, almost double their percentage of the labour force.

But these may only have been straws in the wind, and in any case were hardly representative of the views of large argibusiness outfits, of the Cattleman's Association, the Dairy Farmers of Canada, etc. There is, as Don Mitchell has argued in his excellent study, *The Politics of Food*, no single class interest among farmers, while the politics of independent farmers, in particular, are unpredictable.[57] The fact that most of the capital invested in agribusiness is Canadian, rather than American,[58] further lessens the appeal of nationalism as a focus of farmer discontent. (The one exception may have been the Kraft boycott organized by the National Farmers Union, where foreign ownership was raised as an issue.[59])

The political economy of both agriculture and agribusiness explains the relative unimportance of a farmer-based nationalism by the 1970s. It was in the urban centres, where some four-fifths of the Canadian population congregated, that nationalism received its main support.

The other component of the traditional petty bourgeoisie, the self-employed professionals, is relatively small in number (some 0.7 per cent of all occupations in 1972 according to Table 2.12), but not unimportant to the issue at hand. On the contrary, lawyers, architects, doctors, engineers, writers and artists were extremely prominent in the CIC when it was being organized, as the following list based on Appendix 2 would suggest:*

Pierre Berton, Author
Earl Birney, Poet
John Blansche, Engineer
Molly Lamb Bobac, Artist
Christopher Chapman, Film Producer
Henry Comer, Actor
E. Delsotto, Delsotto, Zorzi, Andrews & Applebaum, Toronto
N.R. Fischbuch, Consulting Geologist
Edwin A. Goodman, Q.C., Lawyer
Judy LaMarsh, Lawyer
S. Loschiaco, Physician
Michael D. MacDonald, Lawyer
Michael Meighen, Lawyer
Farley Mowat, Author
Christina Newman, Author
Eric Nicol, Author
Alden Nowlan, Author
John C. Parkin, Architect
Al Purdy, Poet
John Reeves, Photographer
Harold Town, Artist

(N.B. There are also several French Canadian lawyers who figure

*Not all of these were exclusively self-employed, indicating the blurred line separating self-employed professionals from salaried professionals whom we have classified in the new petty bourgeoisie.

on the list of 120, who, had they been included, would have brought the self-employed professional component on the CIC's Steering Committee up to approximately 25/120).

That writers and artists should have been attracted to nationalism in this period is not surprising, given the revulsion against the American involvement in Vietnam that swept the intelligentsia of most Western countries, including the United States itself. There was no lack of collections and works, from Al Purdy's *The New Romans* to Dennis Lee's *Civil Elegies* to Margaret Atwood's *Survival*, that articulated the new anti-Americanism and cultural nationalism springing up in English Canada. Indeed, as one observer of cultural trends in the early 1970s argued:

> Oddly, or perhaps characteristically, English Canada had to wait until the economy was virtually captured before experiencing the type of introspection which logically should have preceded it . . . Contemporary Canada then presents the contrasts of a nation in which political sovereignty is being slowly but surely eroded, but in which cultural identity has at last become a reality.[60]

"The owl of Minerva takes flight in the gathering dusk."

It is difficult to assess to what extent English Canadian intellectuals (including academics) created the new nationalism, much as their *confreres* had done in the Quebec of the early 1960s (and at least one strong nationalist, Barry Lord, made a conscious parallel[61]), or to what extent they themselves were merely responding to a political force let loose by the waning influence of the United States. In any event the climate for Canadian cultural activity—literature, theatre, film—became vastly more encouraging in the 1965-75 decade than before, public response far greater, and the activity of the state—simultaneously patron and repository of national loyalty—ever more important.

> Where once artists and critics earnestly searched for greatness, now Canadian cultural activity in its own right is a first goal . . . theatre groups now . . . present Canadian plays, worthwhile or not . . . the Canadian Film Development Corporation pours money into backing a feature film in-

dustry . . . The Canadian Radio and Television Commission
has stiffened its rules for Canadian content . . . The Canada
Council, which has been supporting Canadian art for some
twenty years, has extended the scale of its activities.[62]

The nationalism of other self-employed petty bourgeois
professionals—e.g., lawyers, architects, doctors—was more
equivocal; indeed there was also a fair amount of anti-
nationalism.

On the nationalist side, a corporate lawyer and Tory power
broker like Eddie Goodman could tell a Toronto conference in
1971:

> As a strategy for planned, proper growth for Canada,
> economic nationalism is a far superior stratagem than
> uncontrolled foreign investment.[63]

An independent economic consultant like D.W. Carr could write
that "the decay and weakening of the United States economy and
its society (was) now only beginning," calling for the emergence
of "a group of angry young Canadian entrepreneurs" demanding
a high degree of competence from themselves and appropriate
support from the Canadian government.[64] A chartered
accountant, reviewing the Foreign Investment Act in 1974, could
write that notwithstanding objections from those who wished to
sell their businesses, many Canadians would "welcome the
legislation as necessary to achieving some degree of future
economic independence."[65]

On the anti-nationalist side, *The Canadian Chartered
Accountant* editorialized at the time of the formation of the CIC
that "independence is a relative proposition." "Rational
arguments," it suggested, would be "low on the list of factors
brought to bear on the decision-making process" regarding
foreign investment.[66] A. John Marshall, writing in the same
journal in 1974, went considerably further, arguing the need for
chartered accountant firms to go multinational, to service
multinational firms in the international economy. Accountants
had to help "eliminate the fears of the international firms which
is (*sic*) based primarily on economic and ethnic jealousies," while
striving to develop "common professional standards with

worldwide application" in the developed and developing, countries.[67]

The Canadian Bar Association, in its brief to the Standing Committee on Finance, Trade and Economic Affairs regarding Bill C-132 (the Foreign Investment Review Act), objected to the degree of ministerial discretion in the bill, and to threatened interference with "the rights of Canadians to dispose of their holdings as they saw fit."[68] Its suggested amendments to protect the right of the seller and provide for appeal of the Review Agency's decisions to Federal Court won strong editorial backing from *The Financial Post*.[69] Nationalism was not the bread and butter of the Canadian legal profession. As a *Financial Post* editorial had suggested in 1968:

> Bankers, lawyers, chartered accountants and others have foreign-owned branch-plants as their clients or they hope to woo such a client.[70]

Overall, then, there was considerable difference of opinion regarding nationalism in the ranks of self-employed professionals ranging from those who saw both nationalism and the state as a fillip to their own ambitions (e.g., writers and artists) to those professionals allied with the large multinational corporations.

THE NEW PETTY BOURGEOISIE

Turning to the new petty bourgeoisie, we come to the class which played *the decisive role* in the eruption of English Canadian nationalism after 1965. As we argued in Chapter Two, this class—embracing salaried professionals, many of them working for the state, for universities and schools, in research institutes, as well as the student estate, i.e., those in training for future positions as salaried professions—came into its own with the fantastic take-off of the state sector and of higher education in the 1960s (cf. Tables 2.14-15, 2.19-20). Members of the new petty bourgeoisie dominated two key nationalist organizations that sprang up, the centrist CIC and the left-wing Waffle, while publications by members of this class gave ideological direction and coherence to the nationalist movement.

The growth of nationalism among the new petty bourgeoisie was slow at first, given the strong anti-nationalism in both the academic world and civil service (discussed in the previous chapter). 1966, for example, saw the publication by the University League for Social Reform (a Toronto-based group of academics) of a collection of articles, *Nationalism in Canada*. Liberal anti-nationalism prevailed in a majority of the pieces included:

> For Canada, unlike the heroic nation-state of old, national survival is not the highest priority of foreign policy . . . There are many things more important to us than resisting our absorption, as a minor but influential entity, into an Atlantic state or even our national extinction through annexation by the United States.[71]

> English-speaking Canadian intellectuals, impressed by the progress of the Quiet Revolution's ideological conquest of Quebec, are strongly tempted to reply in kind with counter-ideologies of English-Canadian nationalism . . . This is a dangerous exercise . . .[72]

> . . . the withdrawal of nationalist sentiment from national politics will facilitate Canada's contribution to the growth of world government, international law and global scientific, technological and economic cooperation . . . To cease loving one's own nation is also to cease hating other nations.[73]

The odd article, in particular that by Abe Rotstein, did, however, point to the new stirrings:

> Between the views of Harry Johnson, who claims that there is no problem with regard to foreign investment, and the view of George Grant, who claims that it is already too late, there is a viable middle course. . . . The democratic nation increasingly embodies the values and purposes of our society.[74]

By 1967-68, academics and students were signing petitions, marching and occupying university placement offices in opposition to American policy in Vietnam and to Canadian complicity, e.g., through arms sales. Liberal academics could argue:

> (Quiet Diplomacy) is no longer suitable for Canadian foreign policy in the late sixties . . . its view of the world is ten years out of date. The alternative . . . is developing an independent foreign policy. [75]

Socialist academics could state:

> We are nationalist because, as socialists, we do not want our country to be utterly absorbed by the *citadel of world capitalism.* [76]

Activists in the student movement were to point their guns against both American imperialism and a branch-plant Canadian capitalism:

> Canada no longer has an independent economy in any important way. Our economy, especially in the extractive industries, and the highly technologized manufacturing industries is largely owned by foreigners, especially Americans. . . . The Americans refer to this as "interdependence"; perhaps a more accurate, if less polite term, is imperialism. [77]

> . . . if the Canadian university is beginning to resemble the United States ones structurally, it is even less distinguishable in educational content. *Canadian universities are thus becoming yet another chapter in our emasculation as a nation and servitude to the American empire.* [78]

A form of anti-imperialism was in the air.

The other crucial factor making for nationalism in the late 1960s was the steady growth of government expenditure (cf. Chart 2.3), for health, education, pension plans and other social services. As Michael Pitfield, now Clerk of the Privy Council, then an official in the Prime Minister's Office, stated it several years ago:

> In terms of the social policy in the sixties, there was in the countries of the world a marked increase in state interventionism. Call it "communism" or "socialism" or just the "welfare state," what it really amounted to is the government were and are doing what people as individuals or in private sector corporations couldn't do . . .[79]

Many in the new petty bourgeoisie benefited from these changes, and came to see statism, by which we mean a strong interventionist state, as in their interests. A strong state was a central theme for nationalists, like Mel Watkins:

> The nationalists must see that the only effective alternative to high and rising foreign ownership is the steady expansion of Canadian public ownership. The creation of crown corporations—which governments of the old parties were once prepared to do, albeit in a modest way—is the means by which we can halt and reverse American economic penetration.[80]

And it was echoed years later by Robert Page, another academic, and 1974-75 Chairman of the CIC:

> The public enterprise tradition in Canada differs from the U.S. Due to geography and the power of transnational corporations, Canadians have had to resort to public ownership and will probably do so even more in the future.[81]

It was perfectly logical then that the two main nationalist movements in English Canada, the Waffle, formed in August 1969, and the Committee for an Independent Canada, formed in September 1970, should both, for all their ideological differences, have been emanations of the class whose interests were directly linked to the existence of a vigorous nationalist state.

Where the Waffle was concerned, fully 21 per cent of its members were students, 8 per cent teachers, 10 per cent professors and 19 per cent professionals, many of these presumably salaried professionals in either the private or public sectors (cf. Appendix 3). Its main leaders—Mel Watkins, James Laxer—were from this same class.

Where the Committee for an Independent Canada was concerned, as one of its co-founders defensively argued:

> This is not the know-nothing reaction of professional malcontents but a sober middle class movement . . .[82]

Its original steering committee included 32 academics, 10 students, 10 journalists and broadcasters, and 5-6 professional politicians, in itself a near-majority of the 120-member committee (cf. Appendix 2). Two of its three god-fathers, Peter Newman and Abe Rotstein, were from the new petty bourgeoisie, with only Walter Gordon representing the dominant class in Canada.*

The emergence of the Waffle and the CIC did not mean that anti-nationalism lacked stalwarts in the ranks of the new petty bourgeoisie in the late 1960s or early 1970s. A Harry Johnson could continue his crusade of an earlier day, deriding "the defense of small national enterprises" against multinational corporations as interfering with "the development of international scale," and seeing the multinational corporation as the harbinger of "a more humane, equitable and non-discriminatory civilization."[83] Salvation lay in a world run by Exxon.

An overwhelming majority of Carleton University faculty could reject the attempt by Robin Mathews and James Steele in late 1968 to get a) a two-third Canadian quota for faculty members of all university departments and b) a policy of only Canadian citizens in all administrative positions from chairman up to chancellor.[84] On the contrary, they urged that "academic competence" rather than citizenship be the sole criterion employed in making academic appointments.[85]

Many academics through the following years denied any validity to the nationalist call. Some denounced "empty gestures

---

*The intellectual origins of the CIC can be traced back to "An Open Letter to Canadian Nationalists" that appeared in the May-June 1967 issue of *Canadian Dimension* signed by Gad Horowitz, C.W. Gonick and G. David Sheps arguing: "To mobilize the majority nationalist sentiment in Canada, we propose the formation of an alliance for independence. It would be politically non-partisan and would cross racial, regional and class lines to include all Canadians who wish to preserve their country's independence." All three were academics who defined themselves as socialists, and though none actually joined the CIC—Gonick, in fact, was quite active in the Waffle—this letter further underlines a symbiosis between many members of the new petty bourgeoisie and nationalism in the late 1960s that transcended ideological differences.

of cultural nationalism that try to lead us to cultural separatism";[86] others, the harnessing of history in the service "of what brand of nationalism . . . is currently popular";[87] still others the "cult of the nation" reminiscent of the 1930s, "and no less dangerous."[88]

Yet in a moderate way, nationalism did begin to take hold. Margaret Prang, while denying the validity of Gad Horowitz's left-nationalist arguments, could nonetheless acknowledge "the intensification of nationalism in English Canada" by 1968, as a response to the nationalisms of French Canada and the United States. She suggested, furthermore, that Canada pursue economic and foreign policies that would reduce Canada's dependence on the United States.[89] Claude Bissell, while fulminating against the student movement threatening the serenity of his Parnassus, or against the Waffle, could in 1971 argue, in convoluted fashion, the case for a defensive Canadian nationalism, "not explosive and aggressive," but looking to a Canada flourishing, side by side with the United States, "in our own sovereign right."[90] And the quite moderate Canadian Association of University Teachers, under the twin onslaught of nationalist agitation in its ranks [91] and the shrinking job market for Canadian graduate students, could by 1975 adopt a series of guidelines on hiring, suggesting preference for qualified Canadians in academic appointments. [92]

To give a comprehensive account of the explosion of nationalism among academics, students, journalists, and intellectuals in the period around 1970 could constitute a study in its own right. A number of illustrations representative of the principal orientaions will have to suffice.

Works like *Close the 49th Parallel etc.* or *Silent Surrender,* both published in 1970, spoke for a left nationalism percolating its way through the ranks of the University League for Social Reform, the student movement or the Waffle, and bringing together economists, historians, political scientists and others. Many of these writers were influenced by "dependency" theory as it had been applied to Latin America by economists such as Andre Gunder Frank, and many on the left sought to make a connection between anti-imperialism and opposition to the Canadian bourgeoisie:

To get a proper perspective of Canada's relationship to the

United States, we should bear in mind that capitalism is an international rather than a national system; . . . What distinguishes Canada (and Latin America) within this international system is the extent to which we have become tied to the American metropolis.[93]

Canada's dependency is a function not of geography and technology but of the nature of Canada's capitalist class. . . . The need for Canadian independence to end the exploitation of Canada by the American empire has given birth to new strategies and a new institutional framework for Canadian working class politics.[94]

Yet how much of a working class base this left nationalism itself had was highly problematical, as a former member of the Waffle, Cy Gonick, would later acknowledge:

The nationalism of the left, growing out of the deepening consciousness of Canada's subordinate place in the American empire, had little or no class connection. This is one of the reasons why the Waffle, for example, was never able to penetrate the Canadian working class to any extent. And because of its preoccupations with the question of Canadian survival, groups like the Waffle were unable to come to terms with the class basis of the Canadian state.[95]

Where the mainstream of the nationalist movement was concerned—liberals, conservatives, right-wing social democrats —ideology was less explicit. Magazines like *Maclean's* could churn out article after article supporting un undifferentiated nationalism:

"The Heartening Surge of a New Canadian Nationalism"[96]
"The Canada Firsters March on Ottawa"[97]
"Canada's Independence Inventory: The cupboard is ours, but the stock is fast becoming theirs"[98]
"Growing Up Reluctantly"[99]

The Committee for an Independent Canada, in its publication, *The Independencer*, addressed a whole series of topical concerns:

"Canadian Publishing in Crisis"[100]
"End Oil Exports in Three Years"[101]
"*Time*—A privileged Non-Canadian"[102]

Its February-March 1975 issue listed those who had made the CIC's "All Canada Team" for 1974, from Dave Barrett for his realistic resource pricing to Stompin' Tom Connors for his songs and stories about Canada; from Pauline Jewett on her appointment as president at Simon Fraser to Pierre Juneau for his excellent leadership of the Canadian Radio and Television Commission.[103]

This celebration of Canada, which in a number of ways recalled the "celebration of America" which C. Wright Mills had so sharply criticized in the United States some twenty years before,[104] was not, however, without ideological content. It spoke to a new petty bourgeois concern for economic or resource independence, for science or cultural policy.

It was an Eric Kierans, back at his old perch at McGill, who could accuse the United States of "*folie de grandeur*" and advocate Canada pursuing her own economic and political priorities.[105] A group of academics at Dalhousie opposed the dominant position of foreign energy corporations in the Canadian oil industry and the implications for exploitation of Canada's diminishing reserves.[106] An academic, Vice-President of the Canadian Society for Chemical Engineering, could call for a science policy "worthy of the name," capable of assuring technological innovation, Canada's economic health and perhaps "our continued existence as a nation."[107] Other academics and writers could call for more "Canadian Studies,"[108] and for a communications system worthy of "a mature nation-state."[109]

Though one of the ideologues of the new nationalism could claim that it spoke "for the national interest, for national survival, not for a class interest,"[110] Marxist analysis would underline the class interests of most of those articulating this so-called classless nationalism. It was the new petty bourgeoisie that stood to be the chief beneficiary of the symbolic investment now called for in "science policy," "cultural policy," "independent foreign policy" and so on. Members of this class would be its interpreters, and in all likelihood, the policy-makers engaged in turning nationalist ideology into state policy. Such a petty bourgeois nationalism need not for a moment challenge the underlying capitalist nature of the Canadian economy—and none of the "moderate" nationalists did. Such were the ideological limits of the "new Canuckism."

Nationalism was also a growing value in the 1965-75 period for the whole government sector. True, a John Deutsch, speaking for many of the older veterans of the civil service, could still write in 1971:

> There is no country where the blind forces of nationalism could be more dangerous (than Canada). Nationalism has constructive uses, but mindless exploitation of these passions could destroy our country.[111]

But the statement quoted above by Michael Pitfield spoke to the new statism prevalent among younger civil servants, which in conjunction with changes in Canadian-American relations, entailed a new nationalism.

Trudeau's chief advisor on foreign policy, Ivan Head, could significantly title a 1972 article in *Foreign Affairs*, "The Foreign Policy of the New Canada," and quote extensively from Trudeau's various statements since coming to office (which Head presumably had helped to draft) speaking to a new nationalism.[112]

The Science Council of Canada published a number of studies by staff researchers calling into question the traditional continentalism of Canadian economic policy and, by extension, the logic of the multi-national corporation:

> . . . we are the world's largest producer of nickel, but we are net importers of stainless steel and manufactured nickel products, including "cold climate" nickel-cadmium batteries; we are the world's second largest producer of aluminum, but we import it in its more sophisticated forms . . . we are the world's largest exporter of pulp and paper, but we import much of our fine paper . . .[113]

> *. . . in no case did we find a Canadian subsidiary that felt it had the freedom to enter foreign markets at will with a product which it thought could be produced in Canada and*

competitively exported. [114]

And a whole range of government reports from The Gray Report to others on communications or defence policy reflected the new nationalism that had crept into the civil service in this decade. As was indicated in Chapter Two (cf. Table 2.18 and the text immediately preceding and following), the state was a soaring area of recruitment for salaried professionals in the new petty bourgeoisie. These clearly stood to benefit from increased state interventionism which nationalism reinforced.

Crown corporations were another incubator of nationalism. For example, in a study on *Theories of Ideology in Advanced Capitalist Society* carried out by Koula Mellos in 1973 (with extensive interviews of a representative cross-section of English-speaking Montrealers from bank vice-presidents to welfare cases), the one strongly nationalist comment registered came from a CBC musician:

> Certain things are best managed by crown corporations, certain things better managed by private individuals . . . but, just keep them Canadian whatever they are. I would say that an American company in Canada is a leech on the body corporate of Canada whereas a Canadian company in Canada is a valid organ of the body corporate. [115]

To go one step further, there is a recent book by Herschel Hardin, *A Nation Unaware*, which elevates the crown corporation tradition into a mythology, arguing that it is the very basis of the Canadian economic culture:

> Public enterprise is indigenous to the Canadian demography . . . Canada, in its essentials, is a public enterprise country, always has been, and probably always will be . . . [116]

Hardin, of course, fails to realize that what he thinks is unique to Canada is in fact characteristic of *all* capitalist societies *except* the United States. What is true, however, is that those working for the state, e.g., in crown corporations, will come to identify their interests with the maintenance of a strong state sector and

nation state. A certain national pride comes through even such
dreary documents as the Annual Reports of Atomic Energy of
Canada Ltd.

> Pickering is an important milestone, and to get the nuclear
> power programme in Canada to this point has taken a good
> deal of work by many people over a number of years. [117]

> The international interest in CANDU is gratifying and sales
> opportunities that result in future contracts will be of benefit
> to the Canadian economy. [118]

An analogy can be made with the pride which French Canadian
managers and technicians, members of what Brazeau called "les
nouvelles classes moyennes," experienced at the time of the
nationalization and takeover of private electricity companies by
Quebec Hydro. [119]

The final component of the new petty bourgeoisie, not yet
mentioned—salaried professionals working for private corporations—are less likely candidates for nationalism. Yet here too
there is some evidence of the same forces at work as in the
universities or state sector.

In December 1971, Peter Desbarats wrote an article in *The
Montreal Gazette* entitled "Many managers are nationalist—but
very silent":

> In a recent poll of 47 members of the Canadian Institute of
> Management—more than 60 per cent of CIM's total
> membership, incidentally, is employed by U.S.-owned
> companies—half of those polled agreed that "the massive
> take-over of industry in Canada would not have been
> possible without the inside help of Canadian managers." . . .
> 80 per cent "thought that foreign control generally works to
> Canada's disadvantage" while 75 per cent "were in favour
> of legislation to curb and control take-overs." [120]

The article goes on to talk about managers unable to get approval
of projects critically needed to keep the Canadian operation
going, because people in New York or Pittsburgh said "no," and
about interference with Canadian managers' bargaining with

workers as examples of what was turning Canadian managers into economic nationalists.

> "But he's also forced to temper it. He's not living on a foundation grant.
> He's got to produce. He's just like any other piece of equipment in that plant.
> If he gives too much trouble, then he's replaced.
> If he starts rocking the boat, if he starts stomping around and saying—well, dammit, we're running this show . . . then he's in trouble." [121]

It may be dangerous to generalize from just one article, but at a minimum it suggests that nationalism does have some attraction for managers, especially in foreign-owned branch-plants, even though they may have to keep their sentiments under wraps. In a general way they were influenced by the same trends which J. Douglas Gibson, a bank economist whose anti-nationalist sentiments we cited in the previous chapter, analyzed in 1973:

> Economic nationalism has been growing in Canada. It is partly an anti-American phenomenon . . . partly the result of a developing belief among Canadians that they are too dependent on the United States. . . . The days when Canadians supported and joined with enthusiasm in the policies of General Marshall and President Truman are unhappily long past. [122]

THE WORKING CLASS

The organized trade union movement, for its part, experienced winds of change as intense as those which embraced the new petty bourgeoisie. At the end of Chapter Four we left the Canadian Labour Congress immured in its defence of "international" unionism. Over the next decade, the changing composition of the membership of the Congress coupled with external phenomena such as the decline in American power and the rise of American protectionism were to weaken the hold of American-based unions, leading to subtle changes in both policy and leadership of the Canadian trade union movement.

The bold secular trends were sketched in Tables 2.24-26. Of particular importance where power relations within the CLC were concerned was the displacement by the Canadian Union of Public Employees (CUPE) of the International Steelworkers as the largest union in Canada in 1974, and the emergence of the Public Service Alliance of Canada and various provincial civil service unions alongside CUPE as new power brokers. Inevitably these Canadian-based unions were more supportive of nationalism than their international counterparts, all the more since their members worked in the state sector and, much like their counterparts in the new petty bourgeoisie, saw a strong nation state as in their class interest.

Yet the nature of the CLC was such that international unions still accounted for some two-thirds of total membership in 1974[123] —a fact which served to dampen a too strident nationalism on the part of the Canadian-based public sector unions. On the other hand, the trend from the late 1960s on was toward greater nationalism on the part of the Canadian membership of the international unions themselves. One expression of this was the guidelines on autonomy which the CLC adopted in 1970 and reaffirmed at its 1974 convention. Another was the breakaway movement, symbolized by the Council of Canadian Unions formed in 1969, which though small in numbers (some 20,000 members in 1974), served as a goad to the international unions to clean up their act or face the consequences. In British Columbia, in particular, with the highest rate of union organization in Canada, international unions such as Steel were to lose several thousand workers to breakaway unions. A third example of the diminishing appeal of international unions was the 1974 decision by the 55,000 member strong Canadian Pulpworkers to sever their ties with the international union to which they had been affiliated, setting up separate shop as the Canadian Paperworkers Union.[124]

Let us first examine the overall change in CLC policy during this decade, then turn to a more careful analysis of the politics of a union such as CUPE, and finally, to examples of working-class based nationalism outside the mainstream of the CLC.

In the later 1960s, the CLC leadership toughened its attitude on foreign investment and multinational corporations, and somewhat in advance of official Canadian foreign policy (paralleling in this the NDP), became a good deal more critical of the United States. In July 1966, for example, the Executive Council of the CLC called for a royal commission to investigate among other things the nature of capital flows between the U.S. and Canada; the extent of U.S. ownership and control of Canadian industries; the policy relationships between parent companies and susidiaries.[125] The same Council meeting also decried the Winters guidelines on good corporate behavior of March 1966[126] as "belated and inadequate." The public was in need of complete information, not least on the effects American guidelines on investment were having on Canada.[127]

In March 1967, in a brief to Cabinet, the CLC argued for a national water policy, opposing any Canadian commitment on water exports until full information on future needs was available.[128]

At its 7th Convention in 1968, the CLC formally endorsed the Watkins Report, arguing that its proposals "would do much to increase Canada's control over the Canadian economy."[129] An issue of *Canadian Labour* that November contained a two page summary by Mel Watkins of the main points in his Report, [130] while the official CLC publication once again called for its implementation. 1968 also saw rising opposition to Canada's continental defence alliance, with the Congress calling for Canadian withdrawal from NORAD and for an end to weapons shipments destined for Vietnam. Taking the longer view, it stated:

> The Congress believes that we may be on the threshold of one of the great periodic historical realignments, caused by shifting national and international loyalties . . . It may therefore be incumbent upon us to critically re-examine the whole structure of Canadian foreign policy of the past quarter of a century and labour's attitude toward it.[131]

Where international unions were concerned, however, the official Congress line remained highly favourable. Relations between the CLC and the AFL-CIO were fraternal, not structural ones, with the CLC's policies "made in Canada by Canadians and for Canadians living in a world dominated by giant corporations."[132]

Through the early 1970s, in the face of nationalist attacks, e.g., from the CIC or from breakaway movements, the CLC leadership reaffirmed the validity of international unionism, now linking their case to the supposed strength of multinational corporations which only international unions could combat, or otherwise challenging their critics' motives.[133] (It was never explained, however, why trade unions in the Common Market could cooperate against capital without fusing their memberships into pan-European unions.)

Nonetheless, the CLC leadership felt obliged to make some gesture in the direction of "national identity" and did so at its 8th Convention in 1970:

> Whereas the international labour unions have contributed to establishment, growth and success of the trade union movement in Canada;
> Whereas there is a growing tendency towards a Canadian identity in the social and economic sectors of our society;
> Be it resolved that the Canadian Labour Congress adopt a firm policy supporting minimum standards of self-government of the Canadian sections of international unions; and
> Be it further resolved that these standards include: election of Canadian officers by Canadians; policies to deal with national affairs to be determined by the elected Canadian officers and Canadian members; Canadian elected representatives to have authority to speak for the union in Canada; and
> Be it further resolved that the Canadian Labour Congress do all in its power to assist the affiliated unions in the attainment of these objectives.[134]

This was enough to allow David Lewis and other defenders of the "international" unions to express their pleasure at the growing autonomy of international unions as compared to branch-plants in this country.[135] But as Ed Finn, Research Director for the Canadian Brotherhood of Railway, Transport and General Workers, had pointed out, the CLC guidelines were a good deal weaker than ones which had been proposed by a group of reform nationalists at the convention. These had called for retaining sufficient dues in Canada to finance distinctively Canadian services, and for the right of Canadian branches to amalgamate, without having to wait for their U.S. parents to do so first. Moreover, the guidelines were voluntary. [136]

The pressure for greater Canadian union autonomy was to continue over the next years. William Mahoney and Eamon Park of Steel, no doubt feeling the need to curry to nationalist sentiment, lent their names to the CIC Steering Committee in late 1970 along with Ed Finn and Stanley Little of CUPE (cf. Appendix 2). (All but Finn, however, subsequently resigned over the CIC's encouragement of exclusively Canadian unions.)

Some 20 per cent of the Waffle's membership were apparently blue-collar and white-collar workers, though this was not true of Waffle activists (cf. Appendix 3).

The increasingly youthful character of the labour force in the early 1970s (28.9 per cent under 25 in 1971 compared to 21.8 per cent of the labour force in 1961) was a further impetus to nationalism and radicalism:

> The young show much more concern than their seniors about social issues like pollution, Vietnam, racism and Canadian nationalism. They question all those high and mighty sanctimonious pronouncements on political morality from their elders. [137]

AFL-CIO support for protectionist legislation such as the Burke-Hartke Bill was still another factor, though the CLC tried to use its influence with U.S. unionists to lobby for Canadian exemption. [138]

By 1974, the CLC's tenth convention saw a so-called reform slate, backed by CUPE, the Public Service Alliance of Canada, B.C. Government Employees' Union, Canadian Brotherhood of Railway, Transport and General Workers, Canadian Union of Postal Workers and the Letter Carriers' Union of Canada (all Canadian-based unions), displace much of the CLC old-guard from key executive positions and impose tougher policy against recalcitrant internationals. It had been found that only 43 of 90 international unions affiliated with the Congress were in full compliance with all the guidelines passed in 1970, 28 with some but not all, and six with none. (Information was not available for thirteen internationals.) Accordingly the CLC, over the vigorous objection of the building trade unions, passed a policy plan giving the Executive Council of the Congress the authority, by a two-thirds vote, to suspend any union not complying with its autonomy guidelines. If the suspension were upheld at a subsequent convention of the CLC, "the Congress should take whatever steps are necessary to maintain the membership of the suspended affiliate in good standing with the Congress."

As the *Labour Gazette* commented:

> This provision . . . gives the Congress power considerably beyond anything it has previously enjoyed. It amounts, in fact, to a threat that unions failing to comply with the standards will risk losing their membership to another Congress affiliate or to the Congress itself.[139]

For some months thereafter, the building trades held back payment of their *per capita* to the Congress, even threatening to secede altogether in protest against this policy. In the end they caved in, in no small part due to rank and file sentiment within their unions in both Ontario and B.C.[140]

A key factor in the growth of nationalist sentiment within the CLC was the increased strength of Canadian-based unions in the public sector, which we have already mentioned. As the public relations director of the Canadian Union of Public Employees, Norman Simon, admits, a good deal of CUPE's appeal in recent years has been a nationalist one, and the union quite consciously pushes its Canadian character.[141] On the other hand, as a loyal member of the CLC, CUPE has been quite careful not to knock the international unions directly, even coming to their defence against those agitating for exclusively Canadian-based unions.

CUPE's *Journal* over the years shows a fair amount of nationalist content where American economic control is concerned. An article in late 1970 entitled "Nixon Drinks Canada Dry" reprints Mel Watkins' testimony to a U.S. Senate Committee on Multinational Corporations, with his argument:

> On the northern periphery of the American empire, a rising nationalism has to a degree unprededented in Canadian history a strong anti-capitalist and socialist component.[142]

It was an open secret that a number of the staff people in CUPE were quite close to the Waffle. [143]

A mid-1971 article in the CUPE *Journal* by Rick Deaton, entitled "Canada's Sell Out," pinpoints the key role of retained earnings "in financing American investment in Canada" and argues the need to channel "Canadian investment in such a way as to meet the needs of Canadian workers." [144]

A 1972 article entitled "Stop Selling Out Our Resources" argued the case for conservation of energy resources in particular and the need to harry governments into firmer action. [145]

More interesting, because emanating from the rank and file, were resolutions submitted, and in some cases voted, at CUPE Conventions in 1971 and 1973. For example:

Resolution No. 80
Submitted by Local 500, Winnipeg, Man.
WHEREAS the major industries of Canada are foreignly owned, and
WHEREAS the wealth of Canada is being lost to foreign countries;
THEREFORE BE IT RESOLVED that the Canadian Union of Public Employees approach the Federal Government to curtail foreign ownership and investment in Canada in order that Canadian monies may remain in Canada. [146]

Resolution No. 81
Submitted by Local 998, Winnipeg, Man.
WHEREAS overtures have been made by the United States to purchase fresh water from Canada, and
WHEREAS these purchases are mainly to maintain or increase their standard of living, and
WHEREAS the effects of diversions of our rivers are unknown as far as wild life, ecology, are unknown, (*sic*)
BE IT RESOLVED THAT the National Office of CUPE make submission to the Canadian Federal Government to retain all the Canadian fresh water for the use of Canadian citizens. [147]

Resolution No. 86
Submitted by the Alberta Division

WHEREAS our economy is in jeopardy of becoming totally American dominated, and

WHEREAS this contributes heavily to the instability of our economy,

THEREFORE BE IT RESOLVED that this Convention, through the CLC, petition the Federal Government to set up a Crown Corporation to keep the key resources Canadian controlled. [148]

Resolution No. 43 [International]
Submitted by Local 1004, Vancouver, B.C.

WHEREAS the U.S. Atomic Energy Commission seems determined to explode an atomic device on Amchitka Island, regardless of possible catastrophic consequences to Pacific Rim Countries, and

WHEREAS the protest of the government of Canada has made no impression upon the government of the United States,

THEREFORE BE IT RESOLVED that this 5th Convention of the Canadian Union of Public Employees send a telegram to Prime Minister Trudeau urgently requesting that he take strong steps to stop the proposed nuclear tests at Amchitka, and

BE IT FURTHER RESOLVED that this convention calls upon the CLC to submit a similar strong request to the Prime Minister. [149]

Equally interesting were occasional comments from the floor at CUPE conventions, venting discontent with international domination of the CLC:

In my opinion the CLC representatives that sit there are largely made up of representatives from locals which are affiliated to U.S. parent unions. And you and I know that the policies of these unions are dictated straight from the United States of America. I don't think that in any way that is the correct body to be representing our Canadian Union of Public Employees either at the federal government level or the provincial government level. [150]

CUPE was quite prepared to use Canadian nationalism in its bid for greater power within the CLC, [151] as a brochure circulated by it and other Canadian-based unions at the 10th CLC Convention in Vancouver in 1974 showed. At the centre of the three-page pamphlet was a picture of a group of workers building a scaffolding with a large Canadian flag on it. The pamphlet talked about the need "to build the kind of Congress that will genuinely and effectively serve the needs of Canadian workers." And further: "Our vision of reform also includes Canadian control of our labour movement and greater concern for broader social issues." The message was clear, even if muted.

The muted part was a result of CUPE's fear of losing its leverage over the internationals in the CLC by seeming to support breakaways. As Stanley Little, President of CUPE, reiterated on a number of occasions:

> I want it known that I in no way endorse the attempts of the CIC to support the efforts of destructive organizations such as the Canadian Workers Union which is trying to dilute the strength of the Steelworkers' Union. [152]

While recognizing that some international unions did not meet the legitimate aspirations of their memberships to be recognized as Canadians, Little argued this was hardly the case with the Steelworkers. There was a pragmatism in relations between CUPE and large international unions that, pushed to its limits, recalled relations between large Canadian-based and foreign-based corporations.

The Public Service Alliance of Canada is, if anything, less overtly political than CUPE, and less influential within the CLC. In a modest way, however, it too reflected the upsurge of nationalism of the last decade. A 1972 article by the Executive Secretary of the Environmental Component argued:

> One thing is certain. Canadians are not prepared to relinquish their identity and independence. . . . Thus it is predictable that most Canadians will reject the philosophy of continentalism. The worrisome thing is that despite the nationalistic feeling of Canadians . . . our government and politicians continue to flirt with the feasibility of some sort of

continental arrangement. [153]

And as was pointed out already, the Public Service Alliance was one of the unions which along with CUPE supported the so-called reform slate at the 1974 CLC Convention, which dominated the new executive.

It is on the fringes of the official labour movement that some of the most interesting developments with respect to nationalism occured. An early example lies in a pamphlet *A Canadian Voice*, "Published by a group of Canadian workers at Vancouver, B.C., July 1967":

> American imperialism, as powerful as it seems today is a sick giant . . . Vietnam provides a view of only a small part of the army of aroused people from many countries that the Americans will soon have to face.
> The first question should be: Do Canadians want to remain independent? We say categorically, Yes! . . . In the circumstances now facing the new Canadian nation, it is very necessary that the trade union movement be free of domination from the United States . . . [154]

Late 1969 saw the publication of a special issue of *The Progressive Worker*, another Vancouver-based publication, [155] entitled "Independence and Socialism in Canada: A Marxist-Leninist View." Though too lengthy a document to be summarized in detail here, a few relevant paragraphs give its flavour and direction:

> It is the position of the Progressive Workers Movement that the development and success of a national independence movement is absolutely vital in our struggle for socialism . . . It is an undeniable fact that broad sections of the Canadian working class are thoroughly disillusioned with the policies and leadership of the "internationals" and would welcome an opportunity of an alternative Canadian labour centre which would provide leadership and a rallying point in the exodus of Canadian workers from the American unions. . . . it is critical that the working class have the leading role in the independence movement, and put forth demands that will

ensure Canada's independence, once achieved, will be lasting and that Canada will ultimately progress into a socialist state.[156]

The Council of Canadian Unions was one attempt to found such an alternative labour centre, and ever since 1969 has represented a small but persistent thorn in the side of theCLC and some of the largest international unions, especially the Steelworkers. The ideology of the CCU is overtly nationalist, aiming to provide Canadian workers with 1) an independent labour movement that is democratically run by Canadian workers and 2) an end to the "business union" philosophy of the American unions. As the CCU sees the situation:

> Canada is the only nation in the world that has a labour movement controlled from a foreign country. The consequences of such a situation have become painfully aware to thousands of Canadian trade unionists: autocratic leaders that say what we can and cannot do; "International" representatives that don't understand and couldn't care less about the Canadian situation; union dues that are shipped off to headquarters in Washington, Pittsburgh or New York. . . . The record of the CCU stands in sharp contrast to (the) business union orientation of the American unions. When it comes to a showdown, the unions in the CCU have shown that they are second to none in fighting for working class principles.[157]

Making allowance for the usual degree of hyperbole in all such pronouncements, the fact remains that the CCU has played a role on the Canadian labour scene out of all proportion to its small numbers. Most of its energy has gone into organizing against companies, not international unions, but it has provided a home for dissident unionists unhappy with organizations such as Steel. Its most famous recruit was the former Alcan local at Kitimat, B.C.,[158] but its affiliates have had a number of other successes in mining communities in B.C. Nationalism is clearly an important factor in its appeal, though not the only one.

The younger workers, because of the environment they've

been brought up under and seeing the fallacies of their society, these have a stronger feeling of anti-Americanism. It's there, let's not kid ourselves, not only in Canada but all over the world. [159]

It does not follow that the CCU will ever be successful in recruiting a majority of English Canadian workers into its ranks. Nor does it follow that some of its wilder charges against the international unions, particularly its argument that CALURA figures show consistent plundering of Canadian workers, are altogether true. [160] Nor, for that matter, does it even follow that CCU affiliates are necessarily left-leaning in their politics. [161] But for purposes of this study the CCU is significant in illustrating the movement to greater Canadian nationalism that existed among workers in English Canada between 1965 and 1975. And that movement, as we have seen, embraced the CLC itself, the international unions, Canadian-based unions in the public sector and a certain number of workers outside the official house of labour.

ENGLISH CANADA VIEWS QUEBEC

Before concluding this chapter, let us consider how different classes in English Canada viewed Quebec nationalism in this period. Opinion polls in the early 1970s indicated that an overwhelming number of English Canadians believed that Quebec would not separate from Canada and supported the federal government's invocation of the War Measures Act. [162] On the other hand, a significant number, more than 40 per cent for English Canada (cf. Table 5.4), opposed the use of force to keep Quebec inside Confederation if a majority of Quebecois wished to secede, a figure which may well have grown since 1971. By and large, the English Canadian bourgeoisie and traditional petty bourgeoisie were least favourable to Quebec's right to self-determination, while there was considerably greater support among the new petty bourgeoisie of English Canada, especially the intellectuals, and more problematically, the working class, after 1970.

Where the big bourgeoisie is concerned, hostility to Quebec's right to independence is clear enough. John Robarts, then Premier of Ontario, subsequently director of a horde of

190   *The Land of Cain*

companies, stated the position of the English Canadian bourgeoisie (and probably traditional petty bourgeoisie) *circa* 1967 succinctly:

> I firmly believe that English-speaking Canadians, by actual practice not just by words, must recognize that Canada is essentially a country of two societies and two founding peoples, in addition to the Indians and Eskimos . . . While we accept that Confederation is a partnership between two basic cultural groups . . . there is only one nation-state for all citizens of our country and that is Canada.[163]

The Official Languages Act was the extent to which they—and the federal government under Trudeau—were prepared to go.

The formation of the Canada Committee and of the General Council on Industry to advise the Quebec government in 1969—both grouping top executives of corporations like Alcan, Bell Canada, Iron Ore of Canada, Seagram's as well as the principal banks—was an indication of the English Canadian bourgeoisie's opposition to further nationalist lurches in Quebec politics. As R.C. Scrivener, Bell President, and a member of both committees, declared in 1969:

> If we don't wake up, tomorrow it will be too late. (An influential minority promotes) the methodical sabotage of our national unity. The country is going through a crisis which could break it up.[164]

The Brinks coup of April 1970, when Montreal Trust transported several million dollars worth of equity across the Ontario border prior to the Quebec provincial election, further symbolized big bourgeois opposition to the idea of independence, e.g., a victory of the Parti Quebecois.

The most interesting evidence, however, lies in the reaction of an English Canadian bourgeois nationalist, Walter Gordon, to the October crisis:

> Surely it is not reasonable to suppose that any part of Canada could separate from other parts without causing grievous harm to all concerned. If this is so, should any group of

Canadians—French Canadians, those French Canadians who live in the Province of Quebec, all Canadian citizens who live in the Province of Quebec irrespective of their origins, or the residents of any province—have the right to self-determination? . . . for better or for worse all Canadians should accept the fact that we are destined to live together for as long into the future as anyone can fortell. [165]

To be sure, then as later Gordon was prepared to offer Quebec a form of special status short of separation. [166] But on the crucial question of self-determination, Gordon, and one can assume *a fortiori* his anti-nationalist confreres in the big bourgeoisie, were resolutely opposed.

Where the traditional petty bourgeoisie is concerned, a few representative opinions will be quoted from sources by no means hostile to forms of English Canadian nationalism. A figure like Eddie Goodman, Chairman of the CIC in 1971-72, rejected the suggestion from Claude Lemelin of *Le Devoir* that the CIC's failure to make inroads in Quebec was because French Canada already had an independence movement—for Quebec.

"That's a lot of b------t" snuffed Goodman. Goodman noted that Claude Ryan, editor of *Le Devoir*, subscribed strongly to the objectives of the Committee and he claimed there was a sympathetic atmosphere in Quebec. . . . within the next year the same roots which now existed in the English-speaking provinces would be established in French-Canada. [167]

(Four years later, at its convention in Vancouver in August 1975, the CIC was still trying to come to grips with Quebec's distinctive nationalism, and had finally come around to proposing a form of special status for Quebec within a new bi-national committee. [168] There were few takers.)

Another petty bourgois nationalist no friendlier to Quebec nationalism in the early 1970s was D.W. Carr, the economic consultant whose views on the need for Canadian entrepreneurship we cited earlier. Like Walter Gordon, Carr interpreted the October Crisis to mean that the separation of Quebec from Canada was clearly impossible.

The majority of Canadians, French or non-French, cannot be convinced that it is in their interests to split the nation in order to placate a misdirected minority.[169]

The urgent need in Canada was for a strong national government to prevent Canada's nationhood from being lost through the breach in Quebec.[170]

Among the intelligentsia, e.g., the artists and writers, views were more mixed. An Al Purdy might lampoon Rene Levesque and the very concept of an independent Quebec,[171] but on the other side a Dennis Lee could confess four years later: "If I were Quebecois, I would be a separatist."[172] In this he was stating a truth which many would-be English Canadian nationalists, especially in the new petty bourgeoisie, had come to realize by the 1970s—that English Canada was one distinct national entity and Quebec another.

The first statement of this idea occurred in the student movement* in the middle and late 1960s, which here, as on the issue of anti-imperialism, played a seminal role. One Canadian Union of Students document reads:

> Quebec, as a sovereign geo-political society, must be allowed to determine its own future course *vis-a-vis* North America.[173]

Another:

> Quebec must have the right of self-determination, and this does not include the idea that this choice is made by the English-speaking majority of Canada who have been oppressing and exploiting them.[174]

And a third:

> I have by and large confined myself in this paper to a

---

*Contrast the complete distortion in James Laxer's "The Americanization of the Canadian student movement" in Ian Lumsden, *Close the 49th Parallel etc.* which gives no recognition to the pioneering role of the Canadian Union of Students and various new left groups in raising the twin issues of imperialism and Quebec in English Canada.

discussion of student unionism as it has developed in the predominantly English-speaking provinces. My use of the terms Canada, Canadian and national should be understood in this light. Whenever I employ the term "Canadian" in reference to student unions, I am in fact referring to student unions—whether local, provincial, or national—outside Quebec.[175]

The Canadian Union of Students and the Union Generale des Etudiants du Quebec began to put into practice the theory of two separate nations—English Canada and Quebec.

Such an idea was of course heresy to a *Canadian* nationalist like Donald Creighton, for whom the menace to Canada in the late 1960s and early 1970s came as much from French Canada as from the United States:

> . . . the movement to reconstitute Canada in the interest of bilingualism and biculturalism can have only one possible outcome—the creation of a separate Quebec.

> Canadian nationalism can be preserved only by a comprehensive program in which resistance to excessive particularism and defence against aggressive continentalism is each an integral part.[176]

Creighton was not alone. A social democrat like Kenneth McNaught showed scarcely greater sympathy, equating French-Canadian nationalism with "racialism," not to speak of "introverted racial totalitarianism."[177] A liberal like Ramsay Cook had little sympathy for any nationalism tending towards the nation state.[178] The list of English Canadian academics of similar persuasion would be almost endless for the 1960s and might still be impressive in the 1970s.

Yet there were countervailing views. Reference was made in Chapter Four to Gad Horowitz, who in the mid-1960s in *Canadian Dimension*, was arguing the case for an English Canadian nationalism side by side with Quebec's. By 1970-71 such a view had become central to the Waffle which, as a result of the October Crisis, argued at the 1971 NDP convention in behalf of Quebec's right to self-determination up to and including independence. By extension, the argument became one for alliances between left nationalists in English Canada and in Quebec.

> For English Canadians who are concerned with building an anti-imperialist socialist independence movement in English Canada, the struggle in Quebec is enormously significant. In it lies the hope that English Canadians and Quebecois will no longer be victimized by a federal system which has simply handed both parts of the country over to the American corporations. Let us hope that an anti-imperialist alliance is possible. [179]

More moderate English Canadian nationalists in the new petty bourgeoisie were, however, also coming to a self-determination position. Abe Rotstein, one of the co-founders of the CIC and no admirer of the Waffle on most questions, agreed with the latter's position on Quebec. [180] For Rotstein, as for many other English Canadian academics, the October Crisis sparked a *crise de conscience* which led him to conclude:

> Nationalists in (English Canada) must realize that the continued repression of Quebec will only create a society which is not worth inhabiting. . . . Our dialogue must be reopened in a serious vein; our emphasis must be on techniques, on institutions, and strategies that deal evenhandedly with the interests of two emerging nations. [181]

A work published in 1971, *One Country or Two?* showed English Canadian academics of moderate persuasion wrestling with the question of Quebec independence.

> Separation is no longer a remote possibility advocated by a small group of militants. It is a respectable political movement. It may well succeed. [182]

While the author of this quotation, Richard Simeon, made clear his personal dislike for Quebec separation, he also underlined his preference for an amicable, negotiated separation *a la* Levesque's *Option Quebec* over a scenario involving civil war:

If Quebec were to decide, democratically, to opt for separation, my own desire would be for English Canadians to
recognize the legitimacy of such self-determination, to
pursue strategies which would encourage maintenance of
relatively friendly authorities within Quebec, and to use the
considerable bargaining power available to ensure economic
cooperation on beneficial terms. [183]

Entre petits bourgeois, on peut s'arranger.

That same year, Denis Smith, a Canadian nationalist of liberal
persuasion, could formally espouse Quebec's right to self-
determination:

(Is) it permissible for Quebec to secede peacefully from
Canada? For liberal democrats, as opposed to liberal
defenders of vested interests or vested power, the answer
can only be yes. [184]

Three years later the idea had clearly come into its own when a
conservative academic, whose intellectual hero is Edmund
Burke, could argue, even while rejecting the *term* self-
determination:

The claim that Quebec possesses a right to self-
determination is either mistaken or else it is a misleading
and unfortunate way of saying something worthwhile and
important: namely the values of civility to which Canadians
aspire, and which they sometimes achieve, precludes the
application of force to stop a secessionist movement of the
kind contemplated. [185]

Clearly a good number of Canadian academics, if not necessarily
the new petty bourgeoisie as a whole, had come to a form of
recognition of Quebec's right to self-determination—one of the
crucial questions outlined in Chapter One as determining the
progressive or reactionary character of English Canadian
nationalism.

Where the working class is concerned, there is also evidence of
movement towards recognition of Quebec's specificity, if not

necessarily of her right to self-determination. Back in 1965-66, the CLC in its brief to the Royal Commission on Bilingualism and Biculturalism had argued, "Canada must remain a united nation," even while accepting the necessity of aiding the French language to survive [186]

During the October Crisis, the CLC, like the NDP, expressed concern about the proclamation of the War Measures Act, but in the name of due process and civil liberties, not theoretical rights to self-determination.[187]

In 1974, however, for the first time, the CLC leadership was faced squarely with demands from the Quebec Federation of Labour for autonomy within the Congress, and was forced to yield.

> The (QFL)'s resolution sought control over 1) the educational program that is now conducted by the Congress; 2) jurisdiction over labour councils, and control of Congress staff now assigned to service them; and 3) the allocation of funds for use by the Federation. The proposals were based on cultural and language differences, and the presence in Quebec of a competing central labour organization, the Confederation of National Trade Unions. The administration was opposed to the resolution.
>
> There was immediate and vehement objection from the floor. QFL President Louis Laberge maintained that, in Quebec, the CLC was far outstripped by the CNTU, and that large international unions were suffering as a result. He insisted that the CLC presence in Quebec could be properly maintained only by strengthening the Federation.
>
> The delegates' rejection of the administration position, and their support for the Quebec resolution, was overwhelming.[188]

Despite claims by Joe Morris, CLC President, in an interview with the author,[189] that this in no way reduced the QFL's ultimate responsibility to Congress for policies, the die may well have been cast. The QFL has attained a form of special status within the CLC, recognition of its unique national character. The future may well see a repetition of the UGEQ-CUS separation.[190]

The CLC has not, thus far, come out in support of Quebec's

right to self-determination. This position was, not surprisingly, advanced by small left-wing groups such as Progressive Workers in the late 1960s,[191] and has even been proposed at CUPE conventions, though by a local from Quebec.[192] Yet one suspects that in practice the reaction of the CLC as a whole to a hypothetical bid for independence by a Quebec government would be along the same pragmatic lines some of the academics cited above suggest—acceptance in principle, with an attempt to work out the best possible modalities for separation. Only the future will say for sure.

THEORETICAL CONCLUSIONS

The decline in the American empire, by which we mean the weakening of American military, economic and political power, provided the setting for the upsurge of Canadian nationalism between 1965-75.

The relative decline in the American position saw a corresponding improvement in the position of other capitalist powers, including Canada. Paradoxically, this led to less rather than more nationalism on the part of the Canadian big bourgeoisie, whose lingering fear of American domination vanished. Instead, the Canadian big bourgeoisie aspired to multinational status, making it an inveterate enemy of all nationalisms, English Canadian no less than Quebecois. The fact that the major support for nationalism was now coming from the new petty bourgeoisie also turned most of the big bourgeoisie against a concept of the nation, which usually entailed a strong state sector.

The smaller bourgeoisie for its part could not aspire to multinational status, and found its interests increasingly at odds with those of the big bourgeoisie, foreign- and Canadian-controlled, regarding advantages of scale or availability of research and development. Without espousing an unqualified nationalism, many of its members could see the utility of measures that would reduce the size of foreign investment in the monopoly sector and perhaps of the Canadian big bourgeoisie itself relative to themselves. Unlike elements of the new petty bourgeoisie or of the working class, however, the smaller bourgeoisie could not challenge the "free enterprise" assumptions of Canadian capitalism or welcome an increased role for the state in the Canadian political economy.

Farmers and self-employed professionals from lawyers and accountants to writers and artists show no unified class interest, splitting in different directions according to whether their interests were linked to a multinational capitalism or not.

The most important social class behind the rise of a new nationalism was the new petty bourgeoisie. For the intelligentsia in the burgeoning educational sector, American models were losing their attraction. The margin of manoeuvre of the Canadian state meanwhile increased as American power declined. The fact that the social and economic functions of the state were growing by leaps and bounds gave those working directly or indirectly for the state an importance unprecedented in the Canadian political economy. Like their counterparts in Quebec in the early 60s, many members of the English Canadian new petty bourgeoisie came to identify nationalism with a strong state sector, based predominantly in Ottawa, but sometimes in the regions. Some could even envisage a separate Quebec state. Ideologically, the nationalism of the new petty bourgeoisie could range from a socialist anti-imperialism on the left to support for a mixed economy or an independent Canadian capitalism on the centre and right. That important elements of this class also opposed nationalism further underlines the new petty bourgeoisie's vacillating character. Cohesion is at a premium; but some of its members have access to important ideological and political levers of power, which made its nationalist component a force to be reckoned with in the period in question.

As for the working class, the stranglehold of the international unions over the CLC weakened somewhat, without disappearing. There was greater support for nationalism, not only in the public sector unions, but among the members of internationals themselves. This reflected the declining economic appeal for Canadian workers of American imperialism and of its long-time appendage, the American trade union movement, opening the door to an increasingly autonomous and independent Canadian trade union movement, though not necessarily to a more radical one. To speak of a specifically working class-based nationalism, implying a concept of the nation rooted in the working class, would be going to far. Rather one saw fairly widespread support for the kind of nationalism articulated by members of the new petty bourgeoisie, coupled with opposition to nationalism, especially by members of the older trade union bureaucracy.

Chapter Six
SOCIALISM AND NATIONALISM

We have now completed the major part of what we set out to do in Chapter One, namely, to examine the development of national consciousness in English Canada since World War II, relating it to the changing fortunes of American imperialism and to the changing perceptions of the different classes within English Canada over the thirty-year period. We have also made mention of English Canadian attitudes towards Quebec, especially since the so-called Quiet Revolution of the early 1960s.

What now remains to be done is to assess the significance of what we have uncovered "in a world of multinational corporations and national liberation movements," answering at the same time the strategic questions posed in Chapter One.

Regarding the potentially oppressive character of English Canadian nationalism *vis-a-vis* Quebec, we have seen that attitudes range from insistence on unity, i.e., a united Canada embracing Quebec, at almost any price, to support for the principle of self-determination for Quebec. As was argued in Chapter One, the historical basis of English Canadian nationalism was a Confederation from sea to sea, without recognition of two distinctly English Canadian and Quebec nations. Even in the submissions to the Royal Commission on Bilingualism and Biculturalism by English Canadians in the middle 1960s, there was almost no recognition of the bi-national character of the country.

Yet attitudes evolve, and one of the most striking changes, from the author's point of view, has been the emergence of a distinctively *English Canadian* sense of nationhood in the last decade or so. Even while official attitudes, as evidenced by the Royal Commission Report and the Official Languages Act, were moving in the direction of cultural and linguistic bi-nationalism within a single nation state, attitudes among the young, e.g., students, and among the intelligentsia of English Canada were moving to firmer recognition of the political reality of two nations side by side.

The development of a modernizing Quebec nationalism in the early 1960s, based on the French-Canadian petty bourgeoisie, the students and the intellectuals, but embracing with time significant numbers of white-collar and blue-collar workers as well as elements of the traditional petty bourgeoisie, was one important factor.The October Crisis, with its evocation of the possibility of armed intervention by Ottawa against a hypothetical bid for independence by some future Quebec government, was another. Still a third was the development of English Canada's own sense of national identity in the late 1960s and early 1970s, especially among members of English Canada's new petty bourgeoisie, which made these more willing to acknowledge similar rights to national identity—up to and including independence—for Quebec.

To be sure, the process has been an unequal one, and as we have argued, some classes, especially the dominant English Canadian big bourgeoisie, are far from ready to entertain the possibility of Quebec's separation. Nor would the mass of English Canadian opinion, in the working class no less than in the petty bourgeoisie old and new, necessarily welcome or support a move to independence by Quebec, *particularly* if this were on the part of a Quebec government with only a minority of popular support. And here we do not raise the further question of the nature of such a Quebec independence movement, e.g., if it were to the left of the Parti Quebecois' rather technocratic capitalist program.[1]

Potentially, then, an English Canadian nationalism could still be turned against Quebec in alliance with those forces within Quebec itself which oppose independence. These forces can include the predominantly (though not exclusively) English-speaking big bourgeoisie, the smaller bourgeoisie, elements of the traditional and new petty bourgeoisie, and probably more conservative elements of the working class itself. And since the class struggle in Quebec has been sharper in recent years than in English Canada, since there may well be pressure from the left of the trade union movement, from elements of the intelligentsia, etc., to go further than the petty bourgeois independence the Parti Quebecois has in mind, the possibility of armed confrontation both between Quebecois and between the English Canadian military and more radical Quebecois, is by no means a fantasy. Such is the pessimistic scenario.

The optimistic one would point to growing support for Quebec's right to self-determination among the intelligentisia and, to some extent, the trade union movement of English Canada; a revulsion (if only retrospective) against the use of the War Measures Act in 1970; and greater confidence in English Canada's ability to make it on its own. The very parallels we have noted between the class basis of Quebec nationalism after 1960 and of English Canadian after 1965, the opposition of the Canadian big bourgeoisie to both in recent years, the impact of American imperialism on each, make for some possibility of cooperation between a progressive English Canadian and Quebec nationalism.

As was argued at the end of Chapter Two, English Canada was not simply an oppressed or colonized nation in the post-World War II period in the way that third world countries were victims of a more classical colonialism. Indeed, as public opinion surveys bear out,there was strong majority support for continentalism in economic, defence and foreign policy through two decades of Cold War, something which left nationalists may decry, to no avail. It was *only* when American imperialism began to weaken internationally in the 1960s that English Canadian sentiment began to shift, and that anti-imperialism, or simply anti-Americanism, became a potent force.

As was also argued, however, the fact that Canada was not a colony of the classical kind, that her standard of living, class structure, political institutions, levels of education, etc., were very much those of an advanced capitalist country, does not mean that there was not a strong dependency in Canadian-American relations. Though a first world country, Canada was in the peculiar position of having a significant proportion of its economy *directly* controlled by the largest American corporations, and its foreign and defence policies, culture, etc., strongly influenced by the United States.

Canada, to be sure, was not the only country to experience American domination in the post-war period, quite the contrary. But the forms of domination were more direct and threatening to a sense of separate nationhood than in the case of the capitalist countries of Western Europe or of Japan. The colonial mentality of the Canadian bourgeoisie was a contributing factor—i.e., Canada lacked the tradition of strong nationalism that national bourgeoisies of most other capitalist societies had developed over the previous centuries. And other classes—the petty bourgeoisie, the working class—were too weak, or ideologically subservient to the big bourgeoisie, especially in the period of the Cold War, to provide an alternative basis for nationalism.

The result was a mortgaging of Canadian sovereignty in numerous fields, even while the shell of political independence was maintained. American capital sparked much of Canada's development in the post-war years, particularly in the resource field, with Canadian capitalism becoming organically integrated with that of the United States both within Canada and without. Canadian banks helped finance branch-plant expansions at home, while benefiting from the American umbrella in their own activities in the United States, the West Indies, etc. Large Canadian corporations were prepared to work side by side with American- and foreign-controlled ones inside such organizations as the Canadian Manufacturers Association, in turn coming to aspire to multinational status in the international sphere. Canada's external policies mirrored the same approach.

To say that recent English Canadian nationalism has been progressive, then, is true insofar as it challenges the hegemony of American imperialism within Canada's own borders. But it is not necessarily progressive if it simply means supporting Canadian capitalism, a la the Committee for an Independent Canada, supporting national unity a la Expo or the War Measures Act, and racism or oppression at home or abroad. English

Canadian nationalism is not necessarily *progressive*, though neither is it *necessarily* reactionary or oppressive. The determining factor, ultimately, is its ideology and class basis.

This brings us to the class basis of English Canadian nationalism, which we examined empirically in Chapters 3-5.

Regarding the big bourgeoisie, we found strong support for Canada's integration into the American empire throughout the post-war years, coupled with support for *limited* forms of nationalism. If strategically the big bourgeoisie, and with it the Canadian state, saw no alternative to close integration with the United States in a bi-polar world, in practice, there was always a minimum commitment to the preservation of a *formally* sovereign country. *The Canadian bourgeoisie was never entirely comprador in its behavior.*

Some were of course more concerned with sovereignty than others, and we mentioned such names as Vincent Massey, George Drew, Walter Gordon or James Coyne to illustrate our case. But even the most continentalist of bourgeois spokesmen, e.g., C.D. Howe, could insist on Canadian equity and managerial participation in the operation of branch-plants, while effectively furthering the American takeover.

What is interesting, in fact, is to see that the strongest manifestations of nationalism between 1945-65 came from members of the big bourgeoisie—the Massey Royal Commission, the Gordon Commission, Coyne's speeches, Gordon's 1963 budget—and that other social classes reacted to their lead. *The Financial Post* is a more accurate guide to English Canadian nationalism—with all its contradictions—up until 1965 than is *The Canadian Forum* or *The Canadian Unionist/Canadian Labour*. It is only after 1965 that this changes dramatically.

Of course, one should not exaggerate. The majority of the big bourgeoisie was firmly continentalist from 1945 on. *But* a certain residue of an earlier pro-British bourgeois outlook remained— e.g., the Tory nationalism of a George Drew or Henry Bordon—while members of the bourgeoisie, as the dominant class in Canada, may have had the sense of their class interests *being* at the same time the national interest, with certain consequences for nationalism. Hence our observation that, unlike Quebec in the 1950s or 1960s, English Canadian nationalism betweeen 1945-65 was primarily a bourgeois, not petty bourgeois, phenomenon.

Since the middle 1960s, however, this is no longer the case. The development of Canadian-based multinational corporations and banks is one crucial factor, as is the fusion of interests betweeen Canadian- and American-based sections of the big bourgeoisie. Equally important are the challenges to bourgeois hegemony, Canadian no less than American, represented by external developments—e.g., the successful liberation movement of Indo-China, the rise of OPEC—and by internal ones, in particular the development of a strong state sector, provincially and federally, not *exclusively* subordinated to the big bourgeoisie.

The aspiration of the largest Canadian-controlled corporations and banks to multinational status has meant a hesitation on their part to support nationalism, economic or political, that can potentially be turned against their own activities abroad. The speeches and statements of bank and corporate presidents, Canadian Manufacturers Association officials or editorials in *The Financial Post* bear this out.

A minority, to be sure, accepts the reality of the situation, e.g., the need for the Foreign Investment Review Act, but is most careful to couch its nationalism in *moderate* and cautious forms. There is too much dry tinder around to indulge in radical rhetoric.

Externally, the margins of capitalism are shrinking and third world countries have served notice they will no longer put up with "the free flow of capital" which is the other side of capitalist exploitation:

> Every country has the right to exercize permanent sovereignty over its national resources and all economic activities.
>
> i) Every country has the right to exercise effective control over natural resources . . . including the right of nationalization or transfer of ownership to its nationals.
>
> ii) Peoples under foreign occupation, colonial rule, *apartheid* have the right to full compensation for depletion and damage to natural resources.
>
> iii) Nationalization is an expression of the sovereign right of every country to safeguard its resources; in this connexion, every country has the right to fix the amount

of possible compensation and mode of payment, while
possible disputes have to be solved in accordance with
domestic laws of every country.[2]

Internally, the nationalism of other classes, expecially the
statism advocated by members of the new petty bourgeoisie,
challenges the untramelled decision-making power of large
corporations, hemming these in with regulations, controls and, in
some cases, actual government ownership. To be sure, the
interpenetration of big capital and the state continues, and many
of the state's functions, e.g., those of accumulation and
legitimatization outlined by James O'Connor in *The Fiscal Crisis
of the State*,[3] are ultimately supportive of what must be called
monopoly capitalism. (One thinks of ARDA, tax write-offs,
research and development grants, transportation infrastructure,
or export incentives.)

Yet the state in an advanced capitalist society is not merely an
executive committee "for managing the common affairs of the
whole bourgeoisie," as Marx and Engels described it in 1848.[4]
True, the bourgeoisie remains the dominant class in contemporary capitalism, *but* the liberal state must mediate different class
interests, from time to time asserting policies unwelcome to the
big bourgeoisie (though not imcompatible with the maintenance
of the capitalist system, as Ralph Miliband might argue.[5]) One
example of this in Canada was the Foreign Investment Review
Act, weak as it was, which the big bourgeoisie did not support.
Another may be more recent government moves against the tax
status of *Time* and *Reader's Digest*. A third would be the
initiatives taken by social democratic governments provincially,
e.g., Premier Blakeney's partial potash takeover or former
Premier Barrett's mining legislation, bitterly opposed by the big
bourgeoisie, foreign- and Canadian-controlled.

Overall, then, nationalism is by no means a welcome ideology
to many in the big bourgeoisie, who see it associated with left or
centre-left causes in much of the world, and with social classes,
e.g., the new petty bourgeoisie in English Canada, potentially in
competition for political hegemony.[6]

Where the smaller bourgeoisie and traditional petty bourgeoisie are concerned, we found relatively little nationalism on
the part of small businessmen or self-employed professionals

between 1945-65, and very limited examples in the case of farmers. There was not through those years a coherent sense of class interest on the part of these groups, which meant their attitudes on nationalism were passive, rather than active, determined by what the big bourgeoisie was saying and doing.

Since 1965, however, there has been significant development of class consciousness on the part of small business, e.g., the Canadian Federation of Independent Business. Reacting to the twin power of the large corporations and the multinational corporations, small business wants its share of the pie and is prepared to use nationalism to bolster its case. This is not, however, the nationalism of the new petty bourgeoisie looking to the state, but rather one wanting the state to support *its* activities through tax write-offs and so on. Ideologically, then, it is even less friendly to the large state sector than is the big bourgeoisie itself.

Self-employed professionals since 1965 split down the middle regarding nationalism. Those in occupations most closely allied with big business and the corporate sector—lawyers, accountants —oppose it for much the same reasons as the big bourgeoisie or alternatively support moderate courses of action, e.g., the Foreign Investment Review Act. Others, e.g., artists and writers, have a definite stake in the new nationalism, being its cultural custodians and economic beneficiaries.

Farmers, a declining force in Canada, divide between large and small, nationalist and anti-nationalist, without any clear ideological coherence. Even those who are nationalist, however, tend to be influenced by the nationalism articulated by other classes.

The most significant force for English Canadian nationalism since 1965, we have argued, has been the new petty bourgeoisie, i.e., salaried professionals, especially in the state sector. Between 1945-65, however, academics, students, or civil servants were not enthusiastic nationalists. On the contrary, liberal anti-nationalism swept everything before it, while intellectually the United States was seen as the chief market place of ideas, culture, and so on. There were voices in the wilderness so to speak, e.g., Harold Innis, Donald Creighton, Kenneth Mc-Naught, but they were drowned out in the chorus of Hallelujahs to the American empire.

Exceptionally, members of the new petty bourgeoisie might

support limited forms of nationalism in this period, e.g., the cultural concerns articulated by the Massey Commission. The occasional journalist, e.g., G.V. Ferguson, James M. Minifie, James B. McGeachie might speak up. The still more occasional civil servant, e.g., the D.B.S. statisticians C.D. Blyth and E.B. Carty, could lend a little credence to the unsubstantiated (and for this period incorrect) thesis of S.D. Clark that the civil service has been the backbone of Canadian nationalism.[7] But they were the exceptions.

After 1965 it is quite a different ball-game. Influenced by the success of their petty bourgeois counterparts in Quebec, motivated by the same anti-war sentiment as their counterparts in the United States, academics and students, in particular, were attracted to a new Canadian nationalism. To be sure, this was not a universal phenomenon and there was *still* significant resistance in academic quarters to anything smacking of nationalism. But a petty bourgeois form of nationalism did take off, and whether in the anti-imperialist ideology of the Canadian Union of Students or Waffle, the centrist ideology of the CIC or Canadian Association of University Teachers, or more conservative variants, became a central feature of Canadian politics in the early 1970s.

This new nationalism coincided with a tremendous increase in the functions of the state: higher education, health services, the Canada Pension Plan, regional development programs, science policy, environmental concerns. A non-Marxist political scientist observes:

> The emergent national policy is in several important respects congruent with both past Canadian experience and how an increasing number of Canadians are beginning to view the national economy. Like the older national policy, it gives the federal government a crucial role in economic development.[8]

What Donald Smiley fails to realize, however, is that the take-off of the state sector is not confined to Canada, but is a feature of the political economies of all post-war capitalist societies of the West (see Tables 6.1 and 6.2).

We are dealing then with a secular phenomenon that transcends Canada and is in no way a throw-back to an earlier period of Canadian capitalist development, e.g., the national

TABLE 6.1
State Expenditure[1] in Major OECD Countries
Per cent of Gross Domestic Product in 1972

	U.K.	France	West Germany	Italy	USA
Total Expenditure	39.8	36.7	38.0	40.0	34.3

1 Excluding state productive enterprises

Source: Ian Gough, "State Expenditure and Capital," *New Left Review* No. 92, July-August, 1975, Table 1, p. 59, in turn based on OECD National Accounts statistics.

TABLE 6.2
State Expenditure in the UK, 1910-1973
Per cent of GNP in each year

	1910	1937	1951	1961	1971	1973
Total Public Expenditure	12.7	25.7	44.9	42.1	50.3	50.5

Source: Ian Gough, "State Expenditure and Capital," *op. cit.*, Table 2, p. 60, in turn based on British statistical studies, governmental and academic.

policy of 1879. Rather, it is the specific nature of contemporary capitalism that makes the state so central to economic activity, as planner, co-partner to private capital, manager of industrial relations (labour legislation, price and incomes policy), legitimatizer of the system (social security, health insurance, unemployment insurance), promoter of human capital formation (education), scientific research. And in advanced capitalist society, a new social class—scientists, academics, state technocrats—becomes important.

One does not have to buy Galbraith's terminology about the technostructure—itself a throw-back to Veblen's or St. Simon's paeons to the engineers—to recognize the significance of what we have called the new petty bourgeoisie. R. Richta and his school did so well before Galbraith, in their writings in Czechoslovakia before 1968.[9] Alain Touraine and Serge Mallet have done no less for France, pre- and post-May 1968.[10]

The rise of the English Canadian new petty bourgeoisie over the post-war period was documented in Chapter Two; its

ideological impact began to be felt after 1965. The specificity of
Canadian capitalism—i.e., the presence of large-scale American
investment, the fusion between Canadian- and American-
controlled capital—gave the new petty bourgeoisie in English
Canada a more nationalist animus than its counterparts in other
capitalist countries, e.g., the United States, France, West
Germany. Even the Canadian student movement, just like its
counterpart in Quebec, was more sympathetic to nationalism
than were new left movements in other countries. (cf. One of the
slogans of the May 1968 student revolt in France, "Down with
national frontiers.")

The new petty bourgeoisie, to be sure, did not support only
nationalism. Its most significant ideological characteristic, as we
have tried to show, was in the direction of a strong state sector.
This led some to espouse a form of socialism, others the mixed
economy. But state intervention was seen as a positive good.

The new breed of civil servants that has entered the lists over
the last decade, provincially and federally, advanced a similar
philosophy. Without being rigidly hostile to "private enterprise," they wished to see many of its activities, especially where
firms were foreign-controlled, regulated and checked by the
state. They were certainly more prepared for nationalist
departures in economic or foreign policy than were their
predecessors, prisoners of a cold war liberalism. The world of
Lester Pearson and A.D.P. Heeney was dead and gone.

Even salaried professionals in the private sector, e.g.,
journalists or managers, could see nationalism as helping their
cause. For the former, much like for artists and writers, it
provided an ideological prism through which to view the world
and stake out their own place. For the latter, it might provide a
stepping-stone to greater power, especially within foreign-
controlled firms.

Overall, then, the new petty bourgeoisie has been the
strongest supporter of nationalism in recent years and its
greatest beneficiary. Government policy has been unusually
responsive to its demands—perhaps because so many in
government positions are themselves members of this class.
Ideological cohesion has been greater among the salaried
professionals than was the case before—their numbers have
exploded, their organizational skills increased, reinforced by the

increased importance of the institutions—universities, government departments, research institutes, the media—in which they find themselves.

There are, however, real limits to their power. Canada, like other Western societies, remains a capitalist one, with the bourgeoisie very much in control. Our capitalist class is not about to turn power over gracefully to a new group (cf. the venom with which the capitalist class in British Columbia attacked the essentially "new petty bourgeois" government of Dave Barrett). Our relations with the United States, while looser than before, are still enormously restrictive. Moreover, the new petty bourgeoisie in English Canada is by no means united in the objectives it seeks, whether with respect to nationalism, socialism, or what have you. In this they resemble those classical petty bourgeois of yore, the farmers, with an oscillating and indeterminate attitude towards capital and labour.

In other Western societies, e.g., France, Italy, even England, one would be able to put the working class forward as the principal antagonist to bourgeois domination. In English Canada, however, one of the sad but undeniable truths is that this has not been the case over most of the post-World War II period. Whatever Marxism may say in theory, the Canadian working class, by and large, has not behaved like a class-conscious proletariat. The trade union leadership, e.g., the Canadian Labour Congress, is reformist in the extreme, and the rank and file, in a general way, not given to radical political demands.

The situation the trade union movement and, *a fortiori*, the working class found itself in through the years of the Cold War was one of subordination to the bourgeoisie, Canadian and American. This process was only strengthened by the subordination of the Canadian trade union movement to that of the United States and by the strong anti-communism of the time. Bourgeois ideology

tend(ed) to prevail, to gain the upper hand, to propagate itself throughout society—bringing about not only a unison of economic and political aims, but also intellectual and moral unity, posing all the questions around which the struggle rages not on a corporate but on a "universal" plane, and thus creating the hegemony of a fundamental social group over a series of subordinate groups.[11]

To be fair, the labour movement in Quebec overcame even greater obstacles—Duplessis, the ideological power of the Church, the power of capital—in forging its militancy in the post-war years, coming by the early 1970s to a quasi-Marxist type of analysis quite unique on the North American continent.[12] And just possibly, the labour movement in English Canada will follow a similar course. But for the moment, one should not take one's desires to be reality.

If anti-imperialism can be taken as one litmus test of trade union/working class consciousness over the thirty-year period, then it is evident that English Canadian workers have tended to follow rather than lead other social classes. In the late 1940s and early 1950s, the trade union movement was swept up in the wave of Cold War liberalism, accepting uncritically Canadian participation in NATO, the Korean War and various continental projects in the economic and defence fields. If there was a minimal criticism of American domination, it was in such areas as culture, where the Canadian bourgeoisie itself was giving a lead.

Similarly in the mid-1950s, the CLC agreed with the criticism of American branch-plants in Canada voiced by the Gordon Commission or with the joint Conservative-CCF opposition to the Trans-Canada Pipeline Loan. Yet it cooperated readily with CIA-financed labour activities in Latin America, resolutely opposed suggestions of neutralism voiced by people like James M. Minifie, and time and time again defended the role of "international" unions in this country.

If nationalism becomes somewhat more important in the CLC by the middle and late 60s, it is because of its increased importance for Canada as a whole. In no substantial way does the CLC leadership deviate from the moderate criticisms of multinationals voiced by the Watkins or Gray Reports, while within the NDP the CLC has by and large been a force on the right, e.g., its strong opposition to everything the Waffle represented.

Though there have been unmistakable moves towards nationalism within the CLC, for some of the reasons outlined in Chapter Five, the CLC leadership has been uncomfortable with the question and incapable of re-defining it to correspond to working class interests, i.e., socialism. This has been left to small groups outside the CLC, whose relative ineffectiveness to date leaves one fairly sceptical about the immediate prospects for a radical working class politics. An anti-imperialist coalition led by the working class, then, while desirable, would seem almost impossible in the present situation in this country.

Does it follow that nationalism is simply the ideology of the new petty bourgeoisie, and that socialists, even when members of that self-same petty bourgeoisie, should spurn it under all conditions? Nothing could be more erroneous. For just as in Quebec, the raising of the national question in English Canada in recent years may have led to a more radical form of class politics.

If the working class was a mute witness to many of the debates among the politicians and intellectuals of Quebec's *petite bourgeoisie nouvelle* during the Quiet Revolution, this was no longer true in the ensuing years. Separatism opened the door to an interesting type of politics—the questioning of the federal system, true, but for some at least, of the capitalist system itself. If student demonstrations were one form of activity and terrorist bombings another, the most important of all were the militant strikes and occupations that swept Quebec from 1965 on, culminating in the La Presse demonstration and Common Front strike of 1971-72. Working class radicalism was forged in the cauldron of nationalist politics and may yet come to transcend it.

In English Canada there has been greater politicization in the last ten years to the reality of multinational corporations and their power than in previous decades. The fading of the American dream, the weakening of continental ties, inflation and the growing crisis of capitalism have all had their effect. There may now be a greater potential for socialist consciousness in English Canada than has been true at any time since the end of World War II.

Nationalism has helped this process along, even though it has been primarily petty bourgeois in character. The weakening of ties between Canadian and American capitalism makes the possibility of a Canadian socialism greater, rather than smaller. At the minimum it helps remove the permanent cloud which has hung over Canadian economic development ever since the massive American capital inflows began around the beginning of this century.

> The "expropriation of the expropriators" could not be
> successfully carried out in Canada much in advance of a
> similar event in the United States. Or to put it in much more
> immediate and practical terms, a country that is dependent
> to a considerable extent on foreign borrowing must, if it is to
> borrow economically, follow social, economic, and political
> policies that commend themselves reasonably well to the
> relatively small group that controls the money market in
> which it borrows. [13]

To be sure, socialists must at all costs avoid subordinating
socialist principles to some unhyphenated Canadianism. The big
bourgeoisie and elements of the petty bourgeoisie hostile to
socialism can play the game of patriotism far more effectively. So
much the history of Canada through two world wars and the
October Crisis should teach us.

There are, moreover, forms of chauvinism that sometimes
surface in English Canada that must be challenged. Robin
Mathews is one example in his fulminations against all things
American and rejection of the internationalist dimension of
socialism:

> Liberation in the U.S.—liberation of anybody or anything—
> is the liberation of the individual within a society that
> possesses world predominance in power. Liberation in the
> U.S. involves the individual getting loose from a cruel
> imperial monolith, getting loose from it from within . . .
> Liberation in a dependency like Canada has, in contrast, got
> to be liberation with the people for the people and in a way
> that releases in the community the strength to survive and to
> throw off the imperial master while changing the structures
> that support the imperial predominance. [14]

Heather Robertson is another who fails to distinguish between
opposition to American imperialism and hatred for Americans:

> About a year ago I met a member of the Committee for an
> Independent Canada outside a radio station after a hotline

brawl about Canadian nationalism. "Whew," he said, looking guilty, "I almost admitted I was anti-American."

Why not? It would at least be an admission of the truth. I am sick of all the sniveling hand-wringing cant about our good friend and neighbour to the south, the longest undefended border in the world blah blah while this good friend, violent and explosive abroad and corrupt at home, treats us with contempt and robs us blind. I am anti-American. There, it's said. The secret is out. I do not identify with American traditions or sympathize with American values. I feel no comradeship. They are foreigners; I like them less the more they push me around. [15]

Even the Vietnamese and Chinese, with far more reason to hate the United States than we have, could distinguish between regimes and peoples during their national struggles. A socialist must place a class perspective first and foremost in his analysis.

At the same time, there is the need to re-think the strategy of transition to socialism. Socialism, if it is to come to Canada, may not come in a great apocalyptical wave. Instead, we must envisage what Fernand Dumont has called "un socialisme d'ici," [16] not necessarily the semi-Proudhonian model that he outlines for Quebec, but a socialism or Marxism adapted to the realities of Canada in the late 20th Century.

For example, the tendency of late capitalist society may be to ever more intervention by the state in the whole economic process. We have seen this in Canada with Price and Incomes Policy, a significant step beyond the purely Keynesian monetary and fiscal measures outlined in the White Paper on Employment and Income at the end of the Second World War. The state has served notice that salaries and prices are too important to be left to the market place alone.

To be sure, such intervention, just like public ownership of particular industries or services, does not constitute socialism. And there are countries enough, in the third and second, no less than first worlds, whose "socialism" is little more than statism, having precious little to do with direct control and power by the working class and mass of the population. I include in this category the countries of eastern Europe with "socialized" means

of production, no less than many third world countries where
"private" ownership persists. Sixty years after the Russian
Revolution it is no longer good enough to say that things have
gone wrong with the Soviet model. We *must* envisage something
better.

That something better, to be sure, does not rule out an
intelligent use of the state. If anything, the cunning of reason
suggests that the growth in state functions under capitalism may
itself in time lead to quantitative change becoming qualitative.
Monopoly state capitalism, still with predominantly private
control and direction of the means of production, may give way
eventually to an equation where the state, rather than private
capital, is the dominant force. (Is this not the road down which
England seems to be headed?) And this new form of state
capitalism may yet provide, not without struggles, the basis for a
leap into socialism.

In an advanced industrialized society, moreover, socialism, in
addition to public ownership of the principal means of
production, must embrace forms of industrial as well as direct
democracy that would take a society such as Canada considerably
further in the direction of participation and democratization than
liberalism ever can. This will, no doubt, entail a socialist or
Marxist party well to the left of what the NDP is today. It will also
be helped if the international factors leading to socialization in
various third world countries or first world ones such as Italy and
France, intensify rather than diminish.

This brings us back directly to the subject of class and
nationalism. For aspirations to democratization are potentially no
less appealing to members of the new petty bourgeoisie than to
the working class. It is not an accident that the student
movement, a movement of the new petty bourgeoisie *par
excellence*, put participation and direct democracy back on the
agenda of Western societies, and that in some instances these
have found an important echo in the ranks of the working class.
One thinks of the factory occupations in France in May 1968, and
of the concept of *autogestion* or workers' control to which many
trade unions and parties of the left in Europe now give lip service.
Even in Quebec, there have been analogous developments—
taking over the running of factories, e.g., the Regent Knitting
Mill in St. Jerome.

Nationalism can be part of the same process. Just possibly the working class, in alliance with much of the new petty bourgeoisie and even with certain segments of the traditional petty bourgeoisie, can impose a new conception of the nation, as part of a new conception of democracy and of society, on English Canada. It is around such questions that the class alliances of the future may be forged.

If the author may be allowed a closing prediction, it is that nationalism will be of increasing importance in English Canada in the years to come. In a context in which Quebec moves inexorably closer to national self-determination, the survival of English Canada looms ever larger as the dominant question in Canadian politics. For centuries, the land of Cain has been locked into a cycle of resource extraction and capitalist domination. It will be the task of the first generations of *English Canadians* to break that cycle, founding a new nation, side by side with Quebec and with the United States, on the North American continent. English Canada will be socialist, or it will have no reason to exist.

APPENDIX I

MEMBERS OF THE CANADIAN-AMERICAN COMMITTEE
(May 1958)

Co-Chairmen

Robert M. Fowler
President, Canadian Pulp
& Paper Association
2280 Sun Life Building
Montreal

R. Douglas Stuart
Chairman of the Board
The Quaker Oats Company
345 Merchandise Mart Plaza
Chicago 54, Illinois

Arthur S. Adams
President
American Council on Education
1785 Massachusetts Ave. N.W.
Washington, D.C.

William L. Batt
1407 Kenilworth Apartments
Philadelphia 44, Pennsylvania

Ralph P. Bell
President, The Halifax Insurance Co.
Halifax

L.J. Belnap
Chairman
Consolidated Paper Corporation
Sun Life Building
Montreal

Harold Boeschenstein
President
Owens-Corning Fiberglas Corporation
Toledo 1, Ohio

John Brownlee
President
United Grain Growers Ltd.
310 Lougheed Building
Calgary, Alberta

L.S. Buckmaster
General President, United Rubber,
Cork, Linoleum & Plastic Workers
of America
United Rubber Workers Building
High Street at Mill
Akron, Ohio

George Burt
Director, Region No. 7
United Automobile, Aircraft & Agri-
cultural Implement Workers of
America
AFL-CIO-CLC
1568 Ouellette Ave.
Windsor, Ontario

Brooke Claxton
Vice President and General Manager
Metropolitan Life Insurance Company
80 Wellington Street
Ottawa, Ontario

Harold Dodds
President Emeritus
Princeton University
87 College Road West
Princeton, New Jersey

Marriner S. Eccles
Chairman of the Board
First Security Corporation
Salt Lake City, Utah

A. Hollis Edens
President
Duke University
Durham, North Carolina

Marcel Faribault
President and General Manager
General Trust of Canada
80 Notre Dame Street West
Montreal

218

Harold S. Foley
Chairman of the Board
Powell River Company Ltd.
510 West Hastings Street
Vancouver

Clinton S. Golden
Solebury
Bucks County, Pennsylvania

Donald Gordon
Chairman and President
Canadian National Railways
360 McGill Street
Montreal

W.L. Gordon, President
J.D. Woods and Gordon Ltd.
15 Wellington Street West
Toronto

H.H. Hannam, President
Canadian Federation of Agriculture
11 Sparks Street
Ottawa

Peavey Heffelfinger
President, F.H. Peavey & Company
Minneapolis 15, Minnesota

James Hilton
President, Iowa State College
Ames, Iowa

Stanley C. Hope
President, Esso Standard Oil Co.
15 West 51 Street
New York 19, New York

T.V. Houser
Chairman, Sears, Roebuck and Co.
Executive Offices
Chicago 7, Illinois

C.D. Howe
7 Crescent
Rockcliffe
Ottawa

C.L. Huston, Jr.
President, Lukens Steel Company
Coatesville, Pennsylvania

Claude Jodoin
President, Canadian Labour Congress
100 Argyle Avenue
Ottawa

Joseph D. Keenan
International Secretary
International Brotherhood of Electrical
  Workers
1200 15th Street N.W.
Washington, D.C.

R.A. Laidlaw
Secretary and Director
R.A. Laidlaw Lumber Company Ltd.
50 King Street West
Toronto

Maurice Lamontagne
18 Lakeview Terrace
Ottawa

Edward H. Lane
Chairman and Director
Lane Company
Alta Vista, Virginia

H.H. Lank, President
Dupont Company of Canada Ltd.
P.O. Box 660
Montreal

Donald MacDonald
Secretary-Treasurer
Canadian Labour Congress
100 Argyle Avenue
Ottawa, 4

N.A.M. Mackenzie, President
The University of British Columbia
Vancouver

W.A. Mackintosh
Vice Chancellor and Principal
Queen's University
Kingston, Ontario

John McCaffrey, Chairman
International Harvester Company
180 North Michigan Avenue
Chicago, Illinois

James A. McConnell, Dean
School of Business
Cornell University
Ithaca, New York

James L. Madden
Vice President
Scott Paper Company
Chester, Pennsylvania

William Mahoney
National Director, United Steel Workers
  of America
20 Spadina Road
Toronto, Ontario

Jean Marchand
General Secretary
The Canadian & Catholic Confederation
  of Labour
155 Boulevard Charest East
Quebec City, P.Q.

J. Morris, President
District Council No. 1
International Woodworkers of America
AFL-CIO-CLC
No. 4, 45 Kingsway
Vancouver

Herschel Newsom
Master, National Grange
744 Jackson Place N.W.
Washington, D.C.

Charles A. Perlitz
Executive Vice President
Continental Oil Company
Box 2197
Houston 1, Texas

R.E. Powell
Senior Vice President
Aluminium Ltd.
2100 Sun Life Building
Montreal

H.W. Prentis, Jr.
Chairman of the Board
Armstrong Cork Company
Liberty & Charlotte Streets
Lancaster, Pennsylvania

Herbert V. Prochnow
Vice President
The First National Bank of Chicago
Chicago, Illinois

Rhys M. Sale, President
Ford Motor Company of Canada Ltd.
120 Bloor Street East
Toronto

George Schollie
General Vice President
International Association of
  Machinists
1440 St. Catherine Street West
Montreal

H. Christian Sonne
President, South Ridge Corporation
Room 1703, 61 Broadway
New York, New York

J.E. Wallace Sterling
President
Stanford University
Stanford, California

Andrew Stewart
President
University of Alberta
Edmonton, Alberta

James Stewart
Chairman of the Board
The Canadian Bank of Commerce
Toronto

Harold W. Sweatt, Chairman
Minneapolis-Honeywell Company
2747 4th Avenue South
Minneapolis, Minnesota

Robert C. Tait, President
Stromberg-Carlson Company
Division of General Dynamics
  Corporation
100 Carlson Road
Rochester, New York

G.J. Ticoulat
Senior Vice President
Crown-Zellerbach Corporation
343 Sansome Street
San Francisco 19, California

Graham Towers
260 Park Road
Rockcliffe Park
Ottawa

W.E. Williams
President and General Manager
The Proctor and Gamble Company of
  Canada Ltd.
P.O. Box 355, Terminal "A"
Toronto

Francis Winspear
Winspear, Hamilton, Anderson and Co.
303 Mercantile Building
Edmonton, Alberta

David J. Winton
Chairman of the Board
Winton Lumber Company
3100 West Lake Street
Minneapolis, Minnesota

John White, President
Imperial Oil Ltd.
111 St. Clair Avenue West
Toronto

MEMBERS OF THE CANADIAN-AMERICAN COMMITTEE
(September 1964)

Canadian Members	American Members
CO-CHAIRMAN	**CO-CHAIRMAN**
Robert M. Fowler	Harold W. Sweatt
President	Honorary Chairman of the Board
Canadian Pulp and Paper Assn.	Honeywell, Inc.
T.N. Beaupre	I.W. Abel
Chairman of the Board	Secretary-Treasurer
British Columbia Forest Products Ltd.	United Steelworkers of America
	AFL-CIO
L.J. Belnap	
Chairman	William L. Batt
Consolidated Paper Corporation Ltd.	Delray Beach, Florida
George Burt	J.A. Beirne
Canadian Director, Region No. 7	President
United Automobile, Aerospace & Agri-	Communications Workers of America
cultural Implement Workers of	AFL-CIO
America, AFL-CIO-CLC	
	Harold Boeschenstein
A.D. Dunton	Chairman
President	Owens-Corning Fiberglas Corporation
Carlton University	
	Earl L. Butz
Marcel Faribault	Dean, School of Agriculture
President and General Manager	Purdue University
General Trust of Canada	
	John F. Gallagher
Harold S. Foley	Vice President
Vancouver, B.C.	International Operations
	Sears, Roebuck and Company
Donald Gordon	
Chairman and President	Dr. John A. Hannah
Canadian National Railways	President
	Michigan State University
Claude Jodoin	
President	Heffelfinger, F. Peavey
Canadian Labour Congress	Chairman of the Board
	F.H. Peavey & Co.
Vernon E. Johnson	
Director	G.W. Humphrey
Canadian International Paper Company	Chairman
	The M.A. Hanna Company
David Kirk	
Executive Secretary	Charles L. Huston, Jr.
The Canadian Federation of Agriculture	President
	Lukens Steel Company

Canadian Members	American Members
W.S. Kirkpatrick Chairman and President The Consolidated Mining and Smelting Company of Canada Ltd.	Curtis M. Hutchins Chairman of the Board Dead River Company
R.A. Laidlaw Secretary and Director R. Laidlaw Lumber Company Ltd.	Joseph D. Keenan International Secretary International Brotherhood of Electrical Workers, AFL-CIO
Herbert H. Lank President DuPont of Canada Ltd.	Ernest S. Lee Assistant Director Department of International Affairs AFL-CIO
Donald MacDonald Secretary-Treasurer Canadian Labour Congress	Franklin A. Lindsay President Itek Corporation
M.W. Mackenzie Chairman of the Board Canadian Chemical Company Ltd.	James L. Madden Vice President Scott Paper Company
Dr. N.A.M. Mackenzie Vancouver, B.C.	Brooks McCormick Executive Vice President International Harvester Company
Dr. W.A. Mackintosh Vice-Chancellor Queen's University	Herschel D. Newsom Master National Grange
William Mahoney National Director United Steelworkers of America AFL-CIO-CLC	Thomas S. Nichols Chairman of the Executive Committee Olin Mathieson Chemical Corporation
Jean Marchand President Confederation of National Trade Unions	Joseph E. Nolan Executive Vice President Weyerhaeuser Company
Hon. M. Wallace McCutcheon Toronto, Ont.	Herbert V. Prochnow President The First National Bank of Chicago
J. Morris Executive Vice-President Canadian Labour Congress	Charles Ritz Chairman International Milling Company Inc.
R.E. Powell Honorary Chairman Aluminum Company of Canada Ltd.	Henry E. Russell President Carling Brewing Company
L.D. Smithers President Dow Chemical of Canada Ltd.	William F. Schnitzler Secretary-Treasurer AFL-CIO
James Stewart Director The Canadian Imperial Bank of Commerce	Peter T. Sinclair President Crown Zellerbach Corporation

Canadian Members

Graham F. Towers
Ottawa, Ontario

W.O. Twaits
President
Imperial Oil Ltd.

W.E. Williams
President and General Manager
The Proctor and Gamble Company of
  Canada Ltd.

Henry S. Wingate
Chairman
The International Nickel Company of
  Canada Ltd.

Francis G. Winspear
Winspear, Hamilton, Anderson & Co.

American Members

H. Christian Sonne
President
South Ridge Corporation

Allan Sproul
Kentfield, California

Claude O. Stephens
President
Texas Gulf Sulphur Company Inc.

Dr. J.E. Wallace Sterling
President
Stanford University

R. Douglas Stuart
Director
The Quaker Oats Company

Jesse W. Tapp
Chairman of the Board
Bank of America

G.J. Ticoulat
Senior Vice President
Crown Zellerbach Corporation

John R. White
Vice President and Director
Standard Oil Company (New Jersey)

APPENDIX II

COMMITTEE FOR AN INDEPENDENT CANADA
COMITE POUR L'INDEPENDANCE DU CANADA

STATEMENT OF PURPOSE

We believe that Canadians today share a surging mood of self-awareness. But this mood must be translated into effective policies, or we may risk the erosion of Canadian independence by default. Government guidelines and vague political promises are no longer enough.

The Committee for an Independent Canada has been established to speak out with one strong voice for the survival of this country. It represents men and women from every corner of Canada, of all ages, professions and political hues, who believe that meaningful independence can only be secured by an active process that involves the day-to-day participation of concerned citizens which will lead to government action.

We realize the benefits that Canada derives from being part of the western hemisphere and we do not want to close this country to the foreign capital which it may need. But our land won't be ours much longer if we allow it to continue to be sold out to foreign owners. Not if we allow another culture to dominate our information media.

If we are to ensure this country's survival, our governments must adopt legislative policies that will significantly diminish the influence presently exerted by outside powers—their citizens, their corporations and their institutions—on Canadian life. We believe that the federal parliament together with provincial legislatures in relevant areas of their jurisdiction must take urgent measures in the following areas.

1. The present level of foreign ownership is unsatisfactory for Canadians since major decisions affecting our economic life are taken outside this country. We urge the Government to implement policies designed to increase the proportion of Canadian ownership, including the establishment of a federal agency to supervise the conduct of foreign-controlled operations in Canada, and in particular any new take-overs. We draw special attention to the early establishment of a Canada Development Corporation and the policy on sale of our energy resources.

2. To foster a national development program, we urge the greater

allocation of resources—both private and public—to the less well developed regions of the country.

3. Safeguarding Canadian control as well as a reasonable amount of Canadian news and content in our newspapers, magazines, radio, television stations and cable TV networks should form an essential part of Government policy. Adequate financial support must be provided to achieve these objectives.

4. We are convinced that trade unions in Canada must have the autonomy necessary for them to reflect the aspirations of their Canadian membership.

5. Within their respective jurisdictions, governments at all three levels must become more active in the fight against pollution, even when cleaning up our environment infringes on established vested interests. This emphatically includes the protection of Canadian jurisdiction in our Arctic.

6. One of the most important functions of our educational institutions is to enhance our cultural life. This means that without in any way isolating ourselves from the benefits to be obtained abroad, there should be a reasonable degree of information about Canada in curriculum and a reasonable knowledge about Canada on the part of the members of the teaching personnel.

7. Since foreign policy is an extension of domestic policy, the objectives stated here should be reflected and supported in our relations with all other nations. A general foreign policy designed to ensure Canadian independence must be formulated by our Government and its implications followed in our relations abroad.

We are convinced that a majority of Quebeckers prefer to remain within Confederation. With this the case, it is in the best interests of Quebec and Canada as a whole that we should work together to promote genuine independence for Canada.

The Committee for an Independent Canada has been created to enlist the support of all Canadians in urging their MP's and MLA's to make Canada's survival as an independent nation their top priority.

COMMITTEE FOR AN INDEPENDENT CANADA

Honourary Chairman — Hon. WALTER L. GORDON
Co-Chairmen — JACK McCLELLAND, Toronto, CLAUDE RYAN, Montreal

Among those on the steering commitee

Gus Abols — Past President, University of Toronto Students' Council, Toronto
Michael Adams — Social and Environmental Researcher, Environics Research Group Ltd., Toronto
Fred Anderson — Dean, Faculty of Social Sciences University of Saskatchewan, Regina Campus, Regina
Doris Anderson — Editor, Chatelaine Magazine, Toronto
John Archer — Principal, University of Saskatchewan, Regina Campus, Regina
Lloyd Axworthy — Director, Institute of Urban Studies, University of Winnipeg, Winnipeg
Pierre Berton — Author, Kleinburg
Earl Birney — Poet, Vancouver
John Blansche — Engineer, Toronto
Molly Lamb Bobac — Artist, Fredericton
Bernard Bonin — École des Hautes Études commerciales, Université de Montréal, Montréal
Louis-Philippe Bonneau — Vice-Recteur, Université Laval, Ste-Foy
Jean Brunelle — Directeur général, Centre des dirigeants d'entreprises, Montréal
Marcel Bureau — Directeur général, SSJB du diocèse de Sherbrooke, Sherbrooke
Donald Cameron — Department of English, University of New Brunswick, Fredericton
Harold Cardinal — President, Indian Association of Alberta, Edmonton
John Carter — President, Mt. Scio Farms Ltd., St. Johns, Newfoundland
Marc Carrière — Président général, Dupuis Frères, Montréal
Donald A. Chant — Pollution Probe, Toronto
Christopher Chapman — Film Producer, Markham
Tim Christian — President of Students' Union, University of Alberta, Edmonton
Adrienne Clarkson — T.V. commentator, Toronto
Bob Cohen — Editor and Journalist, Winnipeg
Emile Colas, C.R. — Lawyer, Montréal
Henry Comar — Actor, Edmonton
Yves Cousineau —Montréal
Keith Davey — Senator, Ottawa
Elvio Delzotto — Delzotto, Zorzi, Andrews & Applebaum, Toronto
Hugh Dempsey — Director of History, Glenbow, Alberta Institute, Calgary
Peter Desbarats — T.V. Commentator and Journalist, Montreal
J.-A. Dionne — President, Fédération des magasins coopératifs du Québec, Montréal
Charles Dojack — Publisher and General Manager, National Publishers Limited, Winnipeg
Murray Donnelly — Provost, University College, University of Manitoba, Winnipeg
Léo Dorais — Recteur, Université du Québec à Montréal, Montréal
W. J. Duthie — Duthie Books, Vancouver
George M. Elliott — Advertising Executive, Toronto
Dave Erickson — President of Students' Union, University of Saskatchewan, Saskatoon

Max Ferguson — Author and Commentator, Toronto
Gérard Filion — Président, Marine Industries, Montréal
Ed Finn — Research Director, Canadian Brotherhood of Railway Transport and General Workers, Ottawa
N. R. Fischbuch — Consulting Geologist, Calgary
Yves Fortier — Lawyer, Montréal
G. F. Francolini — President, Livingston Industries Ltd., Tillsonburg
Bruce Gillis — Past President, Students' Council, Dalhousie University, Middleton, N.S.
Jerry Goodis — President, Goodis, Goldberg, Soren Ltd., Toronto
Edwin A. Goodman, Q.C. — Lawyer, Toronto
Walter Gordon — Chairman, Canadian Corporate Management Co. Ltd., Toronto
George Grant — Department of Religion, McMaster University, Hamilton
Alvin Hamilton — T.V. Commentator, Manotick
Malim Harding — Chairman, Harding Carpets Ltd., Brantford
Harry Hays — Senator, Calgary
Henry Hicks — President, Dalhousie University, Halifax
Beland H. Honderich — President and Publisher, Toronto Star Ltd., Toronto
Rod Hurd — President, University of Toronto Students' Council, Toronto
Mel Hurtig — Publisher, M. G. Hurtig Limited, Edmonton
Harry A. Hyde — Chief of Surgery, Royal Alex Hospital, Edmonton
Pauline Jewett — Director of the Institute of Canadian Studies, Carleton University, Ottawa
Jack M. Johnson — Lawyer, Calgary
Leon Katz — Head, Department of Physics, University of Saskatchewan, Saskatoon
Betty Kennedy — Women's Editor, Radio Station CFRB, Toronto
J. R. Kidd — Chairman, Dept. of Adult Education, Ontario Institute for Studies in Education, Toronto
Paul Lacoste — Vice-Recteur, Université de Montréal, Montréal
Judy LaMarsh — Lawyer, Niagara Falls
Maurice Lamontagne — Senator, Ottawa
Laurier Lapierre — Institute of Canadian Studies, McGill University, Montreal
S. A. Little — National President, Canadian Union of Public Employees, Ottawa
Dorothy Livesay — Department of English, University of Alberta, Edmonton
Samule Loschiavo — Physician, Winnipeg
Flora MacDonald — Department of Political Studies, Queen's University, Kingston
Michael D. MacDonald — Lawyer, Edmonton
Hugh MacLennan — Author, Department of English, McGill University, Montreal
Guy Marcil — Président, Fraternité des policiers de Montréal, Montréal
David Margolus — Political Science student, University of Alberta, Edmonton
Robin Mathews — Department of English, Carleton University, Ottawa
William Mahoney — National Director, United Steel Workers of America, Toronto
Jack McClelland — President, McClelland & Stewart Ltd., Toronto
Donald D. McGeachy — Director, Northern Life Assurance Co., London
Kenneth McNaught — History Department, University of Toronto, Toronto
Michael Meighen — Lawyer, Montreal
Alex Mercer — Chairman, Renaissance '71, Toronto
Jim Millar — President, University of Winnipeg Students' Union, Winnipeg
David Milne — Department of Political Science, University of P.E.I., Charlottetown

J. H. Moore — President, Brascan Limited, London
W. L. Morton — Champlain College, Trent University, Peterborough
Farley Mowat — Author, Port Hope
Mrs. M. L. Murray — Editor, Lillooet-Bridge River News, Lillooet
Christina Newman — Author, Toronto
Peter C. Newman — Author, Editor Maclean's Magazine, Toronto
Eric Nicol — Author, Vancouver
T. G. Norris, Q.C. — Pitt Meadows
Alden Nowlan — Author, Fredericton
Allan O'Brien — Mayor, Halifax
Desmond Pacey — Dean of Graduate Studies, University of New Brunswick, Fredericton
René Paré — Président général, La Société des artisans, Montréal
Eamon Park — Assistant to the National Director, United Steel Workers of America, Toronto
John C. Parkin — John C. Parkin, Architects, Planners
Dorothy Petrie — Toronto
Allan Pope — President, Progressive Conservative Student Federation, Toronto
Al Purdy — Poet, Ameliasburg
Paul Racine — Président, Centre d'achats Laurier, Québec
John Reeves — Photographer, Toronto
J. W. Ritchie — Scotia Bond Company Ltd., Halifax
Abraham Rotstein — Department of Political Economy, University of Toronto, Toronto
Claude Ryan — Publisher and Editor, Le Devoir, Montréal
Laura Sabia — Broadcaster, St. Catharines
Jean-Paul Sainte-Marie, C.R. — Lawyer, Montréal
Jean-Jacques Saint-Pierre — Secrétaire général, Université de Sherbrooke, Sherbrooke
D. S. Scott — Faculty of Engineering, University of Waterloo, Waterloo
Harvey Scott — Head Coach, University of Alberta Football Team, Edmonton
Lloyd Shaw — President, L. E. Shaw Limited, Halifax
Arthur R. Smith — President, Cantrans Services (1965) Ltd., Calgary
Denis Smith — Department of Politics, Trent University, Peterborough
Larry Steinman — President, University of Western Ontario Students' Council, London
Thomas H. B. Symons — President and Vice Chancellor, Trent University, Peterborough
Hugh G. Thorburn — Head, Department of Political Studies, Queen's University, Kingston
Harold Town — Artist, Toronto
John Varley — President, Canadian Student Liberals, Ottawa
Norman Ward — Department of Political Science, University of Saskatchewan, Saskatoon
Leon E. Weinstein — Director, Public and Consumer Affairs, Loblaws Groceterias Co. Ltd., Toronto
Jack Webster — Radio and T.V. commentator, Vancouver

APPENDIX III

WHITHER WAFFLE? *

The Waffle is an anomaly in Canadian political history. It began as an ad hoc collection of unconnected individuals rather than a carefully constructed, closely designed group. It did not go through a long planning stage seeking alliances with various groups in the party.

Members of the New Democratic Party met informally in Toronto, April 29, 1969, to discuss the right wing drift of the party and what might be done to reverse it. They decided to draw up a statement to be circulated among other New Democrats. At this stage no thought was given to forming a large organization of the left in the party. The need for a socialist movement functioning both inside and outside the NDP had been expressed in *Dimension* editorials on several occasions, but it was not part of the early strategy of this group.

Jim Laxer, then living in Ottawa, wrote a first draft of the statement. He started from the premise that Canada had become a resources colony within the American Empire. The imperial fact came first. Then came socialism and public ownership of the commanding heights of the economy as an instrument of breaking the chain of economic dependence, providing greater regional equality and ending the rule of the profit system and the giant corporation. Then came statements on Quebec, workers' control, women's liberation and the freeing of politics from the slavery of electioneering and money-raising in favour of extraparliamentary politics.

The statement was overly academic. Mel Watkins, one of the original eleven, re-worked it. Others took a hand, in particular Ed Broadbent, Gerald Caplan, Lorne Brown, Giles Endicott.

Many meetings were held, but debate on the statement never went beyond this small circle. Ed Broadbent bowed out. He didn't like the emphasis. Gerald Caplan later left to manage Stephen Lewis' campaign for Ontario NDP leader. During one discussion, the hedging stand over the extent of nationalization came under heavy fire. Someone, arguing for a stronger position, said: "If we're going to waffle, I'd rather waffle to the left than waffle to the right."

The "Waffle" Manifesto was born.

As the federal convention approached, the group decided to use

Canadian Dimension, Vol. 7, No. 8, April 1971, pp. 24-25.

the Manifesto to try and identify the left inside the NDP. The Manifesto was spread across the country to friends and friends of friends. New Democrats were asked to endorse it. In late August, it was published in *Dimension* along with a preliminary list of prominent New Democrats who agreed to endorse it. The list included names like Charles Taylor who later withdrew and became a foe of the Waffle. A press conference was held in Ottawa, September 4, to announce the existence of the Waffle group and its challenge to the NDP. By this time, several NDP constituency associations had passed the Waffle Manifesto as a resolution for debate at the convention. The October confrontation was assured.

The Waffle really came together as a national group only at the convention itself. It caucused openly and often, attracting 400-500 delegates at each meeting. The Manifesto received the support of a third of the delegates despite the fact that virtually every high ranking spokesman in the party opposed it. But what was more important is that out of the convention the Waffle found its constituency in the party. It agreed to form a continuing left in the party with a national steering committee and it drew up plans for regional branches.

There are about 2,000 New Democrats across the country that now openly identify with the Waffle. About half of these are in Ontario. A large part of the rest are in Saskatchewan. The Waffle leadership numbers about 100. To a large degree they are people connected to universities, either as faculty or students. As our survey indicates, Waffle supporters are broadly representative of party membership: 20% are blue-collar and white-collar workers; 10% are farmers; 10% are university professors; 8% are teachers and 20% are other professionals. The one major difference is that over 20% of the Wafflers are students, whereas for the party as a whole, students are less than 10% of total membership.

About half the Wafflers are under 35. Our survey showed that a large majority of party members in this age bracket are Waffle supporters. Men outnumber women about 3 to 1 in the Waffle; in the rest of the party the ratio is about 7 to 1. Wafflers are somewhat less affluent than non-Wafflers, even when non-income earning students are excluded.

One last statistic. While the Waffle has brought many new people into the NDP, about four-fifths of the Waffle were in the party before 1969. About one-fifth joined the party after the Waffle was formed.

Since its founding at the Winnipeg convention, the major activity of the Waffle group, accounting for perhaps 75% of its energies, has been electoral politics inside the NDP. This means that the Waffle has regarded the NDP itself to be its most important constituency and within the party its most important work has been at provincial and federal councils and conventions winning votes for Waffle resolutions and Waffle candidates.

That this should have become the main focus of the Waffle is, in some ways, paradoxical. A key Waffle tenet is that the NDP is too confined to electoral politics, that it should be helping to organize the unemployed, working with citizens' groups where they exist and setting up new ones where they do not exist, pamphleteering in the schools, plants, offices and neighbourhoods.

The Waffle has failed to move the party to do these things and with a few notable exceptions, the Waffle itself has failed to do them. Three main reasons may be offered for this.

1. The Waffle has a great deal of available potential talent but it has made use of only a small fraction of it. The 100 or so super-Wafflers are totally occupied with Waffle strategy meetings and work at regular party functions. Little energy is left for other things. Even work within the party is often done haphasardly. Educational work at the constituency level is rare and contacts made at conventions are often not followed up.

2. Wafflers have argued that it is not the Waffle's job to organize and agitate at large. This should be urged upon the NDP and the labour movement. But after two years of pressing and waiting, it should now be obvious that this will not happen. The Waffle cannot wait until the NDP is transformed into a socialist party before getting seriously involved in these activities, even should it be at the expense of electoral work inside the NDP.

3. The Waffle tends to be incestuous. Waffle activists are a small university-based middle class group enjoying nothing more than talking among themselves and doing intellectual work. Few have first-hand organizing experience, little direct experience with the poor and even less with the blue-collar working class. A first task of the Waffle will have to be to broaden it leadership core.

The Waffle is more than the youth wing of the NDP, despite its virtual monopoly of the under 30 age group of the party. It is also more than the academic wing of the party—although many of the Waffle leaders are connected with the universities. To a large degree, the Waffle has been successful in uniting the traditional left-wing of the New Democratic Party and that includes every occupation and every age group.

The NDP was dull and dying before the Waffle. The Waffle has made the NDP an exciting and vibrant political party. It has given the NDP the opportunity to be the champion of Canadian independence and the spokesman for Canadian socialism. It has shown the NDP how it can be relevant in Quebec and how it cannot be relevant. So far there is little indication that the NDP is ready to seize these opportunities and some Wafflers are becoming impatient.

Mel Watkins, summarizing the purpose of the Waffle after the 1969 convention, said the Waffle is not a party within a party but a movement for the party. The Waffle is *not* a party within the party—much less so than the federal caucus and the provincial caucuses that meet privately and regularly and decide party policy. But neither can the Waffle truthfully be said to be a movement for the party. The Waffle today is a collection of individuals that wants to build a movement for socialism and independence but confines most of its political work to the regular functions and agencies of the New Democratic Party.

While it was the Waffle's strong anti-imperialist emphasis that dominated the 1969 convention, it will likely be the Waffle emphasis on self-determination for Quebec that will dominate the 1971 convention. As the *Dimension* survey demonstrates, the Waffle harbors few New Democrats who actually favor Quebec separatism. But there is a strong sentiment that supports the view that only by recognizing the right of the Quebec people to self-determination, including the right to separate, can there be a feeling of mutual trust and equality between the two nations.

That this view won the endorsement of the Quebec Wing of the NDP stunned and annoyed the party leadership. There was always a strong feeling within the Quebec NDP for this position. It was the major issue of contention at the founding convention of the NDP-Quebec held in the summer of 1963. One group, led by Michel Chartrand, supported a reconstructed Confederation made up of an association of the two nations. This group wanted a fully independent Quebec group operating in both the provincial and federal fields. The other group, led by Charles Taylor and the English Canadian wing of the Quebec party, favored a new constitution which would expand provincial rights and wanted the Quebec party to stay within the federal party. A compromise was reached, suggested by Emile Boudreau: a federal Quebec NDP and the Parti Socialiste de Quebec, limiting its activities to the provincial sphere. The PSQ lasted only a few years. It ran provincially but this was the period of the "Quiet Revolution" and the PSQ never made much headway.

There was constant feuding within the federal wing of the party and little or no co-operation. The separatists within the PSQ split away. The others drifted from formal politics. It is this latter group and individuals allied to them which forms the core of the present Quebec NDP which took the momentous decision to turn the NDP away from provincial politics and to insist that federal candidates for the NDP run on a platform of self-determination for Quebec. This group is also left-socialist and it has in effect become the Waffle of Quebec.

NOTES

FOOTNOTES TO CHAPTER ONE

1. "L'inquietante hesitation de la pensee historique et sociologique devant le phenomene nation, l'emploi discutable ou manifestement abusif des mots "nation," "national," "nationalisme," "patriotisme" ou "patrie" fait de nos jours encore obstacle a la recherche." Pierre Vilar, *La Catalogne dans l'Espagne moderne*, Vol. 1, Paris, 1962, p. 29, cited in Georges Haupt, Michael Lowy & Claudie Weill, *Les marxistes et la question nationale 1848-1914*, Montreal and Paris, 1974, p. 21, Fn. 21.

2. Cf. Donald Creighton, *Towards the Discovery of Canada*, Toronto, 1972, especially the essays "The Decline and Fall of the Empire of the St. Lawrence" and "Canadian Nationalism and Its Opponents."

3. As early as 1961, at its founding convention, the New Democratic Party affirmed its belief in a federal system "which alone insures the united development of the two nations which originally associated to form the Canadian partnership." Significantly, the resolution in question was titled "Co-operative Federalism." *Policies of the New Democratic Party, 1961-1973*, Ottawa, 1974, p.73.

    The Royal Commission on Bilingualism and Biculturalism had as its mandate "equal partnership between the founding races," and proposed the extension of equal language and cultural rights across the country. *Bilingualism and Biculturalism*, ed. Hugh R. Innis, Toronto, 1973, pp. 4-6.

    Writers from Charles Taylor, (*The Pattern of Politics*, Toronto, 1970, p. 142) to John Deutsch (Introduction to R.M. Burns, ed., *One Country or Two*, Montreal, 1971, pp. 13-14) to Donald Smiley (or so at least I read the chapter "Cultural Duality and Canadian Federalism" in his book *Canada in Question: Federalism in the Seventies*, Toronto, 1972) accept the logic of a revamped Confederation, while rejecting independence for Quebec.

4. Eugene Forsey made his support for a cultural/sociological use of the term two nations, as opposed to a political one, the central point of his 1962 presidential address to the Canadian Political Science Association. See his *Freedom and Order, Collected Essays*, Toronto, Carleton Library, 1974, pp. 247-269. He broke with the NDP over their "two nations" theory, yet one wonders how many social democrats, or for that matter liberals at the time, ever understood "two nations" or "two founding peoples" in other than a cultural/sociological sense. Since 1970, however, as will be argued in Chapter Five, there has been some movement towards a political interpretation of the two nations by English Canadian writers.

5. Acton started the ball rolling with his denunciation of nationalism, "a theory more absurd and criminal than the theory of socialism," in his famous essay on "Nationality" of 1862, reprinted in *Essays on Freedom and Power*, London, 1962. For Trudeau, the multinational state, i.e., federalism, is "a product of reason in

politics," while nationalism is a "cheap and powerful tool" which addresses the emotions, rather than reason. *Federalism and the French Canadians,* Toronto, 1968, pp. 195, 175. Ramsay Cook beats much the same drum in his *The Maple Leaf Forever,* Toronto, 1971, especially the first and third essays.

6. Cf. Maurice Seguin, *L'Idee d'independance au Quebec,* Trois Rivieres, 1968.

7. Cf. Hubert Guidon, "Social Unrest, Social Class and Quebec's Bureaucratic Revolution," *Queen's Quarterly,* Vol. 71, pp. 150-162; Jacques Brazeau, "Les Nouvelles classes moyennes," in Fernand Dumont and Jean-Paul Montminy, eds., *Le Pouvoir dans la societe canadienne-francaise,* Quebec, 1966, pp. 151-163; Gilles Bourque and Nicole Laurin-Frenette, "Social Classes and Nationalist Ideologies in Quebec, 1760-1970," in Gary Teeple, ed., *Capitalism and the National Question in Canada,* Toronto, 1972, pp. 186-210; Marcel Rioux, *Les Quebecois,* Paris, 1974; Louis Le Borgne, *La CSN et la question nationale, 1960-73,* these de maitrise, l'UQUAM, 1975.

8. Douglas LePan, "The Old Ontario Strand in the Canada of Today," *Queen's Quarterly,* Vol. LXXIII, 1966, pp. 483-495, p. 487.

9. The percentage of Canada's population of neither British nor French origin increased from 21.3 per cent in the 1951 census to 26.7 per cent in that of 1971. *Canada Year Book, 1973,* Ottawa, 1973, p. 215. Deducting the French Canadian component would leave the non-British element at 37 per cent of the remaining total. By way of comparison, non-British and non-French constituted a mere 8 per cent of the total Canadian population in 1871. *Perspectives Canada,* Statistics Canada, Ottawa, 1974, p. 257.

10. Desmond E. Henn, "The Canadian Dilemma," *The Spectator,* London, February 27, 1953.

11. Cf. Donald Creighton's *The Empire of the St. Lawrence,* Toronto, 2nd edition, 1956; John Bartlet Brebner, *North Atlantic Triangle,* Carleton Library Edition, Toronto, 1966; and Harold A. Innis, *Essays in Canadian Economic History,* Toronto, 1956, and other writings. In his essay, "Great Britain, the United States and Canada" in this latter volume, Innis observes that "American imperialism has replaced and exploited British imperialism." *Essays,* pp. 394-412, p. 395.

12. "Our position in Canada is perhaps more serious because of our counter-revolutionary tradition. In Quebec the French population largely escaped the influence of the French Revolution and in the older English-speaking provinces immigrants arrived from the United States because of their definite hostility to the revolutionary tradition." Innis, "The Church in Canada," in *Essays in Canadian Economic History,* pp. 383-393, pp.383-4.

13. Cf. W.L. Morton, *The Canadian Identity,* Toronto, 1973, especially Chapter III "Canada and the United States."

14. "The existence of a nation is a plebiscite of every day, as the existence of the individual is a perpetual affirmation of life." Ernest Renan, "The Meaning of Nationality" in Hans Kohn, ed. *Nationalism,* New York, 1955. p. 139.

15. Royal Institute of International Affairs, *Nationalism,* London, 1939, p. 336.

16. Hans Kohn, *The Idea of Nationalism,* New York, 1944, p. 576.

17. *Ibid.* Cf. also K.R. Minogue's more recent tract *Nationalism*, London, 1967, which concludes: "The good it (nationalism) does could all be done in other ways; but equally, it has contributed little more than a new vocabulary to the history of political evil." p. 155.

18. For a representative comment by Pearson, compare the Reith Lecture he gave over the BBC after he had left office in 1968: "The fact is that the sovereign state is virtually obsolete as a satisfactory basis for rational economic growth, at least in industrially developed societies." Cited in *Canadian Labour*, Ottawa, May 1969, p. 30. For Trudeau, cf. the last three essays in *Federalism and the French Canadians.*

19. Karl Marx and Frederick Engels, *The German Ideology*, New York: International Publishers, 1970, p. 64.

20. Cf. Christopher Hill's discussion of "The Norman Yoke," in his *Puritanism and Revolution*, Panther Edition, London, 1968, Chapter Three. For the use of nationalism by a triumphant Cromwell see Chapter Four, *Ibid.*, "The English Revolution and the Brotherhood of Man," Section Six.

21. Cf. the language of the Declaration of Independence, "that these united colonies are, and of right ought to be free and independent states"; or the opening words of the American constitution "We the People of the United States." On the class character of the leaders of the revolution, see Charles Beard, *An Economic Interpretation of the Constitution of the United States*, New York, Reprinted 1960. Of the revolution itself, Clinton Rossiter has written: "Perhaps the most remarkable characteristic of this political theory was its deep rooted conservatism . . . More than one hundred and fifty years ago Americans took up their unique role as the world's most conservative radicals, the world's most sober revolutionists." "The Political Theory of the American Revolution," *The Review of Politics*, 1953, Vol. 15, p. 108.

22. Cf. The Abbe Sieyes's famous tract at the opening of the revolution, "What is the Third Estate?" in Peter Campbell's edition, New York, 1964. By Sieyes's calculations there were some 80,000 clergy, 110,000 nobility, and 25-26 million members of the third estate in 1788-9. When he affirms that the nation alone must make the constitution, it is the third estate in particular that he has in mind. Cf. also the Declaration of the Rights of Man of 1789, Article 3: "Le principe de toute souveraineté reside essentiellement dans la Nation."

23. Karl Marx and Frederick Engels, *Manifesto of the Communist Party,* in Marx and Engels, *Selected Works*, Moscow, 1968, p. 51.

24. "If the Commune was thus the true representative of all the healthy elements of French Society, and therefore the truly national Government, it was, at the same time, as a working men's Government, as the bold champion of the emancipation of labour, emphatically international. Within sight of the Prussian army, that had annexed to Germany two French provinces, the Commune annexed to France the working people all over the world." Or further, "Class rule is no longer able to disguise itself in a national uniform: the national Governments are *one* as against the proletariat." Karl Marx, *The Civil War in France,* in the *Selected Works,* pp. 297, 310.

25. "I am normally said to be free to the degree to which no man or body of men interferes with my activity," writes Berlin, arguing the need for a minimum area

of individual rights in which authority is kept at bay. Isaiah Berlin, "Two Concepts of Liberty," in *Four Essays on Liberty*, Oxford University Press, N.Y., 1969, pp. 122, 126.

26. Cf. Rosa Luxemburg, "La question polonaise et le mouvement socialiste," (1905) calling for unity of the Polish and Russian proletariats in overthrowing Tsarism, or her "La question nationale et l'autonomie," rejecting the idea of an independent Poland as an objective of a socialist revolution. Cf. also Anton Pannekoek's "Lutte de classe et nation," (1912). All three essays are in the extremely useful collection edited by Georges Haupt, Michael Lowy, and Claudie Weill, *Les marxistes et la question nationale 1848-1914*, Montreal and Paris, 1974.

27. League for Social Reconstruction, *Social Planning for Canada*, Toronto, new edition, 1975, p. 55.

28. Marx and Engels, *The Communist Manifesto, op. cit.*, p. 51

29. F. Engels, Emigre Literature, 1. *The Polish Proclamation*, 1874, cited in Lenin, *Questions of National Policy and Proletarian Internationalism*, Moscow, 1964, p. 107.

30. Cf. the discussion of Engels' *Po and Rhine* in Horace B. Davis, *Nationalism and Socialism*, New York, 1967, pp. 60-1, or the disparaging comments Engels makes about the Welsh, the Scottish, the Bretons, and the Lapps in his 1866 *Commonwealth* article, "What have the classes to do with Poland?," reprinted in French translation in the Haupt *et al.* reader, *op. cit.*, pp. 90-3.

31. "England has to fulfill a double mission in India: one destructive, the other regenerating—the annihilation of old Asiatic society, and the laying of the material foundations of Western society in Asia," is but one such comment strewn through Marx's newspaper articles of the 1850s. Karl Marx, *Surveys from Exile*, ed. David Fernbach, Penguin Books, 1973, p. 320.

32. Kautsky's *Nationality and Internationalism* of 1907-1908 plumps strongly for the nation state over the multinational state, while Bauer's *The National Question and Social Democracy* of 1907 argues the case for multinational states, respectful of the cultural autonomy of different nationalities. The Haupt reader, *op. cit.*, contains extracts in French from both works.

33. "The right of nations to self-determination implies exclusively the right to independence in the political sense, the right to free separation from the oppressor nation." Vladimir I. Lenin *Questions of National Policy and Proletarian Internationalism*, Moscow, 1964, p. 113.

34. "*Insofar as* the bourgeoisie of the oppressed nation fights the oppressor, we are always, in every case, and more strongly than anyone else, *in favour*, for we are the staunchest and most consistent enemies of oppression. But insofar as the bourgeoisie of the oppressed nation stands for *its own* bourgeois nationalism, we stand against. We fight against the privileges and violence of the oppressor nation, and do not in any way condone strivings for privileges on the part of the oppressed nation." *Ibid.*, p. 62.

35. "We *must* support *every* revolt against our chief enemy, the bourgeoisie of the big states, provided it is not the revolt of a reactionary class," *Ibid.*, p. 137, or again, "A blow delivered against the power of the English imperialist bourgeoisie

by a rebellion in Ireland is a hundred times more significant politically than a blow of equal force delivered in Asia or in Africa.'', p. 160. (Hardened anti-nationalists take note!)

36. "It would be an unpardonable opportunism if, on the eve of the debut of the East, just as it is awakening, we undermined our prestige with its peoples, even if only by the slightest crudity or injustice towards our own non-Russian nationalities." *Ibid.*, p. 170.

37. "Can a Communist, who is an internationalist, at the same time be a patriot? We hold that he not only can but must be. The specific content of patriotism is determined by historical conditions. There is the "patriotism" of the Japanese aggressors and of Hitler, and there is our patriotism . . . To bring about the defeat of the Japanese aggressors and of Hitler by every possible means is in the interests of the Japanese and the German people, and the more complete the defeat the better . . . China's case, however, is different, because she is the victim of aggression. Chinese Communists must therefore combine patriotism with internationalism . . . The victory of China and the defeat of the invading imperialists will help the people of other countries. Thus in wars of national liberation patriotism is applied internationalism." "The Role of the Chinese Communist Party in the National War," October 1938, Mao Tsetung, *Selected Works,* Vol. II, p. 196.

38. Thus, the "Manifesto of the Chinese People's Liberation Army" of October 1947, has as its first point: "Unite workers, peasants, soldiers, intellectuals and businessmen, all oppressed classes, all people's organizations, democratic parties . . . form a united front; overthrow the dictatorial Chiang Kai-Shek government; and establish a democratic coalition government." Mao Tsetung, *Selected Works,* Vol. V, page 150. See also the article "On the Question of the National Bourgeoisie and the Enlightened Gentry," in the same volume, pp. 207-210.

39. The Corporations and Labour Unions Returns Act Report on Corporations uses the $25 million base line in distinguishing large from small corporations. Cf. the further discussion in Chapter Two below. The most recent *Financial Post* listing of the top 100 Canadian companies at our disposal shows only six of the top 100, and possibly a seventh, with assets of less than $100 million. *The Financial Post*, July 26, 1975, p. 13.

40. Cf. Libbie and Frank Park's *Anatomy of Big Business*, Toronto, 2nd edition, 1973; John Porter, *The Vertical Mosaic*, Toronto, 1965; and most recently Wallace Clement, *The Canadian Corporate Elite*, Toronto, 1975.

41. Karl Marx, *Theories of Surplus-Value*, Part 1, Moscow, 1969, pp. 174-5.

42. *Ibid.*, pp. 300-1.

43. Karl Marx, *Grundrisse*, Penguin Books, London, 1973, p. 709.

44. Christian Baudelot, Roger Establet, Jacques Malemort, *La petite bourgeoisie en France*, Paris, Maspero, 1974, especially Part III "Petite bourgeoisie et partage de la plus-value," and more especially, Section 1 of part III, "Tous les salaries ne sont pas des proletaires."

45. *Ibid.*, pp. 156-7.

46. Karl Marx, *Capital,* Book 1, Part Three, "Production of Absolute Surplus Value," Part Four, "Production of Relative Surplus Value," and Part Five, "Production of Absolute and of Relative Surplus Value," London, Everyman's Library, 1957, Vols. 1 and 2.

47. This idea was first suggested to the author by David Mole.

FOOTNOTES TO CHAPTER TWO

1. Thus even a John Holmes, long-time Director of the Canadian Institute for International Affairs and a frequent apologist for American's post-war role, could by 1968 bring himself to speak about "the Pax Americana," albeit in a positive, and not negative sense. "In its benevolence, and its sense of mission, the Pax Americana resembles the Pax Britannica, but it is more extensive." From an address in September 1968 entitled "The American Problem" in John W. Holmes, *The Better Part of Valour,* Carleton Library, Toronto, 1970, p. 182.

2. *Resources for Freedom, Vol. 1, A Report to the President by the President's Materials Policy Commission,* Washington, June, 1952, p. 3.

3. *Ibid.,* p. 91.

4. *Ibid.,* p. 121.

5. Statistics Canada, Corporations and Labour Unions Returns Act, *Report for 1972, Part 1—Corporations,* Ottawa, 1975, Chart 1, p. 29.

6. *Resources for Freedom,* Vol. 1, p. 122.

7. Organization for Economic Cooperation and Development *Economic Outlook,* No. 16, December 1974, Table 1, p. 13.

8. See Andre Gunder Frank, *Capitalism and Underdevelopment in Latin America,* Paperback Edition, New York, 1969, pp. 12-14. Our reference to Frank does not however mean that we find his metropolis-hinterland framework by any means a perfect fit for Canada.

9. United Nations, Department of Economic and Social Affairs, *Multinational Corporations in World Development,* New York, 1973, Table 3, pp. 130-137.

10. *Fortune,* "The Fifty Largest Industrial Companies in the World," August 1975, p. 163. By comparison, *American* corporations made up *thirty* of the top fifty multinational manufacturing corporations in the UN study using 1971 figures cited above.

11. *Fortune,* "The Fortune Directory of the 300 Largest Industrial Corporations Outside the United States," August 1975, pp. 155-162.

12. The CALURA Report for 1972 reclassified Alcan and Inco from foreign controlled to Canadian controlled. CALURA *Report, Vol. 1,* p. 16. *The Financial Post's* list of the top 100 Canadian non-financial companies, July 1975, however, shows Alcan with 54.6 per cent foreign ownership, of which 44.1 per cent is in the United States and Inco with 50 per cent foreign ownership, 35 per cent in the U.S.

13. *Fortune,* "The Fifty Largest Commercial Banking Companies Outside the United States," August 1975, pp. 164-5. There has been some slippage in the relative position of Canadian banks, however, insofar as the Toronto-Dominion Bank which figured on *Fortune* lists of the top fifty non-American banks several years ago no longer appears on the 1975 list.

14. E.P. Neufeld, *The Financial System of Canada,* Toronto, 1973, 577-8.

15. Wallace Clement, *The Canadian Corporate Elite,* Toronto, 1975, especially pp. 117-122. To be fair to Clement he does not suggest that there is necessarily conflict between the indigenous and comprador elites, as he calls them; but he does make the fractionalization of the Canadian bourgeoisie a central focus for his study.

16. Harold A. Innis, *Essays in Canadian Economic History,* Toronto, 1956, p. 405.

17. John Porter, *The Vertical Mosaic,* Toronto, 1965, Chap. VIII, especially pp. 233 *et seq.,* and Appendix II, pp. 570-96.

18. Clement, *op. cit.,* Chap. Four, pp. 125 *et seq.,* and Appendix VII, pp. 400-428.

19. "In 1972 foreign controlled corporations with assets of over $25 million in the non-financial industries numbered 372 or about 6 per cent of the total number of non-resident controlled corporations. They held $40 billion in assets or 71 per cent of the assets of all non-financial foreign controlled corporations. The 297 Canadian-controlled non-financial corporations in this asset size group represented less than one per cent of the total number of domestically controlled corporations and had assets of $62 billion or 63 per cent of the total assets under Canadian corporate control." CALURA *Report for 1972, Part 1,* p. 19. Statement 1A, reproduced as Statement 2 in Chapter 2, shows the combined assets of foreign and Canadian corporations as $153.27 billion in 1972. The percentage of this held by both foreign and Canadian controlled corporations with assets of over $25 million is 65.4 per cent. If one were to include in the aggregate figure for assets the $8.08 billion in assets held by unclassified corporations, i.e., those too small to report under CALURA, the 65.4 per cent figure would be reduced slightly to 63.2 per cent.

20. The 1971 census showed Quebec's population at 6,027,764, or 27.9 per cent of Canada's 21,568,311. *Canada Yearbook 1973,* Table 5.4, p. 209. Matching the figures in Table 9 "Taxable Returns by Province and Occupation" with the taxable returns (not all the returns that we use elsewhere in Chapter Two) in Table 3 "All Returns by Occupation" gives the following results for Tax Year 1972 (see continuation of Note 20: Table at top of page 240).

21. Census of Canada, 1961, Vol. 111-Part 1, Bulletin 3.1-3, *The Labour Force,* Table 6, p. 6-2.

22. 1971 Census of Canada, *Occupations,* Vol.: 111-Part 2 (Bulletin 3.2-3) p. 2-1. (Bulletin 3.2-13 in the same Volume lists the occupation codes and titles used in 1971.)

23. *Ibid.,* pp. 2-1 to 2-5.

24. *Ibid.,* Bulletin 3.2-13, Introduction, inside front cover.

25. Statistics Canada, *Education in Canada A Statistical Review for the Period 1960-1*

Continuation of Note 20.

	Teachers	Government Employees	Professionals	Business Proprietors	Investors Property
Taxable returns Quebec	76,737	230,016	17,286	73,540	62,959
Taxable returns all of Canada	293,842	1,002,426	66,132	273,027	289,390
Quebec's returns as % of Canada's	26.1	23.0	26.1	26.9	21.9

Source: *Taxation Statistics 1974 Edition* (for 1972), Table 3, pp. 40-51. Table 9, p. 122.

The percentages shown deviate relatively little from Quebec's 27.9% share of Canada's population in *1971*. They justify our argument that the figures for English Canada would be between 70% and 75% of those shown for Canada as a whole between 1946-72, and the ratios among different income categories roughly the same for English Canada and Canada as a whole.

   to 1970-1, Ottawa, 1973, Forward, p. 7.

26. *Ibid.*, pp. 26-7, 52.

27. *Ibid.*, pp. 45-7, 40-41.

28. *Ibid.*, p. 57; Table 55, p. 405.

29. *Ibid.*, pp. 40-1.

30. *Ibid.*, Table 55, pp. 404-5.

31.
Hospital Revenues and Expenditures

	Total Revenues (in million dollars)	Total Expenditures (in million dollars)
1961	763	779
1974	4001	3875

Source: Department of Finance, *Economic Review 1975*, Table 59, p. 166.

32. Hugh Armstrong, *The Patron State of Canada*, M.A. Thesis, Department of Sociology and Anthropology, Carleton University, 1974, Table 5.5, p. 138.

33. J.E. Hodgetts and O.P. Dwivedi, "The Growth of Government Employment in Canada," *Canadian Journal of Public Administration*, 1969, pp. 224-238. In Table 11, Growth of Government Employees in Canada 1946-66, and Table 111, Number of Government Employees per Thousand of Canadian Population and Labour Force, Hodgetts and Dwivedi used only the *taxable* returns for various tax years in arriving at their totals. In our Table 2.17 and in other tables using tax data we have taken special pains to insure that *all* returns are calculated. Thus Hodgetts and

Dwivedi show only 212,390 government employees in 1950; we show 328,360. Fifteen years later, for 1965, they show 649,293; we show 759,021.

34. *Ibid.*, p. 231.

35. Armstrong, *op. cit.*, Chapter Six and more particularly Table 6.1, p. 167.

36. Cf. Hubert Guindon, "Social Unrest, Social Class and Quebec's Bureaucratic Revolution" *Queen's Quarterly*, Vol. 71, No. 1, 1964, pp. 150-62; Jacques Brazeau, "Les Nouvelles Classes Moyennes," in Fernand Dumont and Jean-Paul Montminy, etc., *Le pouvoir dans la societe canadienne-francaise*, Quebec, pp. 151-63.

37. 1971 Census of Canada, Vol.: 111—Part 2 (Bulletin 3.2-3) pp. 2-9 to 2-19.

38. *Ibid.*, pp. 2-7 to 2-9.

39. *Ibid.*, p. 2-7.

40. *Ibid.*, pp. 2-5 to 2-7.

41. Muni Frumhartz, *The Unionization of White-Collar Workers*, prepared for the National Committee on White Collar Organizing of the CLC, March 1963. See also the special issue of *Canadian Labour*, July-August 1966, on white-collar organizing.

42. Louis Le Borgne, *La CSN et la Question Nationale*, these de maitrise, Departement de Science Politique, Universite du Quebec a Montreal, 1975, pp. 126-7.

43. A CUPE Press Release, dated February 25, 1974 begins: "Canada's largest union today said . . ." An Article in the CUPE *Journal* of February-March 1975 noted Stan Little's decision to retire as CUPE's first and only President, and the union's growth over the twelve year period since its birth from 76,000 to almost 200,000 members, Canada's largest.

44. The CALURA *Report for 1964, Part 11*, Ottawa, 1967, Tables 10A-D pp. 30-2, shows 834,949 members of international unions in English Canada or 71.8 per cent of the 1,166,311 total in international, national or government workers unions in 1963.

45. CALURA *Report for 1972, Part 11-Labour Unions*, Table 28-A, p. 71.

46. Such may well be the drift of certain attempts to adapt metropolis-hinterland arguments to Canada. Kari Levitt acknowledges that Canada has high levels of income and education, (*Silent Surrender*, Toronto, 1970, p. 105), but makes implicit comparisons between dollar outflows from Canada to the United States in the 1960s and those from the poorer regions of Latin America, Africa, and Asia in the same period (p. 94). Mel Watkins, in a 1973 article, makes no distinction between levels of development in his outline of metropolis-hinterland relations: "The metropolis is the seat of manufacturing, importing staples—raw materials, food—from the hinterland and exporting manufactured goods. The role of the hinterland, to export staples and import manufactured goods which embody their own staples, is pre-determined." Watkins, "Resources and Underdevelopment," in Robert M. Laxer, ed., *The Political Economy of Dependency*, Toronto, 1973, p.

111.

47. Cf. Andre d'Allemagne's *Le Colonialisme au Quebec*, Montreal, 1966, or the *tiers mondisme* in many of the articles in *parti pris* of the middle 1960s.

48. This is the main argument of Steve Moore and Debi Wells, *Imperialism and the National Question in Canada*, Toronto, 1975.

49. Statistics Canada, *Canada's International Investment Position 1926 to 1967*, Table XXV, pp. 168-9, Table XXIII, pp. 162-3.

50. See for example John Deverell and the Latin American Working Group, *Falconbridge: Portrait of a Canadian Mining Multinational*, Toronto, 1975; Daniel Jay Baum, *The Banks of Canada in the Commonwealth Caribbean—economic nationalism and multinational enterprises of a medium power*, New York, 1974; "The Brascan File," *The Last Post*, March 1973, pp. 28-39; Rishee Thakur, *Imperialism and Nationalism in the Caribbean: The Political Economy of Dependent Underdevelopment in Guyana*, M.A. thesis, U.B.C., Department of Political Science, 1976, especially Chapter 3.

51. Cf. Arghiri Emmanuel, *Unequal Exchange: A Study of the Imperialism of Trade*, New York, 1972, which provides a useful framework, though by no means a full-proof one, for studying economic relations between developed and underdeveloped countries. Some of Emmanuel's conclusions, especially those pointing to a fundamental conflict of interest between the working classes of first world and third world countries, are open to serious question.

52. Moore and Wells, *op. cit.*, p. 116.

FOOTNOTES TO CHAPTER THREE

1. Cf. M.C. Urquhart and K.A.H. Buckley, eds., *Historical Statistics of Canada*, Toronto, 1965 Series F193-207, p. 169, showing a decline in the British share of non-resident investment in Canada from 53 per cent in 1920 to 36 per cent ten years later, and the corresponding American increase from 44 per cent to 61 per cent by 1930.

2. For the text of the Agreement see Roger Frank Swanson, *Canadian-American Summit Diplomacy, 1923-1973*, Carleton Library, Toronto, 1975, p. 71.

3. Frank H. Underhill, "North American Front," *Canadian Forum*, September 1940, reprinted in J.L. Granatstein and Peter Stevens, eds., *Forum*, Toronto, 1972, pp. 191-3.

4. King's statement to the House of Commons of April 28, 1941 is reproduced in Swanson, *op. cit.*, p. 82.

5. Mildred A. Schwartz, *Public Opinion and Canadian Identity*, Berkeley and Los Angeles, 1967, Table 16, p. 74.

6. *Ibid.*, Table 11. p. 67.

7. *Ibid.*, Table 14, p. 70.

8. Canadian Institute of Public Opinion, #248, 1956, UBC Data Library File, breakdown by province.

9. Through the late 1940s and early 1950s the annual rate of growth in American direct investment averaged well over 10 per cent, figures which had only been equalled in the pre-1930 period. Statistics Canada, *Canada's International Investment Position 1926 to 1967*, Ottawa, 1971, pp. 27, 111.

10. Cf. the discussion in John W. Warnock, *Partner to Behemoth*, Toronto, 1970, Chapter 5, or the author's article, "Canadian defence policy and the American empire" in Ian Lumsden, ed., *Close the 49th Parallel, etc.*, Toronto, 1970, pp. 94-115.

11. Lester Pearson, speech at Rollins College, Florida, February 21, 1954 in *External Affairs*, Ottawa, March 1954.

12. William Carswell, Northern Electric, *The Financial Post*, October 6, 1945, p. 7.

13. W.J. Dowler, secretary-treasurer of a Winnipeg investment firm.

14. Leonard Phillips, Calgary Stock Exchange.

15. Cf. Sir Vincent Meredith, President of the Bank of Montreal, speaking in 1926: "I do not share this fear (of American investment), but rather welcome the flow of money, which must assist in the development of our natural resources, give employment to labour, and increase our exports to other countries." Cited in an editorial in the *Canadian Forum* of February 1926, entitled "Peaceful Penetration," and reprinted in Granatstein and Stevens, eds., *op. cit.*, p. 36.

16. Morris Wilson speaking to the 77th annual meeting of the bank, *The Financial Post*, January 19, 1946, p. 16.

17. *The Financial Post*, September 7, 1946, p. 13.

18. L.S. Amery, *The Washington Loan Agreement: A Critical Study of American Economic Foreign Policy*, London, 1946, p. xi, cited in Joyce and Gabriel Kolko, *The Limits of Power*, New York, 1972, p. 65.

19. Cf. for example the comment of G.D. Conant, a former Ontario Attorney-General, to the effect that in foreign policy it would be wiser for Canada to follow the example of Britain than of the United States. *The Financial Post*, May 5, 1951, p. 7.

20. *The Globe and Mail*, Toronto, November 18, 1947, pp. 1,2.

21. Sydney Dobson, President, Royal Bank of Canada, *The Financial Post*, January 17, 1948, p. 20. Cf. also the speech by Douglas Abbott in New York pointing out that $1.75 billion in interest and dividends had been paid out to American investors since the beginning of the war and suggesting Americans find out more about their largest customer, supplier, and field of investment. *The Financial Post*, January 10, 1948, pp. 11-12.

22. "Our governments have agreed to continue for the time being a close working partnership on economic problems . . .In view of the high degree of economic interdependence of the Canadian and American economies, the Government of

the United States desires to assure the Government of Canada that it will consider
and deal with the problems of transition from war to peace in the spirit of the Hyde
Park Declaration . . .", a U.S. official cited in *The Financial Post*, February 21,
1948, p. 13. "What Does Hyde Park Deal Mean For Canada Now?"

23. In an accompanying article incredibly titled "No Threat to Sovereignty,"
February 21, 1948, p. 13.

24. "When my honourable friend says that we are taking orders from another
country, he is talking rubbish." Douglas Abbott to Howard Green, Canada, House
of Commons Debates, Session 1948, Vol. 1, p. 559.

25. Howard Green, *Ibid.*

26. H.W. Timmins, *Debates,* pp. 586-7.

27. T.L. Church, *Debates,* Session 1948, Vol. 2, p. 1567.

28. See Stephen Scheinberg, "The Indispensable Ally: Canadian Resources and the
Cold War," Canadian Historical Association Papers, June 1975, pp. 13-14, for a
discussion of these negotiations.

29. "Life Magazine advocates economic union with Canada," *The Financial Post*,
March 20, 1948, p. 11.

30. T.C. McNabb, replying to the question, "Customs union with the United States?"
The Financial Post, March 27, 1948.

31. George Cockshutt, *Ibid.*

32. *Ibid.*

33. In addition to the two presidents mentioned, the editor of the *Victoria Daily Times*
spoke of the need for early and dispassionate consideration of the customs union
proposal, while the editor of the *Saskatoon Star Phoenix* argued that *Life*
magazine was right, and that Canada would not get along without the U.S., nor
the U.S. without Canada. *Ibid.*

34. Cf. The Economic Council of Canada, *Looking Outward: A New Trade Strategy for
Canada,* Ottawa, 1975 and the study done for the Economic Council by Peyton V.
Lyon, *Canada—United States Free Trade and Canadian Independence*, Ottawa,
1975.

35. *The Financial Post*, October 7, 1950.

36. "How big is the Yankee stake in our oil?" *The Financial Post*, March 19, 1951, p.
19.

37. G.K. Sheils, "Canadians still own Canada," editorial page, *The Financial Post*,
May 30, 1953.

38. *The Financial Post*, Editorial, August 28, 1954.

39. Speech by N.E. Tanner, President, Trans-Canada Pipe Lines to Independent Gas
Association, New Orleans, *The Financial Post*, September 18, 1954, p. 8.

40. December 4, 1954, p. 50.

41. For a typical example of junior partnership at work, compare the following passage from a speech by Louis St. Laurent, Prime Minister of Canada and a corporate lawyer in his own right, to a Convocation at Northwestern University, Illinois, on June 11, 1951: " . . . the United States is, I repeat, inevitably the dominant factor in the free world. We in Canada who are your closest neighbours, know that you have never, in any crisis, failed to uphold the freedom which this nation was founded to preserve. We know you will not fail in this crisis to give our partnership the leadership it must have to uphold the freedom of mankind." *External Affairs*, July 1951, pp. 245-8.

42. Presidential address of N.A. Hesler to the 78th Annual Meeting of the Canadian Manufacturers Association, St. Andrews, New Brunswick, 1949, p. 7.

43. Presidential address of M.A. East to the 79th Annual Meeting of the Canadian Manufacturers Association, 1950, p. 3.

44. Presidential address of W.F. Holding to the 80th Annual Meeting of the Canadian Manufacturers Association, Quebec, 1951, p. 1.

45. *The Financial Post*, Editorial, "Not Just Canadian Defense," April 23, 1955.

46. Presidential address of Hugh Crombie to the 81st Annual Meeting of the Canadian Manufacturers Association, May 1952, p. 8.

47. F.A. Knox, editor, "The March of Events," *The Canadian Banker*, Toronto, Winter 1950, Vol. 57, No. 1, p. 13.

48. See for example *The Financial Post* editorial in the May 9, 1953 issue attacking McCarthyism for destroying people's reputations without evidence. See also the editorial of March 13, 1954 denouncing McCarthy.

49. C.D. Howe had told a New York audience in April 1953: "The St. Lawrence Seaway is and always has been a Canadian seaway," underlining the point that Canada could well go ahead on its own. *The Financial Post*, April 11, 1953, p. 22. In an editorial as late as May 15, 1954, *The Financial Post* could argue: "To build the Seaway ourselves may still be the final and most satisfactory course."

50. Cf. Eisenhower's address to both houses of parliament on November 14, 1953: "Joint development and use of the St. Lawrence-Great Lakes waterway is inevitable, is sure and certain. With you I consider this move a vital addition to our economic and national security." In Swanson, *op. cit.*, p. 154.

51. July 10, 1954, editorial, strongly criticizing U.S. Senate Majority and Minority Leaders, William Knowland and Lyndon Johnson, for threatening U.S. withdrawal from the UN if China were admitted.

52. October 23, 1954. In the same issue, an article by Michael Barkway argued that "Energy determines the location of industry" and that the Americans were coveting Canadian resources, p. 19.

53. October 9, 1954, editorial.

54. Jean Lesage, "The Water Resources of the Columbia River Basin," a speech

delivered in Vancouver, May 9, 1955, reprinted in *External Affairs,* September 1955, pp. 218-223.

55. Speech by St. Laurent to the Economic Club of New York, November 19, 1951, entitled "North America's Place in the World of Today," *External Affairs,* December 1951, p. 401.

56. One of the Commissioners, Hilda Neatby, used the analogy in a talk on Canadianism to the Canadian Historical Association in 1956. Canadian Historical Association, *Papers, 1956,* pp. 74-6. An important part of her argument was the time-honoured theme in English Canadian historiography of the mutual interdependence of English-Canadian and French-Canadian existence. "This obvious fact, that the English-Canadian existence stemmed from French-Canadian survival has been made possible only by English-Canadian existence, seems to me to be the cardinal fact of Canadianism, known to everyone, but too often ignored." p. 75.

57. Canada, *Report of the Royal Commission on National Development in the Arts, Letters and Science 1949-1951,* Ottawa, 1951, p. 373.

58. *Ibid.,* pp. 11, 13.

59. *Ibid.,* pp. 14, 16, 17, 18.

60. *Ibid.,* p. 271.

61. Cf. H.G.J. Aitken, "Defensive Expansionism: The State and Economic Growth in Canada," in W.T. Easterbrook and M.H. Watkins, *Approaches to Canadian Economic History,* Carleton Library, Toronto, 1967, pp. 183-221.

62. *Report of the Royal Commission . . .,* p. 273.

63. The four other commissioners in addition to Vincent Massey were Norman A.M. MacKenzie, President, U.B.C.; Most Reverend Georges-Henri Levesque, Dean of the Faculty of Social Sciences, Laval University; Hilda Neatby, Professor of History, University of Saskatchewan; and Arthur Surveyer, described as a Civil Engineer, *Report,* pp. xi, xii.

64. *Report* , pp. 355, 377.

65. *Ibid.,* pp. 287 *et seq.*
66. *Ibid.,* pp. 308-9.

67. Cf. editorials in the *Ottawa Evening Journal,* June 11, 1951, the *Ottawa Evening Citizen,* June 2, 1951, the *Montreal Herald,* June 2, 1951 and an article in the *Vancouver Daily Province,* June 2, 1951, all very favourable to the Report.

68. "Reservations and Observations by Mr. Arthur Surveyer on Radio Broadcasting, Television and the National Film Board," *Report,* pp. 384-408. Cf. Also Frank W. Peers, *The Politics of Canadian Broadcasting 1920-1951,* Toronto, 1969, Chapter 16, especially pp. 423-7, or the comments of Howard Green, Progressive Conservative, and Solon Low, Social Credit, cited in the *Province,* June 2, 1951.

69. *The Financial Post,* June 15, 1951. Editorial titled "A Medium of Canadianism."

70. Vincent Massey, cited in an editorial in *The Ottawa Journal,* June 11, 1951, "Mr. Massey on Massey Report," included in the files on the Massey

Commission in *The Norman Mackenzie Papers*, Special Collections, U.B.C.

71. Professor George Grant, Special Study, pp. 28-9, cited in the *Report*, p. 272.

72. *Report*, Part 11, p. 275.

73. Harold Innis' "The Strategy of Culture" is subtitled "With Special Reference to Canadian Literature—A Footnote to the Massey Report." *The Strategy of Culture*, Toronto, 1952. A close associate of Innis, the economic historian J.B. Brebner, in a commemorative article, argued: "He (Innis) was from the beginning perturbed by Canada's historical vulnerability and subordination to powers beyond her control. He masked his self-dedication well, subconsciously and perhaps consciously, until his last finished utterance, "The Strategy of Culture," in which he aimed to make up for what he regarded as the timidity of the Massey Report." Canadian Historical Association, *Papers, 1953*, "Harold Adams Innis as Historian," p. 14.

74. Vincent Massey, *On Being Canadian*, Toronto, 1948, p. 115. Massey also writes: "This threat (Communism) which Christianity faces should have the effect of drawing together Roman Catholic and Protestant whatever language they speak, confronted as they are by a common enemy, p. 23. The Cold War was a useful instrument in cementing Canadian federalism.

75. J.M. MacFayden, Prince Edward Island hotel manager, *The Financial Post* survey "Does Canada Need Foreign Capital?" October 6, 1945, p. 7.

76. Major John Barnett, Manager, Ontario Branch, Credit Foncier Franco-Canadien, *The Financial Post*, August 28, 1948, p. 8.

77. *The Canadian Chartered Accountant*, "The Royal Tour," Toronto, Vol. 59, No. 5, November 1951, p. 169.

78. Carl O. Nickle, "Western Canadian Oil and Gas: How Far so Far and How Much Further to Go," *The Canadian Chartered Accountant*, November, 1951, pp. 171-8.

79. Speech by Walter J. Macdonald in Chicago, *The Financial Post*, October 24, 1953, p. 23.

80. Speech by P.C. Wilmott, *The Financial Post*, September 13, 1952.

81. H.R. Sanders, C.A., "Comments on Canada's Foreign Trade," *The Canadian Chartered Accountant*, Vol. 64, No.3, March 1954, p. 146.

82. *The Farmer's Advocate and Home Magazine*, London, Ontario, October 9, 1947.

83. *Ibid.*, December 25, 1947, "Flirting in the Dollar Area."

84. *The Country Guide*, Winnipeg, February 1948. "The restrictions imposed by the government have undesirable features, but they look unimportant compared with some of the consequences which would flow from devaluation." Pp. 12-13. The Conservatives urged dollar devaluation as an alternative to the Abbott Plan.

85. *The Farmer's Advocate* as early as March 11, 1948, after the Communist takeover of Czechoslovakia, had argued that appeasement wouldn't work, while *The Country Guide* of April 1949, in welcoming the Atlantic Pact, argued that neutrality was impossible in the contemporary world.

86. *The Country Guide*, August 1950, p. 50.

87. *The Farmer's Advocate*, July 12, 1951, p. 9.

88. *Ibid.*, April 25, 1955, p. 10.

89. *Ibid.*, March 28, 1953, p. 10. Editorial entitled "Canada is a Good Help to the USA."

90. Lester Pearson in the House of Commons, February 2, 1951. Reprinted as "The Basis for Canadian Far East Policy" in *External Affairs*, February 1951, p. 38.

91. Karl Marx and Frederick Engels, *The German Ideology*, p. 65.

92. In reply to *The Financial Post* question, "Should we teach more Canadianism in our schools?" September 15, 1951, p. 11.

93. J.M.S. Careless, "Canadian Nationalism—Immature or Obsolete?" Canadian Historical Association, *Papers, 1954*, p. 14.

94. R.A. Preston, Canadian Historical Association *Papers, 1956*, pp. 77, 79.

95. Canadian Historical Association *Papers, 1954*, p. 18.

96. F.H. Soward, "Canada in a Two-Power World," Canadian Institute for International Affairs, *Behind the Headlines*, Toronto, August 1948, Vol. VIII, No. 1, p. 3.

97. Frank H. Underhill, "Notes on the Massey Report," *The Canadian Forum*, August 1951, in Granatstein and Stevens, eds., *op. cit.*, p. 273.

98. A.J.W. Dyck, Ph.D. ed., *Canadian Chemistry and Process Industries,* Toronto, January 1951, p. 35, July 1951, p. 551.

99. B.S. Keirstead and S.D. Clark, "Social Sciences" in *Royal Commission Reports: A Selection of Essays on National Development in the Arts, Letters and Sciences,* Ottawa, 1951, pp. 179-189. American academic salaries were roughly twice those of Canadian, leading the authors to the conclusion: "Canadian universities get a small number of first class scholars who are willing to sacrifice both financial advantage and greater scholarship opportunities in order to serve their country and scholarship at one and the same time." P. 180.

100. Cf. Alan C. Cairns, "National Influences on the Study of Politics," *Queen's Quarterly,* Autumn, 1974, Vol. 81, No. 3, pp. 333-347, and "Political Science in Canada and the Americanization Issue," *Canadian Journal of Political Science,* June 1975, Vol. VIII, No. 2, pp. 191-234 for an interesting discussion of American influence in one particular field, political science.

101. George Grant, "Philosophy," in *Royal Commission Reports,* Ottawa, 1951, p. 123.

102. Despite the argument of Daniel Drache in "Rediscovering Canadian Political Economy," Canadian Political Science Association Meetings, 1975, the author is not impressed by the profundity or originality of most of the work in Canadian political science of the 1940s and 1950s that he singles out. (The exception would

be Macpherson's and to a lesser extent Mallory's books on Social Credit in Alberta.) A far better case for indigenous Canadian work in the social sciences can be made for the 1920s and 1930s, the high point of the staple tradition and of classical political economy. As Mel Watkins pointed out at a conference on the significance of Harold Innis held in 1972 at the Innisfree Farm, the 1920s and 30s correspond to the brief interlude in Canadian history between the British and American empires.

103. F.H. Angus, "The Canadian Royal Commission on the Arts, Letters and Science," *Western Political Quarterly*, Vol. IV, No. 4, December 1951, p. 578.

104. In a *Financial Post* questionnaire of December 14, 1946, pp. 12-13, McLennan saw American economic domination as inevitable, but hoped that politically and culturally Canada could remain intact. For Sir Ernest MacMillan, if Canada were to survive, "We must come to an understanding with our French-speaking compatriots and build a synthesis of both French and British traditions, plus those valuable political qualities that we have developed on our own. I cannot feel that we have progressed very far on this path, to persevere will call for courage, intelligence and above all a national rather than a provincial consciousness. Yet either Canadians must follow this path or English-speaking Canada faces increasing Americanization and French-speaking Canada increasing insularity."

105. J.W.T. Spinks, "The Natural Sciences," in *Royal Commission Reports*, pp. 279-80.

106. Wynne Plumptre, "Special Trade Deal with USA is Step Towards Annexation," *Saturday Night*, December 25, 1948, p. 21.

107. A.R.M. Lower, "Canada-Next Belgium?" *Maclean's*, December 15, 1947, pp. 9, 51-3.

108. Arthur R.M. Lower, *Canada Nation and Neighbour,* Toronto, 1952, pp. 39-40. The analogy with India is, of course, exaggerated.

109. Cf. ArthurR.M. Lower, *This Most Famous Stream, The Liberal Democratic Way of Life*, Toronto, 1954, where the common liberal values of Canada, Britain and the United States are stressed as against Marxism. "Within western society, the English-speaking peoples have enough in common to mark them out as a distinct group . . . Building on the original foundations, each has well made its own contribution, different in form alike in spirit . . . Behind them all stands the stubborn notion that somehow the other man must be treated fairly." Pp. 3, 9.

110. Kenneth McNaught (writing under the pseudonym S.W. Bradford), "The CCF Failure in Foreign Policy," *The Canadian Forum*, September 1950, in Granatstein and Stevens, eds., *op. cit.*, p. 262.

111. *The Financial Post*, August 25, 1945, p. 11.

112. Harold A. Innis, "Great Britain, the United States and Canada," in *Essays in Canadian Economic History*, Toronto, 1956, p. 405.

113. Donald Creighton, *Harold Adams Innis, Portrait of a Scholar*, Toronto, 1957, pp. 133-4.

114. Harold A. Innis, *The Strategy of Culture*, Toronto, 1952, p. 2.

115. *Ibid.*, p. 20.

116. Donald Creighton, "Canada and the Cold War," in *Towards the Discovery of Canada*, pp. 245-55, especially pp. 245, 254.

117. Cf. Norman Penner, ed., *Winnipeg, 1919: The Strikers' Own History of the Winnipeg General Strike*, Toronto, 1973. The author might add that he is far from persuaded by the efforts of such writers as Kenneth McNaught and David J. Bercuson, *The Winnipeg Strike: 1919*, Longman, Don Mills, 1974, or David J. Bercuson, *Confrontation in Winnipeg*, Montreal, 1974, to downplay the radical significance of the Winnipeg Strike. Arthur Meighen had a clearer conception of the threat to the bourgeoisie's interests that these latter-day academics.

118. Cf. Mary Elizabeth Wallace, *The Changing Canadian State: A Study of the Changing Conception of the State as Revealed in Canadian Social Legislation: 1867-1948*, Ph.D. thesis, Columbia University, 1950, especially Chaps. XII-XV.

119. Cf. Gad Horowitz, *Canadian Labour in Politics*, Toronto, 1968.

120. Union membership in Canada increased from 359,000 in 1939 to 711,000 in 1945. Urquhart and Buckley, eds., *Historical Statistics of Canada*, Series D412-413, p. 105.

121. In the 1945 federal election, the Liberals polled 2,170,625, the Progressive Conservatives 1,455,453, the CCF 822,661, Social Credit 214,998, the Bloc Populaire 173,427 and the Labour Progressive Party (i.e., Communists) 111,892. Urquhart and Buckley, eds., *op. cit.*, Series W74-164, p. 617.

122. Cf. Ronald Radosh, *American Labor and United States Foreign Policy*, New York, 1969, in particular Chap. XIV "Labor's Cold War: An Evaluation." See also Charles Lipton, *The Trade Union Movement in Canada 1827-1959*, Montreal, 1968, especially pp. 276-7, for a brief discussion of the Canadian government's role in the smashing of the Canadian Seamen's Union.

123. For a by no means unbiased account of the Communist Party in the late 1940s and early 1950s see the recent history by Ivan Avakumovic, *The Communist Party in Canada*, Toronto, 1975, Chap. 7, "The Cold War." For another account, see Norman Penner, *The Socialist Idea in Canadian Political Thought*, Ph.D. thesis, University of Toronto, 1975, Chap. IV.

124. Cf. Irving Martin Abella, *Nationalism, Communism, and Canadian Labour*, Toronto, 1973, Chaps. 5-8.

125. Tim Buck, "Keep Canada Independent," Report to Labour Progressive Party National Committee, January 5-9, 1948, in Tim Buck, *Our Fight For Canada*, Toronto, 1959, p. 278.

126. *Ibid.*, p. 266.

127. "The Dilemma of Canadian Capital," in Buck, *op. cit.*, p. 230.

128. J. Douglas Gibson, "General Review," in Gibson, ed., *Canada's Economy in a Changing World*, Toronto, 1948, pp. 306-7.

129. M.J. Coldwell, Canada, House of Commons Debate, Session 1947, Vol. 1, pp.

392-3.

130. *The Canadian Unionist*, organ of the Canadian Congress of Labour, Ottawa, November 1947, pp. 251-2.

131. Cf. Coldwell's intervention both in the April, 1948 Commons debate and again during the debate on ratification of the treaty in March, 1949, where in the words of R.A. Spencer, *Canada in World Affairs 1946-1949*, Toronto, 1959, he "firmly repudiated the elements in his party which hankered for a neutral position in the cold war, and pledged the CCF's support for Canada's position in the north Atlantic pact." P. 276.

132. Cf. *The Canadian Unionist*, June 1948, "The Rising Tide of Communism," an article strongly supporting St. Laurent's hard line; the CCL Resolution of autumn, 1948 urging Canadian participation in the Atlantic Defence Conference against totalitarianism, *Canadian Unionist*, November 1948, p. 255; or the Congress Memorandum to the federal government supporting NATO, *The Canadian Unionist*, April 1949.

133. *The Canadian Unionist*, editorial, July 1950.

134. *Ibid.*, August 1950, p. 178.

135. Cf. Lipton, *op. cit.*, "1950 TLC Convention: Developments in Foreign Policy, 1950-1953," pp. 287-94.

136. This was the explanation given to the author in an interview he had with David Lewis in Ottawa in late December, 1967.

137. Thus *The Canadian Unionist* featured prominently speeches by N.A. MacKenzie, President of UBC, urging a middle way between socialism and pure laissez-faire capitalism, with maximum respect for individual rights or by F. Cyril James, Principal of McGill, arguing that no liberty was possible without responsibility, in issues between May and September, 1949. Lester Pearson's Cold War speeches were also given great prominence.

138. Cf. Robert H. Babcock, *Gompers in Canada*, Toronto, 1975, Chap. 3, "The rise of branch-plants."

139. Cf. Radosh, *op. cit.*, Horowitz, *op. cit.*, and Abella, *op. cit.*

140. CCL Memorandum to the Federal Government, March 5, 1948, *The Canadian Unionist*, March 1948, p. 55.

141. *The Canadian Unionist,* January 1950, "Canada's Cultural Independence."

142. Address by James B. Carey to the CCL Convention, Toronto, 1952, "What Americans like about Canada," *The Canadian Unionist,* October , 1952.

143. "Milestones in Industrial Progress," *The Canadian Unionist,* September 1954, p. 286.

144. Canadian imports from the United States were never less than 2/3 of all her imports after 1945, while her postwar exports to the U.S. averaged some 60 per cent of all exports. The pre-World War II figure, especially for exports, was far

lower. Urquhart and Buckley, eds., *Historical Statistics of Canada*, Series F348-356, p. 183.

145. "In the present buoyant state of the Canadian economy the argument that keeping raw materials in this country increases jobs is not only academic, it is also fallacious." C.D. Howe, Canada, House of Commons Debates, Session 1956, Vol. VI, p. 5798.

"It seems to me that if a responsible group of men, be they Canadians or Americans, properly financed and having the proper background and experience, apply to this Parliament for incorporation, they are entitled to incorporate." C.D. Howe, cited in Leslie Roberts, *C.D. The Life and Times of Clarence Decatur Howe*, Toronto, 1957, p. 171.

146. *Fortune,* August 1952, p. 91.

147. *Ibid.*

148. Joyce and Gabriel Kolko, *The Limits of Power,* p. 2.

FOOTNOTES TO CHAPTER FOUR

1. Canada, House of Commons Debates, Session 1956, Volume VI, pp. 5800-5802.

2. Cf. the article by James B. McGeachy, "Nationalism Sparked Tory Win," *The Financial Post,* April 12, 1958 or the address by H.V. Lush, President, to the 87th annual meeting of the Canadian Manufacturing Association: "I think I am safe in saying that there is abroad today in this Canada of ours an innate spirit of independence which is characteristic of but sometimes dormant in Canadians . . .," *Canadian Manufacturers Association Meeting,* 1957, p. 3.

3. Annual Shareholders Meeting of the Bank of Toronto, *The Financial Post,* December 25, 1954, p. 20.

4. Cf. the account in Denis Smith, *Gentle Patriot,* Edmonton, 1973, pp. 31-4, of C.D. Howe's absence from the Cabinet meeting that decided to establish the Gordon Commission and of his consistent opposition to it thereafter.

5. The Order in Council, P.C. 1955—909, dated June 17, 1955, in Canada, Royal Commission on Canada's Economic Prospects, *Final Report,* 1957, Appendix A, P. 472.

6. Cited in a *Financial Post* editorial, "Mr. Coyne is a Bold Prophet," May 14, 1955.

7. *The Financial Post,* October 22, 1955, p. 25.

8. On Coyne's pedigree, compare John A. Stevenson, "J.E. Coyne: Bank Governor Stirs a Tempest," *Saturday Night,* March 29, 1958, pp. 14-15, 39. Coyne's grandfather had been a prominent lawyer in St. Thomas, Ontario and his father a Justice of the Manitoba Supreme Court.

9. Cited in *Financial Post* editorial, November 5, 1955.

10. *The Financial Post*, November 5, 1955, p. 7.

11. *Ibid.*, January 7, 1956, p. 19, and again March 17, 1956, "Dependence on U.S. Goes on Growing," April 14, 1956 "The Great American Flood."

12. *Ibid.*, Editorial, April 1956.

13. Speech of March 20, 1956 cited in James Eayrs, *Canada in World Affairs, October 1955 to June 1957*, Toronto, 1965, Paperback edition, p. 126.

14. House of Commons, Session 1956, Vol. II, pp. 2171-2.

15. *Ibid.*, Vol. IV, p. 3924.

16. Donald Fleming, *Ibid.*, p. 3935.

17. Speech by George Drew, *Ibid.*, Vol. VI, p. 5777.

18. *Ibid.*, p. 5780.

19. *Ibid.*, p. 5773.

20. *Ibid.*, p. 5792.

21. *The Financial Post*, October 13, 1956. The whole episode is further discussed in a speech by Michael Barkway to the Society of Industrial Editors, Toronto, November 14, 1957, p. 6, kindly made available to the author by Mr. Barkway.

22. Cited by Barkway in his 1957 speech, *op. cit.*, pp. 5, 7.

23. James Muir, President, Royal Bank of Canada, Speech in Denver, Colorado, cited in *Financial Post* editorial, November 3, 1956.

24. C. Sydney Frost, President, Bank of Nova Scotia, address to the annual meeting of shareholders, *The Financial Post*, December 8, 1956, p. 21.

25. *The Financial Post*, October 20, 1956, p. 28.

26. Royal Commission . . ., *Final Report*, p. 390. See also the Preliminary Report, pp. 90-93.

27. *Final Report*, Table 18.2, p. 381.

28. *Ibid.*, p. 392.

29. *Ibid.*, p. 393.

30. *Ibid.*, p. 389.

31. *Ibid.*, pp. 399-400.

32. *The Financial Post*, June 22, 1957.

33. *External Affairs*, September 1957.

34. *The Financial Post*, editorial October 5, 1957, article, p. 3.
   The British came prepared to discuss free trade between the two countries, but the Canadian Cabinet refused to take a position.

35. Cf. Philip Sykes, *Sellout: The Giveaway of Canada's Energy Resources*, Edmonton, 1973, e.g., p. 92, where Sykes cites NEB "solicitude for consumers in California" as influencing its decisions on gas exports as late as 1970.

36. There were verbal protestations to be sure. Thus Diefenbaker, in reporting to the Commons on his talks with President Eisenhower during the latter's visit to Ottawa in July 1958, stated: "I raised with the President the question that some Canadian subsidiaries of United States companies may have been prevented from accepting orders from communist China, or from people in that country, by the application of United States foreign assets control regulations, even though acceptance of such orders would be permitted by the policy of the Canadian government. The President expressed the view that the United States regulation should not be applied in anyway to the disadvantage of the Canadian economy. If cases arose in the future where the refusal of companies operating in Canada might have any effect on Canadian economic activity, the United States government would consider favourably exempting the parent company in the United States from the application of the foreign assets control regulations with respect to such orders . . . It was made perfectly clear, and I want to underline the fact, that there is no question at any time that, with respect to the operations of United States companies, Canadian law shall govern and Canadian wishes shall be respected." Roger F. Swanson, ed., *Canadian-American Summit Diplomacy 1923-1973*, p. 185. Ten years later, the Watkins Report would still be placing extra-territoriality high on the list of Canadian grievances against American multi-national corporations. *Foreign Ownership and the Structure of Canadian Industry*, Ottawa, 1968, pp. 407-410.

37. Cf. *The Financial Post*, October 18, 1958, p. 25. "How $2 billion of assets have changed ownership since 1945"; November 1, 1958, p. 3, "U.S. Stake Here Grows and Grows as Investment Capital Still Flows In."

38. *External Affairs*, November, 1958.

39. *The Financial Post*, November 22, 1958, p. 3, "No Anti-Americanism Theme of Canadian Talk."

40. Cf. John Alexander Sweetenham, *McNaughton, Vol. 3*, Toronto, 1969, Chap. 6, "The International Joint Commission."

41. Eayrs, *op. cit.*, pp. 153-60; also A.D.P. Heeney, *The Things that are Caesar's: Memoirs of a Canadian public servant*, Toronto, 1972, p. 144: . . . the senators' activities produced a wave of anti-Americanism in Canada which Pearson told me exceeded anything in his experience."

42. Michael Barkway, "The Fifties: An Ottawa Retrospect," *The Waterloo Review*, Issue No. 5, Summer 1960. In this review of James Eayrs' *Canada in World Affairs, 1955-57*, Barkway goes on to disparage Canada's groveling to Washington in all areas, especially in the personal relations between Canadian ministers and their American counterparts.

43. Speech by Walter Gordon in New York, "We Must Work at Being Friends," *The Financial Post*, February 15, 1958, p. 20.

44. Canadian Manufacturers Association, 87th Meeting, 1958, Speech by H.V. Lush, President, pp. 3-4.

45. Cf. John W. Warnock, *Partners to Behemoth,* Toronto, 1970, Chaps, 5-8, or the author's "Canadian Defence Policy and the American Empire," in Lumsden, ed., *op. cit.*, pp. 94-115.

46. Cf. Larratt Higgins, "The alienation of Canadian resources: the case of the Columbia River Treaty," in Lumsden, ed., *op. cit.*, pp. 224-40.

47. Cf. Isaiah A. Litvak and Christopher Maule, *Cultural Sovereignty: The Time and Reader's Digest Case in Canada,* New York, 1974, for an extended discussion of the exemption.

48. Cf. Charles Taylor, *Snow Job: Canada, the United States and Vietnam, 1954 to 1973,* Toronto, 1974; also Claire Culhane, *Why is Canada in Vietnam?,* Toronto, 1972.

49. Lester Pearson, Press Conference, Camp David, Maryland April, 1965, in Swanson, ed., *op. cit.*, p. 256.

50. *The Financial Post,* February 7, 1959.

51. William Hamilton, *Ibid.,* June 11, 1960.

52. *The Canadian Annual Review for 1960,* Toronto, 1961, p. 180.

53. "The Royal Bank, according to its general manager, received $8.8 million for its Cuban assets; the Bank of Nova Scotia did not immediately announce what it had received although its president described the arrangements as 'satisfactory.'" Libbie and Frank Park, *Anatomy of Big Business,* Toronto, 2nd edition, 1973, p. 127.

54. Green's commitment to disarmament, rather than nationalism, seems to have been the determining element in his opposition to nuclear weapons, though in retrospect, the nationalist element has come to seem more important. Cf. George Grant, *Lament for a Nation,* Toronto, Carleton Library Edition, 1970, Chap. 3.

55. The text is in Swanson, ed., *op. cit.*, pp. 251-4. To be sure, Pearson's speech was larded with numerous references to the honourable character of the American intervention in Vietnam and to the necessity not to "compromise on points or principle, nor . . . weaken . . . resistance to aggression in South Vietnam." Even his limited suggestion for a bombing halt was too much for Lyndon Johnson, in the prime of his power, who flew off his handle at such insolence from dependent allies, *Ibid.,* pp. 220-21.

56. Canadian Manufacturers Association, 85th Annual Meeting, Toronto, 1956, speech by T.A. Rice, President, p. 9.

57. Cited in *Canadian Chemical Processing,* Toronto, March 1961, Editorial, p. 4.

58. Canadian Manufacturers Association, 86th Annual Meeting, 1957, speech by J.C. Whitelaw, General Manager of the CMA.

59. Address of the President, J.N.T. Bulman, *Ibid.,* p. 9.

60. Minutes of the First Meeting of the Canadian-American Committee, Seigniory Club, Montebello, Quebec, November 15-16, 1957, in the N.A.M. Mackenzie Papers, U.B.C., Special Collections.

61. Interestingly, Walter Gordon's biographer, Denis Smith, breathes not a word about his hero's membership in this committee during its first years. Cf. *Gentle Patriot.*

62. Letter to N.A.M. Mackenzie and other members of the Committee dated March 9, 1961 and signed by Robert M. Fowler and R. Douglas Stuart, Co-chairmen: "On the instructions of the Committee, the Carnegie Foundation, which made the initial grant of $100,000 over a three-year period to start the work of the Committee, has been approached for a further grant. The Carnegie officals seem to be well impressed by our performance to date, and are receptive to a "phasing out" request for foundation assistance—perhaps $40,000 this year, $30,000 next year, and $20,000 the following year." P. 4. Mackenzie Papers, Special Collections.

63. *Ibid.,* p. 1.

64. See the Statement by the Committee in *The Financial Times* of October 7, 1963 and the strong editorial reply, probably written by Michael Barkway.

65. Cf. "A Model Plan for a Canada-United States Free Trade Area" by Arthur J.R. Smith, Sperry Lea and Theodore Geiger, a Draft Memorandum for the Canadian-American Committee dated September 2, 1963, Mackenzie Papers, U.B.C. See also the study by Ronald and Paul Wonnacott, *U.S. Canada Free Trade: The Potential Impact on the Economy, Ibid.,* sponsored by the Canadian-American Trading Relations Sub-committee of the Canadian-American Committee. See also *The Financial Post*, November 1, 1958, p. 24, indicating the Committee was already discussing the possibility of free trade as early as 1958.

66. *The Financial Post,* September 21, 1957, p. 38.

67. A.C. Ashworth, President, The Toronto-Dominion Bank, *The Financial Post*, December 10, 1960, p. 38.

68. Speech by George W. Bourke, President, Sun Life Assurance Co. to the Annual Meeting, *The Financial Post*, February 18, 1961, p. 28.

69. Canadian Manufacturers Association, 90th Annual Meeting, Vancouver 1961, Speech by T.R. McLagen, President, p. 7.

70. Speech to the Canadian Chamber of Commerce, Calgary, *The Financial Post*, October 8, 1960, pp. 25-7.

71. Speech to The Canadian Club, Toronto, *The Financial Post*, November 19, 1960, p. 25.

72. Denis Smith, *op. cit.*, pp. 71-2.

73. House of Commons, 1963 Session, Vol. 2, pp. 1000-1001.

74. *Ibid.,* p. 1006.

75. See Peter C. Newman, *The Distemper of Our Times*, Toronto, 1968, Chapter 2, *The Canadian Annual Review for 1963*, Toronto, 1964, pp. 195-204.

76. Walter L. Gordon, *A Choice for Canada*, Toronto, 1966, p. 97: "Many people were unhappy about the exemption for *Time*. Its preferred position makes the establishment of new Canadian magazines more difficult. The matter came up at a time when the automobile agreement was under heavy attack in Congress. Approval of the agreement might have been jeopardized if a serious dispute with Washington had arise over *Time* . . ."

77. Cf. the account by the American business historical John Fayerweather in his *The Mercantile Bank Affair: A Case Study of Canadian Nationalism and the Multi-national Firm*, New York, 1974, especially Chaps. 3 and 4.

78. Gordon, *A Choice for Canada*, p. xix.

79. *The Financial Post*, October 13, 1956. See also "Bridging the Vital Gap," April 28, 1956; "No Simple Choice, " May 26, 1956.

80. *The Financial Post*, January 12, 1957.

81. *The Financial Post*, May 4, 1957.

82. *The Financial Post*, November 16, 1957.

83. *The Financial Post*, July 19, 1958.

84. *The Financial Post*, November 1, 1958, "A Vital Move in Nation Building."

85. *The Financial Post*, November 29, 1958, "U.S. Tries Imposing U.S. Laws Here."

86. *The Financial Post*, August 8, 1959; August 29, 1959.

87. *The Financial Post*, October 8, 1960, "The Big Challenge"; February 11, 1961, "The Fifty-First State?" This editorial attacked American media that had taken to speaking of "Fidel Coyne."

88. *The Financial Post*, July 1, 1961.

89. *The Financial Post*, June 24, 1961, p. 7.

90. *The Financial Post*, July 28, 1962, August 11, 1962.

91. *The Financial Post*, February 16, 1963, pp. 1, 6.

92. *The Financial Post*, June 29, 1963, p. 6.

93. *The Financial Post*, July 6, 1963, p. 6. "Politics are Cooler Up Here," replying to *U.S. News and World Report* which had compared Canada to Mexico regarding policy on foreign investment.

94. *The Financial Post*, July 27, 1963.

95. *The Financial Post*, August 10, 1963, "Banks Go Next."

96. *The Financial Post*, February 29, 1964.

97. *The Financial Post*, July 20, 1963, "Columbia Deal Needs Pushing."

98. For example editorials on October 5, 1963 or November 20, 1965, where the paper regretted Gordon's departure from the Cabinet, and predicted history would accord him a place of distinction.

99. *The Financial Post*, April 17, 1965: "The opportunities the new corporation (the CDC) offers for well-intentioned bungling are alarming to contemplate."

100. *The Financial Post*, May 29, 1965.

101. *The Financial Post*, October 16, 1965.

102. *The Financial Post*, November 6, 1965.

103. Cf. for example Kari Levitt, *Silent Surrender,* Table 6, p. 122, showing 51 per cent foreign control of mining and manufacturing and 69 per cent of petroleum and natural gas, by 1954.

104. Park and Park, *op. cit.*, Chaps. 4 and 5.

105. Maurice Strong, then President of Power Corporation, expressed something of this pro-Canadian ownership sentiment in a 1965 speech to the Canadian Club of Winnipeg: "I would like to see a massive mobilization of our capital for investment in the ownership and control of Canadian corporations. We should use our capital to maintain control of those key companies which are still Canadian owned, to assure substantial Canadian ownership of important new enterprises and to repatriate control of some of our major companies which are now controlled by non-residents." *The Financial Post,* March 27, 1965, p. 6.

106. Cited by Michael Barkway, "How Independent Can We Be?", speech to the Liberal Party's Conference on National Problems, Kingston, Ontario, September 1960, p. 2, kindly made available to the author by Mr. Barkway.

107. *The Financial Post,* February 8, 1964, p. 6.

108. Canadian Manufacturers Association, 93rd Annual Meeting, May 1964, address by H. Roy Crabtree, President, p. 4.

109. Roy A. Matthews, "Canada, 'The International Nation,'" *Queen's Quarterly*, Vol. 72, No. 3, Autumn 1965, pp. 499-523.

110. *The Globe and Mail* of September 23, 1969 and October 23, 1969 has articles discussing the Canada Committee, whose 500 members included senior executives of Bell Canada, Alcan, Northern Electric, Domtar, the Royal Bank, the Bank of Montreal. Andrew Brichant published a book *Option Canada* for this group in reply to Rene Levesque's *Option Quebec.* One of his main arguments was that Montreal should secede from Quebec if separatism continued to grow.

111. *The Financial Post,* July 24, 1961, p. 6.

112. *The Financial Post,* December 8, 1962.

113. Canadian Manufacturers Association, 91st Annual Meeting, Montreal, June 1962, address by F.D. Mathers, President, p. 6.

114. *The Financial Post*, July 1, 1961, editorial entitled "Legislating Language."

115. *The Financial Post,* February 23, 1963, p. 6.

116. James B. McGeachy, *The Financial Post,* August 14, 1965, p. 7. The paper itself would hardly have disagreed.

117. *The Financial Post*, March 20, 1965, "Get Out and Sell the Idea," an editorial following the publication of the *Preliminary Report* of the Royal Commission on Bilingualism and Biculturalism.

118. Lucien Rolland, President, Rolland Paper Company, *The Financial Post,* April 13, 1963, p. 6.

119. Canadian Manufacturers Association, 98th Annual Meeting, 1969, address by John R. O'Dea, President, p. 4.

120. *The Financial Post,* August 31, 1957, p. 29.

121. *The Financial Post*, January 31, 1959, p. 8.

122. *The Financial Post,* December 30, 1961, p. 6.

123. *The Financial Post,* November 3, 1962, pp. 26-7.

124. *The Financial Post,* July 7, 1962, p. 1, "Watch for Sparks from new Canadian 'Rebs'."

125. See for example the Canadian Manufacturers Association, 93rd Annual Meeting, 1964, p. 38, for a picture of Earl K. Browridge, President of American Motors (Canada) Ltd. at the CMA reception in the company of the Deputy Minister of Economics and Development for Ontario and R.J. Waxman, President of Kelvinator of Canada Ltd. There are similar pictures in the reports of most of the annual meetings of the 1960s and 1970s.

126. Speech in Kitimat, B.C., *The Province*, April 27, 1956.

127. Cited by G.W. McLeod, Social Credit, in House of Commons Debates, Session 1956, Vol. IV, May 21, 1956, p. 4157.

128. House of Commons Debates, Session 1963, Vol. II, June 25, 1963, pp. 1165-6.

129. *The Farmer's Advocate,* London, Ontario, April 14, 1956, p. 10.

130. *Ibid.,* March 9, 1957, p. 10.

131. *Ibid.,* April 9, 1960, p. 12.

132. *The Country Guide*, Winnipeg, March 1960, p. 4, editorial entitled "All that Glitters is not Gold."

133. Cf. Vernon C. Fowke, *The National Policy and the Wheat Economy,* Toronto, 1957 and C.B. Macpherson, *Democracy in Alberta,* Toronto, 1953, for two classic accounts of the one-time importance of agriculture in the Canadian political economy and of farmer-based political movements.

134. *Canada Month,* Forerunner, Vol. 1, July 1961, p. 18.

135. *The Financial Post,* September 30, 1961, p. 27.

136. Reproduced in *The Financial Post,* March 23, 1963, p. 6.

137. George Grant does not, to be sure, describe Diefenbaker or Green as traditional petty bourgeoisie, but it is implicit in his description of their nationalism in *Lament for a Nation*: "Diefenbaker was committed to a Canadian populism . . . As a criminal lawyer, he had learnt that the interests of the small need defending against the powerful." (P. 13) "Diefenbaker spoke with telling historical sense when he mentioned the Annexation Manifesto in his last speech to Parliament before the defeat of his government in 1963. He pointed out the similarity between the views of the Montreal merchants in 1849 and the wealthy of Toronto and Montreal in 1963. In neither case did they care about Canada." (P. 69) On the incompatibility between this nostalgic traditional petty bourgeois nationalism and the new petty bourgeoisie, i.e., the civil service and the intelligentsia, see Grant's Chapter 2.

138. "Canadian Defence Policy and the American Empire" in Lumsden, *op. cit.*, p. 105. Grant places the emphasis on Diefenbaker's free enterprise assumptions in explaining some of his anti-nationalist actions. Grant, *op. cit.*, Chap. 2.

139. C.D. Blyth and E.B. Carty, "Non-Resident Ownership of Canadian Industry," *Canadian Journal of Political Science and Economics*, Vol. XXII, November 1956, No. 4, pp. 449-460, pp. 449-451.

140. *Ibid.,* pp. 452-4.

141. *Ibid.,* pp. 458, 460.

142. G.V. Ferguson, "Likely Trends in Canadian-American Political Relations," *Canadian Journal of Political Science and Economics,* Vol. XXII, No. 4, November 1956, pp. 437-448, p. 438.

143. *Ibid.,* pp. 441-2.

144. *Ibid.,* p. 444.

145. Michael Barkway, "How Independent Can We Be?, 1960, *op. cit.*, pp. 4, 11.

146. James M. Minifie, *Peacemaker or Powder-Monkey: Canada's Role in a Revolutionary World*, Toronto, 1960.

147. *The Financial Post,* March 26, 1960, p. 7. McGeachy said he was partly, though not wholly, convinced, criticizing Minifie's failure to discuss ways of getting rid of economic satellitism.

148. *The Financial Post,* June 9, 1962, p. 7.

149. *The Financial Post*, November 17, 1962, p. 7.

150. *The Financial Post*, May 29, 1965, p. 7.

151. *The Financial Post,* October 16, 1965, p.7.

152. Cf. J.W.T. Spinks, "The Natural Sciences" in *Royal Commission Studies*, Ottawa, 1951, pp. 261-288, especially the sub-sections "Dependence of Canadian Science on Foreign Countries," "Dependence of Canadian Industry on Foreign Countries," "Export of Scientists," pp. 277-81.

153. *The Financial Post*, January 9, 1960, p. 31.

154. *Canadian Chemical Processing*, Toronto, March 1961, p. 4.

155. *Canadian Annual Review 1960*, Toronto, 1961, p. 179.

156. *The Financial Post,* November 3, 1962, pp. 26-7.

157. Kenneth McNaught, "Foreign Policy," in Michael Oliver, ed., *Social Purpose for Canada*, Toronto, 1961, pp. 445-72.

158. *The Financial Post,* March 31, 1962, p. 25. Text of an address by MacLennan on the subject of Canadian periodicals.

159. Grant, *op. cit.*, pp. 31, 68.

160. See Kay Macpherson and Meg Sears, "The Voice of Women: A History" in Gwen Matheson, ed. *Women in the Canadian Mosaic*, Toronto, 1976.

161. Gad Horowitz, "Creative Politics," *Canadian Dimension*, Vol. 3, No. 1, November-December, 1965, p. 28.

162. Gad Horowitz. "Mosaics and Identity," *Canadian Dimension*, Vol. 3, No. 2, January-February, 1966, p. 19.

163. *The Financial Post,* March 5, 1955, p. 26, article by F.W.P. Jones, Dean of the School of Business Administration, University of Western Ontario, London, Ontario.

164. J. Douglas Gibson, "The Changing Influence of the United States on the Canadian Economy," *Canadian Journal of Political Science and Economics*, Vol. XXII, No. 4, November 1956, pp. 421-36, pp. 424, 428, 431, 436.

165. *The Financial Post,* March 4, 1961, p. 21.

166. Letter from Norman A.M. Mackenzie to Robert M. Fowler, March 30, 1961 in the Mackenzie Papers, Special Collections, U.B.C.

167. The Ottawa Citizen, April 8, 1971, cited in D.W. Carr, *Recovering Canada's Nationhood*, Ottawa, 1971, p. 60.

168. Lower's views are cited in an article by James B. McGeachy, *The Financial Post*, November 18, 1961, p. 7, describing a Canadian-American Seminar in Windsor,

Ontario.

169. "Canada and the North Atlantic Triangle," in Frank H. Underhill, *In Search of Canadian Liberalism*, Toronto, 1960, p. 255. To be fair to Underhill, he does go on to say "that the American people are, as yet, far from being mature enough to provide the wise leadership that is needed." But the thrust of his talk, delivered at Michigan State University in 1957, is pro-American, and disparaging of Canadian eggheads, e.g., the Massey Commission, who see American influences as "alien" (p. 259).

170. Frank H. Underhill, *The Image of Confederation*, CBC Publications, Toronto, 1964, p. 66.

171. Cf. Morton's *The Canadian Identity*, Toronto, 2nd edition, 1972, especially pp. 80-87, "Canada and the United States: The Years of Friction, 1952-19--."

172. *The Globe and Mail*, September 8, 1964, cited in Ramsay Cook, *Canada and the French Canadian Question*, Toronto, 1966, p. 160.

173. Cook, *Canada and the French Canadian Question*, p. 4.

174. Of the English-speaking Commissioners, both A. Davidson Dunton, Co-Chairman, and F. R. Scott, can be characterized as members of the new petty bourgeoisie.

175. Royal Commission on Bilingualism and Biculturalism, *Preliminary Report*, Ottawa, 1965, pp. 138-9.

176. R.E. Grose, Deputy Minister of Industry and Commerce, Manitoba, *The Financial Post*, April 27, 1963, p. 1.

177. Arnold Heeney, *The things that are Caesar's*, p. 164.

178. *Ibid.*, p. 166. Heeney's views of Green are also symptomatic of how little loyalty Tory nationalists could expect from anti-nationalist civil servants. "Green, the most pleasant and good simple man, is an innocent abroad, and what is more, obstinate and underneath inclined to a sort of pacific-isolationism.", p. 162.

179. *Ibid.*, p. 198.

180. Cited by Maureen Appel Molot, "The Elephant, the Mouse and the Financial Relationship," *Queen's Quarterly*, Vol. 78, No. 1, 1971, p. 73.

181. *Ibid.*

182. The *Canadian Annual Review for 1960* cites a letter by H. Scott Gordon and 16 other economists to *The Globe and Mail* on December 8, 1960 arguing for a change in the management of the Bank of Canada due to incompetent economic analysis, pp. 179-80.

183. H. Scott Gordon, *The Economists versus the Bank of Canada*, Toronto, 1961, pp. 45, 47.

184. Harry Johnson, "Problems of Canadian Nationalism" in his *The Canadian Quandry*, Toronto, 1963, pp. 11-12.

185. Cf. the Memorandum, *A Model Plan for a Canada-United States Free Trade Area* by A.J.R. Smith, Sperry Lea and Theodore Geiger for the Canadian-American Committee, September 2, 1963 and the Memorandum by Smith alone, *Recent Canadian and United States Governmental Actions Affecting U.S. Investment in Canada* of September 5, 1963. Draft Memoranda M-45 and M-46, Mackenzie Papers, Special Collections, U.B.C.

186. Drafts of these studies are also included in the Mackenzie Papers, though both were later published by their authors.

187. Melville H. Watkins, "Economic Nationalism," a Review Article of Robert Craig Brown's *Canada's National Policy,* in the *Canadian Journal of Political Science and Economics,* Vol. XXXII, No. 3, August 1966, pp. 388-92, 391-92.

188. *Canadian Labour,* Vol. 1, No. 1, April 1956, p. 30.

189. *Ibid.*

190. *Ibid.,* p. 35.

191. *Ibid.,* p. 66.

192. *Ibid.,* p. 66.

193. *Canadian Labour,* July 1956, Editorial, pp. 4-5, "United States Investment in Canada."

194. *Ibid.,* October 1956, p. 22.

195. *Ibid.,* February 1959, p. 39.

196. *Ibid.,* April 1960, p. 11.

197. *Ibid.,* April 1961, p. 39.

198. *Ibid.,* January, 1961, Donald Macdonald, "International Unionism in Canada."

199. *Ibid.,* December 1963, Address by Joe Morris to the AFL-CIO Convention in New York, November 1963.

200. *Ibid.,* February 1961, from the Congress brief to the Federal government.

201. *Ibid.,* April 1961, Editorial.

202. On the channeling of funds from the CIA to the Regional Organization of the Americas and to the International Confederation of Free Trade Unions itself, see Philip Agee, *Inside the Company: CIA Diary,* London, 1975, p. 244. He does, however, indicate that there was a limit as to how much money could be funneled through these groups. See also "AFL-CIA" by Lenny Siegel, reprinted in Steve Weissman et al., *The Trojan Horse,* Ramparts Reader, 1975, pp. 117-136, for a discussion of the CIA-Latin American trade union connection. The author is in no position to state whether the leadership of the CLC, or individual staff members of the organization, had any knowledge of covert CIA activity in ORIT and the ICFTU or, to go one step further, whether there was any infiltration of the CLC itself. But there is a murky pattern, particularly when one thinks of the visits of

American Embassy labour attaches to CLC Headquarters, that needs further exploration and airing.

203. *Canadian Labour*, June 1961, reporting the decision by the CLC Executive Council to support Canadian membership in the OAS. The same Council meeting coupled an attack on the "dictatorial nature of the Castro regime" with opposition to the Bay of Pigs Invasion. This would suggest that the CLC was not *simply* in the AFL-CIO's, let alone CIA's, backpocket, though hardly a radical critic of American policy in Latin America.

204. *Ibid.*, January 1961, CLC Submission to the O'Leary Commission.

205. *Ibid.*, February 1961, Submission to the Federal Government; April 1963, article arguing the possibility of a non-nuclear role for Canada within NATO and NORAD.

206. *Ibid.*, September 1964, pp. 37-8.

207. *Ibid.*, Editorial, September 1965.

208. *Policies of the New Democratic Party 1961 to 1973*, Ottawa, 1974, Resolution on Foreign Ownership, 1965, rejecting a policy of buying back the economy as opposed to using the CDC to direct the course of future investment in Canada and diminish the foreign component, pp. 8-9; Resolution on Vietnam, 1965, calling for an end of the U.S. bombing of North Vietnam, for a resumption of the Geneva negotiations, for eventual reunification of Vietnam through free elections, and for an end to Canadian support of the United States on the International Control Commission. Pp. 81-82.

209. Cf. Mildred A. Schwartz, *Public Opinion and Canadian Identity*, Table 11, p. 67.

210. *Ibid.*, Table 12, p. 68.

211. *Maclean's*, "The U.S. and US," June 6, 1964, p. 13.

212. *Ibid.*

213. *The Financial Post*, May 30, 1964, p. 7.

214. Royal Commission, *Preliminary Report*, p. 122.

215. An inhabitant of Yarmouth, N.S., cited *Ibid.*, p. 93.

216. An inhabitant of Sudbury, Ontario, cited *Ibid.*, p. 93.

217. A university professor in Kingston, Ontario, cited *Ibid.*, p. 94.

FOOTNOTES TO CHAPTER FIVE

1. *Newsweek* magazine re the October Crisis, cited in *The Financial Post*, November 28, 1970, p. 5.

2. Cf. Harry Magdoff, *The Age of Imperialism*, New York, 1969 or Raymond Vernon,

Sovereignty at Bay, New York, 1971.

3. Cf. the resolution proposed by the Group of 77 at the United Nation's General Assembly, Sixth Special Session, May 1974, which is reproduced in part in Chapter Six below.

4. Cf. the 1973 War Powers Act, passed over the veto of Richard Nixon, or subsequent Congressional action regarding arms shipments to Turkey, Chile, or anti-Communist forces in Angola.

5. Cf. the account in Peter Newman, *The Distemper of our Times*, Toronto, 1968, p. 415 or John and Graham Fraser, eds., *Blair Fraser Reports*, Toronto, 1969, pp. 83-4.

6. Canada, *Report of the Task Force on the Structure of Canadian Industry*, Ottawa, 1968. Only *The Toronto Star*, Feb. 16, 1968, pp. 23-30 and the NDP, e.g., Max Saltsman, House of Commons, 27th Parliament, 2nd Session, March 6, 1968, p. 7342, strongly supported the various recommendations of the Watkins Report for a special agency to coordinate policies with respect to multinationals, a government export trade agency to deal with extra-territorial impingements on American-owned subsidiaries, or establishment of the Canadian Development Corporation.

7. For the government rationale *re* Denison Mines, see statements by P.E. Trudeau, 28th Parliament, 2nd Session, March 2, 1970, p. 4255 and J.J. Greene, *Ibid.*, March 19, 1970, p. 5250.

8. *Canadian Annual Review for 1971*, Toronto, 1972, pp. 7-9. Interestingly, in early 1970 Trudeau had told a student audience that the CDC was 74th on a list of 74 government bills in terms of priority. *The Financial Post*, editorial, April 11, 1970.

9. From the text of Bill C-132, cited in Maureen Boyd, *The Making of the Foreign Investment Review Act: Sources of Influence on Bill C-132*. Honours Essay, U.B.C., Department of Political Science, 1975, pp. 3-4.

10. Transcript of Questions and Answers at the Prime Minister's Accountability Session, Liberal Party Convention, Ottawa, November 20, 1970, p. 11. Our translation.

11. *Canadian Annual Review for 1970*, Toronto, 1971, p. 347. W.A.C. Bennett, Premier of B.C., was calling for free trade with the United States in 1971, *Canadian Annual Review for 1971*, p. 180; Premier Hatfield of New Brunswick, future champion of the Bricklin car, opposed the Foreign Investment Review Act in 1973, *Canadian Annual Review for 1973*, pp. 336-7.

12. Canada, White Paper on Defence, *Defence in the 70s*, Ottawa, 1971, p. 16. To be sure, "the defence of North America in cooperation with U.S. forces" remained a major priority, immediately after the "surveillance of our own territory and coast-lines."

13. Department of External Affairs, Ottawa, Statements and Speeches 71/73, Mitchell Sharp, *Implications for Canada of the "Nixon Doctrine,"* Address to the Centre for Inter-American Relations, New York, September 21, 1971.

14. Cf. the press conference of Prime Minister Trudeau, Washington, D.C., December

7, 1971, Swanson, ed., *op. cit.*, p. 287, reporting Nixon's sympathy for Canada not wanting to be a colony of the United States; address by Richard M. Nixon to both Houses of Parliament, April 14, 1972, Swanson, ed., *op. cit.*, pp. 298-9.

15. Mitchell Sharp, "Canada-United States Relations: Options for the Future," *International Perspectives,* Department of External Affairs, Ottawa, Autumn 1971, p. 1.

16. *Ibid.,* p. 17.

17. Notes for a Speech by the Secretary of State for External Affairs, Allan J. McEachen, to the Winnipeg branch of the Canadian Institute of International Affairs, January 23, 1975.

18. Robert M. Reford, "Canadian Nationalism—Does it make the border more visible?", an Address to the Chicago Council on Foreign Relations, April 18-19, 1975, p. 6.

19. *Canadian Annual Review,* 1970, pp. 219, 348.

20. A Gallup poll in late 1970 showed 89 per cent of English-speaking Canadians (and 86 per cent of French-speaking) approving the bringing in of the War Measures Act. Canadian Institute of Public Opinion, December 12, 1970.

21. A 1973 poll showed 17 per cent of respondents in the Maritimes, 25 per cent in Quebec, 8 per cent in Ontario and 15 per cent of the West holding Quebec's separation from Canada to be likely "in about five years." 68 per cent of respondents in the Maritimes, 63 per cent in Quebec, 77 per cent in Ontario and 72 per cent in the West thought separation unlikely. Canadian Institute of Public Opinion, June 16, 1973.

22. Robert W. Bonner, Vice-Chairman, MacMillan-Bloedel, "The Future Role of Canadian Companies in International Trade," Address to the University of Western Ontario 15th Annual Business Conference, London, June 4, 1971, pp. 9-10. Cf. also *The Financial Post,* Second Section, October 2, 1971, "B.C.'s multinational giant moves in new directions," discussing MacMillan-Bloedel's activities in Britain, Belgium, Holland, Spain, Indonesia, Malaysia, Australia, and the United States.

23. *The Toronto Star,* March 19, 1971, "Canadian Bankers urge Americans to step up investment in Canada," pp. 1, 8.

24. Canadian Manufacturers Association, 96th Annual Meeting, 1967, Address by H.W. Joly, President, p. 4.

25. *The Financial Post,* September 12, 1970, Address by A.G.W. Sinclair, President, Canadian Manufacturers Association, p. 6.

26. Interview with Gerard Filion, new CMA President, *Industrial Canada,* CMA monthly publication, June 1971, p. 113.

27. Boyd, *op. cit.,* p. 19, citing the briefs of the Canadian Chamber of Commerce and the Canadian Manufacturers Association to the Standing Committee considering Bill C-132.

28. Canadian Manufacturers Association, 100th Annual Meeting, Toronto, 1971, Report by J.C. Whitelaw, Vice-President and General Manager, p. 19. Whitelaw is quoting from a submission by the CMA to the Prime Minister in April, 1971.

29. Canada, *Foreign Direct Investment in Canada*, Ottawa, 1972, p. 302.

30. CMA, 100th Annual Meeting, p. 27.

31. *The Financial Post*, January 30, 1971, p. 6.

32. *Ibid.,* October 5, 1974, p. 7.

33. *Ibid.,* Alexander Ross, "Prophet becoming honored at last," March 21, 1970, p. 7.

34. *Ibid.,* December 10, 1966, p. 6.

35. Cf. Tim Draimin and Jamie Swift "What's Canada Doing in Brazil?" *This Magazine*, Vol. 8, No. 5-6, January-February, 1975, pp.3-8; "The Brascan File," *The Last Post*, March 1973, pp. 28-39.

36. *The Globe and Mail,* Report on Business, May 29, 1970, "Brascan president urges Ottawa to spell out controls."

37. Speech by David Kinnear to the 79th meeting of the Canada-U.S. Committee of the Canada and United States Chamber of Commerce, Florida, News release by the Canadian Chamber of Commerce, Montreal, dated March 24, 1972.

38. Duff Roblin, "A new national policy and Canadian nationalism," The W. Clifford Clark Memorial Lecture, *Canadian Journal of Public Administration*, 1973, pp. 542-56, p. 542.

39. *Ibid.,* p. 556.

40. *Industrial Canada,* July 1971, p. 49.

41. Thus Carl A. Pollock, President of Electrohome, Kitchener, Ontario, and a former President of the CMA, could declare in a November 18th, 1971 speech to the Canadian Institutional Investor Conference, Montreal, that there had been too much Canadian dependence on the United States in the post-war years and that one must seek to sell Canada to Canadians. "Economic nationalism becomes an enlightened policy because it is enlightened private enterprise." V.O. Marquez, Chairman of Northern Electric, could tell a 1972 panel of maufacturers that multinational corporations mean that most entrepreneurial decisions are made elsewhere. The main thrust of his argument, however, was the need for Canadian industry to acquire an international marketing outlook. *Industrial Canada*, April, 1972, p. 38.

42. *The Financial Post*, February 24, 1968, Editorial, p. 1, "We must stay friends."

43. *Ibid.,* editorial, p. 6, "Tensions are mounting."

44. *Ibid.,* editorial, p. 1, July 11, 1970.

45. *Ibid.,* July 11, 1970, p. 29. Floyd S. Chalmers, former Chairman and President of

Maclean-Hunter Ltd.

46. *Ibid.*, August 13, 1966, editorial, p. 1, "Midget can't cope now."
    Ibid.. p. 1, March 15, 1969.

47. Paul Audley, Executive Director of the Independent Publishers Association,
    "Book Publishing in Canada" in A. Rotstein and G. Lax, editors, *Getting It Back*,
    Toronto, 1974, pp. 201-21, p. 215.

48. The Canadian Federation of Independent Business, *The Programmes and
    Objectives.*

49. Letter from James R. Conrad, Director, Policy and Research, The Canadian
    Federation of Independent Business, to the author, dated May 20, 1975.

50. Brief by the Canadian Federation of Independent Business to Commons
    Committee considering Bill C-2, an act to amend the Combines Investigation Act,
    pp. 9-10.

51. John F. Bullock, President, Canadian Federation of Independent Business,
    "Incentives for what?," speech to National Conference on Incentives, Halifax,
    May 28, 1975, p. 2. For the Waffle de-industrialization thesis, see Jim Laxer,
    "Canadian Manufacturing and U.S. Trade Policy" in Robert M. Laxer, editor,
    Canada Ltd., pp. 127-52. For a critique of this thesis based on careful empirical
    investigation see Fred Caloren, "Layoffs, Shutdowns, and Plant Closures in
    Ontario: The Economics of Misery," *Our Generation*, Vol. 10, No. 4, pp. 61-75. It
    is interesting to note that similar arguments about de-industrialization are being
    made in the United States. Cf. Richard J. Barnet and Ronald E. Muller, *Global
    Reach*, New York, 1974, Chapter 9, "The Latin Americanization of the United
    States."

52. Bulloch, "Incentives for What?" pp. 2, 4.

53. *Ibid.*, p. 3.

54. *Ibid.*, p. 7.

55. Letter from James R. Conrad, dated May 20, 1975.

56. Alexander Ross, "Who's for nationalism? Well, almost everybody." *The
    Financial Post*, April 24, 1971, p. 7.

57. Don Mitchell, *The Politics of Food*, Toronto, 1975, Chapter 2, "Farmers: A Class
    Divided," especially pp. 25-30.

58. Mitchell, *op. cit.*, p. 34.

59. Marc Zwelling, "The Kraft Boycott," *Canadian Dimension*, Vol. 8, No. 4-5,
    January, 1972, pp. 8-9, 64.

60. Brian Stock, "A culture in search of an economy," *Times Literary Supplement*,
    "Canadian Writing Today," October 26, 1973, pp. 1311-13.

61. Barry Lord, " 'mericans" in Al Purdy, editor, *The New Romans,* Edmonton, 1968.
    "Let us answer Quebec by developing an equally strong struggle aimed at freeing

Canada from U.S. domination," p. 150.

62. Peter Morris, "Declaration of Independence," *The North American Review*, Spring 1972, p. 4.

63. *The Globe and Mail*, June 25, 1971.

64. D.W. Carr, *Reclaiming Canada's Nationhood*, Ottawa, 1971, pp. 144, 154.

65. Richard J. Cole, C.A., "Reviewing the Foreign Investment Review Act," *CA*, February, 1974, p. 28.

66. *The Canadian Chartered Accountant* (afterwards *CA*), editorial June, 1971, p. 389.

67. A. John Marshall, C.A., "Public Accounting and Multinationalism," *CA*, December 1974, pp. 35-40, p. 40. Marshall is described as a partner in Price Waterhouse & Co., Toronto, who spent a number of years in his firm's Mexican and Central American offices. He is also a member of the Trade Committee of the Canadian Association for Latin America, a corporate-oriented association.

68. Boyd, *op. cit.*, p. 15.

69. *The Financial Post*, editorial, June 30, 1973, p. 6, "Does the Minister always know best?"

70. *Ibid.*, February 24, 1968, p. 1, "We must stay friends."

71. John Homes, "Nationalism in Canadian Foreign Policy," in Peter Russell, editor, *Nationalism in Canada*, Toronto, 1966, pp. 203-220, p. 218.

72. Kenneth McNaught, "The National Outlook of English-speaking Canadians," in Russell, ed., *op. cit.*, pp. 61-71, pp. 62-3.

73. Charles Hanley, "A Psychoanalysis of Nationalist Sentiment," in Russell, ed., *op. cit.*, p. 303-19, p. 318.

74. Abraham Rotstein, "The 20th Century Prospect: Nationalism in a Technological Society," in Russell, ed., *op. cit.*, pp. 341-63, pp. 356, 362.

75. Stephen Clarkson, "The Choice to be Made" in Stephen Clarkson, ed., *An Independent Foreign Policy for Canda?*, Toronto, 1968, pp. 253-69, pp. 260-1.

76. Gad Horowitz, "On the Fear of Nationalism," reprinted in *Nationalism, Socialism and Canadian Independence*, Canadian Dimension Pamphlet, Winnipeg, no date, p. 7.

77. Tony Hyde, *Economics: Large Questions, Short Answers*, Canadian Union of Students, Ottawa, 1968, p. 9, written for the C.U.S. Secretariat "who take full responsibility for the determination of its content."

78. *From What Happened? A History*, a publication of the Canadian Union of Students, no date, p. 14.

79. P. Michael Pitfield, "Canada in the Seventies," April 1972, reprinted in *Canadian*

American Relations—Towards a Better Understanding, St. Lawrence University, New York, 1974, p. 48.

80. Mel Watkins, *Gordon to Watkins to You*, Toronto, 1971, p. 127.

81. Robert Page, Speech to the Chemical Institute of Canada, December 3, 1974. The first part of the statement in the text is a paraphrase of Page's remarks, while the remainder is a direct quotation.

82. Peter C. Newman, "The Thawing of Canada," *The Atlantic Community Quarterly*, Vol. IX, Summer 1971, pp. 219-28, p. 222.

83. Harry G. Johnson, *International Economic Questions facing Britain, the United States and Canada in the 70s*, British-North America Committee, London, 1970, pp. 19-20; Harry G. Johnson, "Economic Benefits of the Multinational Enterprise" in H.R. Hahlo, J. Graham Smith, Richard C. Wright, editors, *Nationalism and the Multinational Enterprise*, Leiden, 1973, pp. 166-67.

84. Robin Mathews and James Steele, editors, *The Struggle for Canadian Universities*, Toronto, 1969, pp. 19-20.

85. Cf. the minutes of the Carleton University Academic Staff Association general meeting, December 11, 1968, *Ibid.*, pp. 35-6.

86. S.P. Rosenbaum, "The Canada Goose—The Canadianization of our literature departments," *The Candian Forum*, March 1972, p. 25.

87. Ramsay Cook, *The Maple Leaf Forever*, Toronto, 1971, p. 164.

88. George Woodcock, "A plea for the anti-nation," *The Canadian Forum*, April 1972, pp. 16-19, *passim*.

89. Margaret E. Prang, "Nationalism in Canada's First Century," Canadian Historical Association, *Historical Papers 1968*, pp. 114-25, pp. 122-25.

90. Claude Bissell, *The Financial Post*, July 3, 1971, p. 6.

91. The minutes of the Canadian Association of University Teachers Council Meetings contain numerous references to the Canadianization question. It was not until 1973-1974, however, that a Committee on Canadianization was formed, and not until May 1975 that a resolution was finally voted.

92. *University Afairs*, July 1975, p. 2, Lynda Woodcock, "CAUT council tackles difficult issues."

93. C.W. Gonick, "Foreign Ownership and political decay," in Ian Lumsden, editor, *Close the 49th Parallel etc.*, pp. 44-73, p. 46.

94. James Laxer, "Introduction to the Political Economy of Canada," in Robert M. Laxer, editor, *Canada Ltd.*, pp. 26-41, pp. 28, 41.

95. Cy Gonick, "A Dimension Editorial Statement: A New Beginning," *Canadian Dimension*, Vol. 10, No. 1, April 1974, p. 5.

96. *Maclean's*, February 1970.

97. *Ibid.*, December 1970.

98. *Ibid.*, December 1971.

99. *Ibid.*, August 1972.

100. *The Independencer*, February-March, 1975, p. 2.

101. *Ibid.*, Vol. III, No. 1, 1974, p. 1.

102. *Ibid.*, Vol. III, No. 3, June-July, 1974, p. 1.

103. *Ibid.*, February-March, 1975, p. 1.

104. C. Wright Mills, *The Power Elite,* New York, 1956, pp. 334-5, "The Conservative Mood."

105. Eric Kierans interviewed in *The Financial Post*, November 6, 1971, p. 7. Kierans was by now back at his old perch at McGill's School of Business Administration.

106. Philip Sykes, *Sellout: The Giveaway of Canada's Energy Resources,* Edmonton, 1973, p. 222. The central heroes of his book are four academics at Dalhousie, described as the Dalhousie four, out to reverse the giveaway.

107. Letter by Donald S. Scott, Vice-President, Canadian Society for Chemical Engineering and Professor of Chemical Engineering, University of Waterloo, in *Science Forum* 20, April 1971, p. 2.

108. Robert Page, "Canadian Studies: The Current Dilemma" in A. Rotstein and G. Lax, editors, *Getting It Back,* pp. 175-91, p .190.

109. Gary Lax, "Cable television and the Canadian Broadcasting System," in Rotstein and Lax, editors, *op. cit.*, pp. 222-50, p. 250.

110. Abraham Rotstein, "The Multinational Corporation in the Political Economy—A Matter of National Survival" in H.R. Hahlo *et al.*, editors, *Nationalism and the Multinational Enterprise,* p. 191.

111. John J. Deutsch, "Agenda for the Seventies," *Queen's Quarterly,* Vol. 78, No. 1, p. 5.

112. Ivan L. Head, "The Foreign Policy of the New Canada," *Foreign Affairs,* January 1972.

113. Pierre L. Bourgault, *Innovation and the Structure of Canadian Industry*, Background Study for the Science Council of Canada No. 23, October 1972, p. 51.

114. Arthur J. Cordell, *The Multinational Firm, Foreign Direct Investment, and Canadian Science Policy*, Background Study for the Science Council of Canada No. 22, December 1971, p. 57.

115. Stephen, a 35 year old musician and program producer for the CBC, cited in Koula Mellos, *Critical and Empirical Perspectives on Theories of Ideology in Advanced Capitalist Society,* Ph.D. thesis, Queen's University, 1974, pp. 98-9.

116. Herschel Hardin, *A Nation Unaware,* Vancouver, 1974, Jacket Cover.

117. Atomic Energy of Canada Ltd., *Annual Report 1971-72,* Covering Letter from J.L. Gray, President, to Donald S. Macdonald, Minister of Energy, Mines and Natural Resources dated June 2, 1972.

118. Atomic Energy of Canada Ltd., *Annual Report 1973-74,* Covering Letter from J.L. Gray to Donald Macdonald dated May 17, 1974.

119. Jacques Brazeau, "Les nouvelles classes moyennes," in Dumont and Montminy, editors, *Le Pouvoir dans la societe canadienne-francaise,* pp. 151-63, p. 157.

120. *The Montreal Gazette,* December 21, 1971, p. 25.

121. Ken Whittington, national publicity director of the Canadian Institute of Management, cited *Ibid.*

122. J. Douglas Gibson, "Canada's declaration of less dependence," *Harvard Business Review,* September-October, 1973, pp. 69-79.

123. *The Labour Gazette,* published by the Department of Labour, Ottawa, gives the following breakdown of the CLC membership in 1974:
   Total CLC membership   1,615,833
   International unions   1,152,843
   National unions   462,990
   August 1974, p. 554.

124. The lead article in the *Canadian Paperworkers Journal,* February-March 1975, begins: "More than 300 delegates to the Canadian Paperworkers Union's First National Policy Conference rose in thundering applause as C.P.U. President L.H. Lorrain inaugurated the union's first official meeting since its founding with the words, 'We're here. The Canadian Paperworkers Union—we've made it—collectively we've made it happen.'"

125. *Canadian Labour,* July-August, 1966, p. 30.

126. For the text of the guidelines, see *Gordon to Watkins to you,* pp. 52-3.

127. *Canadian Labour,* July-August 1966.

128. *Ibid.,* March 1967, p. 23.

129. *Ibid.,* May 1968, p. 37.

130. *Ibid.,* November 1968, pp. 14-16.

131. *Ibid.,* June 1968, "International Affairs Report on Convention," p. 37.

132. *Ibid.*, May 1969, editorial, p. 5.

133. Donald Macdonald, Address to the CLC's 8th Convention, *Canadian Labour*, June 1970, p. 6. See also the interview with William Mahoney of the Steelworkers in *The Labour Gazette*, August 1973, p. 527 in which he attacks the CIC and the Council of Canadian Unions.

134. *The Labour Gazette*, September 1970, p. 640.

135. David Lewis, Address to the CLC's 9th Convention, *Canadian Labour*, June 1972, p. 20.

136. Ed Finn, "The Struggle for Canadian Labour Autonomy," *The Labour Gazette*, November 1970, pp. 767-74, p. 767.

137. Gil Levine of CUPE, "The Coming Youth Revolt in Labour," *The Labour Gazette*, November 1971, pp. 722-30, p. 727.

138. Mel Watkins, "The Trade Union Movement in Canada" in Rober Laxer, ed., *Canada Ltd.*, pp. 178-96, pp. 193-94.

139. "The CLC Convention: New Faces New Direction for the Congress," *The Labour Gazette*, August 1974, pp. 552-60.

140. Interview with Ron Lang, Legislative Director of the CLC, May 21, 1975.

141. Interview with Norm Simon, publicity director of CUPE, Ottawa, May 22, 1975.

142. CUPE *Journal*, November-December, 1970.

143. Interview with Norm Simon.

144. CUPE *Journal*, May-June 1971.

145. *Ibid.*, December 1972.

146. *Proceedings,* 5th CUPE Convention, 1971, p. 30.

147. *Ibid.*

148. *Ibid.*, p. 32.

149. *Ibid.*, p. 17.

150. L. McClintock, Local 1238, Chatham, Ontario, *Proceedings*, 5th CUPE Convention, 1971, p. 98.

151. In 1973-74 CUPE was trying to gain jurisdiction over some of the weaker provincial civil service federations, at one point even threatening to leave the CLC on the question. The 10th CLC Convention decided to encourage provincial federations of civil services to ally inside a new Canada-wide union of provincial civil servants,

but not under CUPE's banner.

152. CUPE Press Release, June 16, 1973.

153. Bill Brassington, "Continentalism—One Option," *Canadian Labour*, November-December, 1972, p. 32.

154. *A Canadian Voice*, pp. 2, 7, 9, 14. This pamphlet is available in the Department of Labour Library, Ottawa. *Apparently* the authors were without any organizational affiliation.

155. Jack Scott, a veteran Communist, who broke with the Canadian CP in the early 1960s to adopt a pro-Chinese position (though never slavishly so like the later CPC-ML associated with Hardial Bains), was one of the key influences on Progressive Worker.

156. The Progressive Worker, *Independence and Socialism in Canada*, inside front cover, pp. 47, 49.

157. Confederation of Canadian Unions, *Canadian Union News*, May 1975, "The CCU—A Real Alternative," p. 1.

158. Cf. Paul Knox, "Breakaway Unionism in Kitimat," in P. Knox and P. Resnick, editors, *Essays in B.C. Political Economy*, Vancouver, 1974, pp. 42-51.

159. Bob Kiever, former President of the Steelworkers Local 480 at Trail, B.C., cited in the author's "The Breakaway Movement in Trail" in Knox and Resnick, editors, *op. cit.*, pp. 52-59, p. 54.

160. For an example of Kent Rowley, Secretary-Treasurer of the CCU, attacking the internationals on this score see *The Montreal Gazette,* March 19, 1971: "A net total of $80 million has been poured into the United States trade union movement in the last seven years by Canadian union members." For a reasoned counter-argument see Ken Eaton, economist in the Economics and Research Branch of the Canadian Department of Labour, "Financial aspects of international unions," *The Labour Gazette*, August 1972, pp. 413-423.

161. The author was present at a Western regional conference of the Council of Canadian Unions, held in Vancouver in January 1973, where a fair number of the delegates, e.g., those from the newly accredited Canadian Aluminum Smelter and Allied Workers Union (CASAW) at Kitimat, voted against or abstained on a resolution condemning the U.S. resumption of bombing of North Vietnam. (N.B. The Canadian House of Commons had just passed an all-party resolution to the same effect.) For a criticism of the Canadian Association of Industrial, Mechanical and Allied Workers (CAIMAW), one of the CCU's main affiliates, see Alvin Finkel "Winnipeg's CAIMAW: Business Unionism Replaces Business Unionism" in *Canadian Dimension*, Vol. 8, No. 1, June 1971, pp. 45-6.

162. Cf. the figures cited in footnotes 20 and 21 above.

163. John Robarts, *Report of the Montmorency Conference*, Progressive Conservative Advisory Conference of the Centennial Convention, Courville, Quebec, August

7-10,1967, pp. 108-9.

164. *The Globe and Mail*, January 20, 1969.

165. Walter Gordon, "The Right to Self-Determination," *The Canadian Forum*, April-May, 1971, pp. 27-28.

166. *Ibid.*, p. 28. Also "Walter Gordon on Giving Quebec its Due," *Maclean's*, September 1972, pp. 72, 76-77.

167. Paul Kidd, "Committee for an Independent Canada ignores Quebec," *The Montreal Gazette*, December 14, 1971, p. 7, reporting on the CIC's first national conference at Thunder Bay.

168. The author was present as an observer at the CIC's 5th Convention held between August 1-3, 1975 in Vancouver, and recalls that the Francophone Quebecois participation was all of one, the initiator of the proposal for a bi-national committee, Normand Paquin.

169. Carr, *op. cit.*, p. 7.

170. *Ibid.*, p. 111.

171. A.W. Purdy, "Levesque: The executioner of Confederation?," *Maclean's*, October 1971, pp. 28-9, 83.

172. Denis Lee, on the program "Le Nationalisme au Canada Anglais," *Present National*, 20 fevrier, 1975, kindly made available to the author by the producers of *Present*.

173. Colin Leonard, *Relations with l'Union Generale des Etudiants du Quebec*, C.U.S., Ottawa, 1968, p. 1.

174. Don I. Ray, *Political Thought of C.U.S.*, Ottawa, 1968, p. 10.

175. Brian Hutchison, Associate Secretary of C.U.S., *CUS and Student Unionism*, Address to the XXXIInd Congress of C.U.S., Guelph, Ontario, August 28-September 4, 1968, p. 3.

176. Donald Creighton, *Towards the Discovery of Canada*, pp. 269-270, 285.

177. McNaught, "The National Outlook of English-speaking Canadians," *op. cit.*, p. 63, p. 71.

178. See especially "Nationalism and the Nation-State," the lead essay in Cook's *The Maple Leaf Forever*, pp. 1-11.

179. Jim Laxer, "Quebec in the Canadian Federal State," in R. Laxer, ed., *op. cit.*, pp. 232-49, p. 248.

180. Abe Rotstein, "After the Fall" in *The Precarious Homestead*, pp. 118-24, p. 124.

181. *Ibid.*, pp. 119-22, *passim*.

182. Richard Simeon, "Scenarios for Separation" in R.M. Burns, editor *One Country or T⋅ ⋅o?*, Montreal, 1971, pp. 73-94, p. 73.

183. *Ibid.*, pp. 93-4.

184. Denis Smith, *Bleeding Hearts . . . Bleeding Country*, Edmonton, 1971, p. 141.

185. David Cameron, *Nationalism, Self-Determination and the Quebec Question,* Toronto, 1974, pp. 155-56.

186. CLC brief to the B & B Commission, *Canadian Labour,* January 1966, p. 23.

187. *Canadian Labour*, November 1970.

188. *The Labour Gazette*, August 1974. "New Faces New Directions for the Congress," p. 558.

189. May 21, 1975, at CLC Headquarters, Ottawa.

190. In the early 1960s, the Union Generale des Etudiants du Quebec was set up by Francophone Quebec Students no longer prepared to be part of a federalist organization, the Canadian Union of Students. The UGEQ-CUS scission was the first carrying through of the two nation principle to the establishment of two quite separate national organizations of students.

191. "English Canadians must support the right of the Quebec people to secede from Canada if they so desire . . . There will never be any possibility of solidarity between the peoples of English-Canada and Quebec if English-Canadians support the forcible retention of Quebec within the Canadian state." *Progressive Worker, op. cit.*, p. 57.

192. Resolution No. 85, submitted by Local 2500 in Quebec in 1971 reads: "BE IT RESOLVED that this Convention goes on record as being in favour of the right of self-determination for each of the Canadian provinces." *Proceedings*, 5th CUPE Convention, 1971, p. 32.

FOOTNOTES TO CHAPTER SIX

1. Cf. the Parti Quebecois's 1972 manifesto, *Quand nous serons vraiment chez nous,* whose inspiration takes a good deal more from the type of economic planning practiced in France under the Vth Republic, than from socialism.

2. From the Report of the Ad Hoc Committee of the 6th Special Session of the UN General Assembly, proposed resolution of the Group of 77, May 1, 1974.

3. James O'Connor, *The Fiscal Crisis of the State*, New York, 1973, p. 6.

4. Marx and Engels, *Manifesto of the Communist Party,* in Marx and Engels,

Selected Works, p. 37.

5. Cf. Ralph Miliband, *The State in Capitalist Society*, London, 1969, especially Chapter 4, "The Purpose and Role of Governments."

6. In an interview with the author, in May 1975, R.H. Catherwood, a senior editor of *The Financial Post*, stated that many businessmen lamented the fact that they had lost contact and influence on government policy. While we must treat such laments with grains of salt, it is nonetheless significant that big business subjectively perceived itself as having less input on government. As our study tends to argue, the main beneficiary of this "shrinking" bourgeois power has been the new petty bourgeoisie.

7. Cf. S.D. Clark, "Canada and the American Value System," in *The Developing Canadian Community*, Toronto, 2nd edition, 1968, pp. 233-42.

8. Donald V. Smiley, "Canada and the Quest for a National Policy," *Canadian Journal of Political Science*, Vol. VIII, No. 1, March 1975, pp. 40-62, p. 59.

9. Radovan Richta and associates, *Civilization at the Crossroads: Social and Human Implications of the Scientific and Technological Revolution*, New York, 1969.

10. Alain Touraine, *The May Movement: Revolt and Reform*, New York, 1971; *The Post-Industrial Society*, N.Y., 1971. Serge Mallet, *La nouvelle classe ouvriere*, Paris, 1963.

11. Antonio Gramsci, *The Modern Prince*, in Quinton Hoare & Geoffrey Nowell Smith, editors, *Selections for the Prison Notebooks*, London, 1971, pp. 181-82.

12. Cf. the manifestoes of the three Quebec centrals, the CNTU, QFL and CEQ in D. Drache, editor, *Quebec—Only the Beginning*, Toronto, 1972. See also *Ecole et lutte de classes au Quebec*, CEQ document, 1974.

13. Herbert Marshall, Frank A. Southard and Kenneth W. Taylor, *Canadian-American Industry*, New York, 1936, p. 291.

14. Robin Mathews, "Canadian Culture and the Liberal Ideology," in R. Laxer, ed., *op. cit.*, pp. 213-31,pp. 217-218. Cf. also the critique of Mathews by Leo Panitch and Reg Whitaker in their ariticle "The New Waffle: From Mathews to Marx," *Canadian Dimension*, Vol. 10, No. 1, April 1974. To be fair to Mathews, he does deserve credit for having helped raise the Americanization question in Canadian universities. But nationalism certainly predominates over socialism in his analysis.

15. Heather Robertson, "Confessions of a Canadian Chauvinist Pig," *Maclean's*, April 1975, cited by Robert Reford, *op. cit.*, p. 1.

16. Fernand Dumont, *La Vigile du Quebec*, Montreal 1971, Section 3. This book has been translated as *The Vigil of Quebec*, Toronto, 1974.

BIBLIOGRAPHY

GOVERNMENT DOCUMENTS

British Columbia, Department of Lands, Forests and Water Resources, Lands Service, *Annual Report, 1973*, Victoria, 1974.
    Opening Statement of the Province of British Columbia to the Federal-Provincial Conference of First Minister, Ottawa, April 9-10, 1975.
Canada, Atomic Energy of Canada Ltd., *Annual Reports*, 1965-1975.
Economic Council of Canada, *Looking Outward: A New Strategy for Canada*, Ottawa, 1975.
    "   Lyon, Peyton V., *Canada-United States Free Trade and Canadian Independence, Study for the Economic Council*, Ottawa, 1975.
External Affairs, Dept. of, *External Affairs*, monthly publication, 1947-1965.
    "   *International Perspectives*, monthly publication, 1972-75.
    "   *Statements and Speeches*, various years.
Finance, Dept. of, *Economic Review, 1974, 1975*, Ottawa, 1974, 1975.
Foreign Direct Investment in Canada, Ottawa, 1972.
Labour, Dept. of, *The Labour Gazette*, monthly publication, 1970-75.
Manpower and Immigration, Dept. of, Meltz, Noah M., *Manpower in Canada 1931-1961*, Ottawa, 1969.
National Revenue, Dept. of, *Taxation Statistics for 1946, 1950, 1955, 1960, 1965, 1970, 1972* Ottawa, various years.
Parliament, House of Commons, *Debates*, various years, 1945-1975.
    "   *Report of the Standing Committee on External Affairs and Defence, 1970*.
Privy Council Office, *Foreign Ownership and the Structure of Canadian Industry*, Ottawa, 1968.
Royal Commission on Bilingualism and Biculturalism, *Preliminary Report*, Ottawa, 1965.
Royal Commission on Canada's Economic Prospects, *Final Report*, Ottawa, 1957.
Royal Commission on National Development in the Arts, Letters and Science, 1949-1951, *Report*, Ottawa, 1951.
Royal Commission Reports: A Selection of Essays Prepared for the Royal Commission on National Development in the Arts, Letters and Science, Ottawa, 1951.
Science Council of Canada, Cordell, Arthur J., *The Multinational Firm, Foreign Direct Investment, and Canadian Science Policy*, Background Study No. 22, Ottawa, December 1971.
    "   Bourgault, Pierre L., *Innovation and the Structure of Canadian Industry*, Background Study No. 23, Ottawa, October 1972.
Statistics Canada, Annual Report of the Minister of Industry, Trade and Commerce under the Corporations and Labour Unions Returns Act, *Part 1—Report on Corporations, Part 2—Report on Trade Unions*, Ottawa, various years.

Statistics Canada,*Canada Year Book, 1973*, Ottawa, 1973.
,,   *Canada's International Investment Position 1926 to 1967*, Ottawa, 1971.
,,   Census of Canada, 1951, *The Labour Force*, Bulletin 4-2.
,,   Census of Canada, 1961, *The Labour Force*, Vol. 111, Part 1, Bulletin 3.1-14.
,,   Census of Canada, 1971, *The Labour Force*, Vol. 111, Part 1, Bulletin (3.1-3).
,,   Census of Canada, 1971, *Occupations*, Vol. 111, Part 2, (Bulletin 3.2-3).
,,   *Education in Canada: A Statistical Review for the Period 1960-1 to 1970-1*, Ottawa, 1973.
,,   *The Labour Force*, monthly publication, various years.
,,   *White Paper on Employment and Income*, Ottawa, 1945.
,,   White Paper on Defence, *Defence in the 70s*, Ottawa, 1971.
Japan, *Economic Survey of Japan 1970-71*, Tokyo, 1971.
Ontario, Royal Commission on Book Publishing, *Background Papers*, Toronto, 1972.
      Select Committee on Economic and Cultural Nationalism, *Attitudes of Community Leaders and the General Public in Four Ontario Communities*, Background Study, Toronto, 1973.
Organization for Economic Cooperation and Development, OECD *Economic Outlook*, Paris, 1967-1975.
Organization of European Economic Cooperation, *Statistics of National Product and Expenditure 1938, 1947-55*, Paris, 1957.
United Nations, Dept. of Economic and Social Affairs, *Multinational Corporations in World Development*, N.Y., 1973.
      General Assembly, Sixth Special Session, May 1, 1974.
United States, *Resources for Freedom, Vol. 1*, A Report to the President by the President's Materials Policy Commission, Washington, June 1952.

NEWSPAPERS, PERIODICALS AND SIMILAR PUBLICATIONS

Canada Month, Toronto, 1961-65.
The Canadian Banker, most issues, 1945-1955, 1965-1970.
The Canadian Chartered Accountant, later *CA*, most issues, 1945-1974.
Canadian Chemistry and Process Industries, later *Canadian Chemical Processing*, Toronto, most issues, 1950-1965.
Canadian Dimension, Winnipeg, all issues, 1965-1975.
Canadian Federation of Independent Business, *Mandates*, 1973-75.
The Canadian Forum, all issues, 1970-75 (and Granatstein and Stevens, eds., *Forum*, for before 1970).
The Canadian Institute of Public Opinion, *Gallup Polls*, 1950-1974.
Canadian Labour, monthly publication of the Canadian Labour Congress, all issues, 1956-1974.
The Canadian Manufacturers Association, *Report of Annual General Meeting*, 1946-1973.
The Canadian Paperworker's Journal, 1975.
Canadian Union News, publication of the Council, later Confederation, of Canadian Unions, 1972-1975.
Canadian Union of Public Employees, *Journal*, Ottawa, 1967-1975.
The Canadian Unionist, monthly publication of the Congress of Canadian Labour, all issues, 1945-1955.
The Country Guide, monthly farm paper, Winnipeg, all issues, 1945-1965.

The Farmer's Advocate, London, Ontario, all issues, 1945-1965.
The Financial Post, weekly, Toronto, all issues, 1945-1975.
The Financial Times of Canada, occasional issues, 1963-1974.
Fortune Magazine, New York, occasional issues.
The Globe and Mail, Toronto, occasional issues.
The Halifax Chronicle Herald, occasional issues.
The Independencer, bi-monthly publication of the Committee for an Independent Canada, all issues, 1972-1975.
Industrial Canada, monthly publication of the Candian Manufacturers Association, 1965-1974.
The Last Post, occasional issues, 1970-1974.
Maclean's, most issues, 1960-1975.
The Montreal Gazette, occasional issues.
The Province, Vancouver, occasional issues.
Saturday Night, Toronto, most issues, 1945-1960.
Science Forum, Toronto, most issues, 1968-1973.
This Magazine, Toronto, all issues, 1972-1975.
The Toronto Star, occasional issues.
University Affairs, all issues, 1970-1975.
The Vancouver Sun, occasional issues.

PRINCIPAL SOURCES

Acton, Lord, "Nationality" in *Essays on Freedom and Power*, London, 1962 edition.
Angus, H.F., "The Canadian Royal Commission on the Arts, Letters and Science," *The Western Political Quarterly,* Vol. IV, No. 4, December 1951.
Barkway, Michael, "The Fifties: An Ottawa Retrospect," *The Waterloo Review,* Summer 1960.
Baudelot, Christian, Establet, Robert & Malemort, Jacques, *La petite bourgeoisie en France,* Paris, Maspero, 1974.
Blyth, C.D. & Carty, E.B., "Non-Resident Ownership of Canadian Industry," *Canadian Journal of Economics and Political Science,* Vol. XXII, November 1956, pp. 449-460.
Brebner, J.B., "Harold Adams Innis as Historian," Canadian Historical Association, *Papers, 1953,* pp. 14-24.
Brichant, Andrew A., *Option Canada: A preliminary essay on the economic implications of separatism for the Province of Quebec,* Montreal, Canada Committee, 1968.
Buck, Tim, *Our Fight for Canada,* Toronto, 1959.
Burns, R.M. editor, *One Country or Two?,* Montreal, 1971.
Cameron, David, *Nationalism, Self-Determination and the Quebec Question,* Toronto, 1974.
Canadian Annual Review, 1960-1973, Toronto, 1961-1974.
Canadian Union of Public Employees, *Proceedings,* 5th and 6th Conventions, 1971, 1973.
Careless, J.M.S., "Canadian Nationalism—Immature or Obsolete?" Canadian Historical Association, *Papers, 1954.*
Carr, D.W., *Recovering Canada's Nationhood,* Ottawa, 1971.
Clark, S.D., "Canada and the American Value System" in *The Developing Canadian Community,* Toronto, 2nd edition, 1968.
Clarkson, Stephen, ed., *An Independent Foreign Policy for Canada?,* Toronto, 1968.
Clement, Wallace *The Canadian Corporate Elite,* Toronto, 1975.
Cook, Ramsay, *Canada and the French-Canadian Question,* Toronto, 1966.

Cook, Ramsay, *The Maple Leaf Forever,* Toronto, 1971.

Creighton, Donald, *Harold Adam Innis, Portrait of a Scholar,* Toronto, 1957.

Creighton, Donald, *Towards the Discovery of Canada,* Toronto, 1972.

Davis, Horace B. *Nationalism and Socialism,* New York, 1967.

Deutsch, John J., "Agenda for the Seventies," *The Queen's Quarterly,* Vol. 78, 1971, pp. 1-6.

Eayrs, James, *Canada in World Affairs: October 1955 to June 1957,* Toronto, 1965.

Ferguson, G.V., "Likely Trends in Canadian-American Political Relations," *Canadian Journal of Economics and Political Science,* Vol. XXII, 1956, pp. 437-448.

Fraser, John and Graham, *Blair Fraser Reports,* Toronto, 1969.

Gibson, J. Douglas, ed., *Canada's Economy in a Changing World,* Toronto, 1948.

Gibson, J. Douglas, "The Changing Influence of the United States on the Canadian Economy," *Canadian Journal of Economics and Political Science,* Vol. XXII, 1956, pp. 421-436.

Gibson, J. Douglas, "Canada's declaration of less dependence," *Harvard Business Review,* September-October, 1973, pp. 69-79.

Godfrey, Dave & Watkins, Mel, eds., *Gordon to Watkins to You,* Toronto, 1970.

Gordon, H. Scott, *The Economists versus the Bank of Canada,* Toronto, 1961.

Gordon, Walter L., "Foreign Control of Canadian Industry," *Queen's Quarterly,* Vol. 73, 1966, pp. 1-12.

Gordon, Walter L., *A Choice for Canada,* Toronto, 1966.

Gough, Ian, "State Expenditure and Capital," *New Left Review,* London No. 92, July-August, 1975.

Gramsci, Antonio, *Selections from the Prison Notebooks,* eds., Quinton Hoare and Geoffrey Nowell Smith, London, 1971.

Granatstein, J.L. and Stevens, Peter, eds., *Forum, Selections from the Canadian Forum 1920-1970,* Toronto, 1972.

Grant, George, *Lament for a Nation,* Toronto, Carleton Library Edition, 1970.

Hahlo, H.R., Smith, J. Graham, Wright, Richard C., eds., *Nationalism and the Multinational Enterprise,* Leiden, 1973.

Haupt, Georges, Lowy, Michael, Weill, Claudie, eds., *Les marxistes et la question nationale, 1848-1914,* Montreal and Paris, 1974.

Head, Ivan, "The Foreign Policy of the New Canada," *Foreign Affairs,* Vol. 50, January 1972.

Heeney, A.D.P., *The things that are Caesar's: Memoirs of a Canadian public servant,* Toronto, 1972.

Henn, Desmond, E., "The Canadian Dilemma," *The Spectator,* London, February 27, 1953.

Hodgetts, J.E. & Dwivedi, O.P., "The Growth of Government Employment in Canada," *Canadian Journal of Public Administration,* 1969, pp. 224-238.

Holmes, John W. *The Better Part of Valour,* Toronto, 1970.

Innis, Harold, *Essays in Canadian Economic History,* Toronto, 1956.

Innis, Harold, *The Strategy of Culture,* Toronto, 1962.

Innis, Hugh, ed., *Bilingualism and Biculturalism,* Toronto, 1956.

Johnson, Harry, *The Canadian Quandry,* Toronto, 1963.

Johnson, Harry, ed., *Economic Nationalism in Old and New States,* Chicago, 1967.

Johnson, Harry, *International Economic Questions facing Britain, the United States and Canada in the 70s,* London, British-North American Committee, 1970.

Johnson, Harry, *On Economics and Society,* Chicago, 1975.

Knox, Paul and Resnick, Philip, eds., *Essays in B.C. Political Economy,* Vancouver, 1974.

Kohn, Hans, *The Idea of Nationalism,* New York, 1944.

Kolko, Joyce and Gabriel, *The Limits of Power,* New York, 1972.

Laxer, Robert M. ed., *Canada Ltd.: The Political Economy of Dependency,* Toronto,

1973.

League for Social Reconstruction, *Social Planning for Canada,* Toronto, new edition, 1975.

Lenin, Vladimir, I., *Questions of National Policy and Proletarian Internationalism*, Moscow, 1964.

LePan, Douglas, "The Old Ontario Strand in the Canada of Today," *Queen's Quarterly,* Vol. 73, 1966, pp. 483-495.

Levitt, Kari, *Silent Surrender,* Toronto, 1970.

Lipton, Charles, *The Trade Union Movement of Canada 1827-1959,* Montreal, 1968.

Lower, A.R.M. *Canada—Nation and Neighbour,* Toronto, 1952.

Lower, A.R.M. *This Most Famous Stream: The Liberal Democratic Way of Life,* Toronto, 1954.

Lower, A.R.M., *History and Myth,* articles by Lower edited by Welf H. Heick, UBC Press, Vancouver, 1975.

Lumdsden, Ian, ed., *Close the 49th Parallel etc.,* Toronto, 1970.

Mao Tsetung, *Selected Works,* Peking, Vols., II, V.

Marshall, Herbert, Southard, Frank A., Taylor, Kenneth, W., *Canadian-American Industry,* New York, 1936.

Marx, Karl and Engels, Frederick, *The German Ideology,* New York, 1970.

Marx, Karl and Engels, Frederick, *Selected Works,* One Volume, Moscow, 1968.

Marx, Karl, *Surveys from Exile,* ed., David Fernbach, London, 1973.

Marx, Karl, *Theories of Surplus Value,* Part 1, Moscow, 1969.

Marx, Karl, *The Grundrisse,* ed., M. Nicolaus, London, 1973.

Marx, Karl, *Capital,* Vol. 1, London, 1957.

Massey, Vincent, *On Being Canadian,* Toronto, 1948.

Mathews, Robin and Steele, James, *The Struggle for Canadian Universities,* Toronto, 1969.

Matthews, Roy A., "Canada, 'The International Nation'," *Queen's Quarterly,* Vol. 72, 1965, pp. 499-523.

McNaught, Kenneth, "Foreign Policy," in Michael Oliver, ed., *Social Purpose for Canada,* Toronto, 1961, pp. 445-472.

Minifie, James M., *Peacemaker or Powder-Monkey: Canada's Role in a Revolutionary World,* Toronto, 1960.

Mitchell, Don, *The Politics of Food,* Toronto, 1975.

Molot, Maureen Appel, "The Elephant, the Mouse and the Financial Relationship," *Queen's Quarterly,* Vol. 78, 1971, pp. 71-82.

Moore, Steve and Wells, Debbi, *Imperialism and the National Question in Canada,* Toronto, 1975.

Morris, Peter, "Declaration of Independence," *The North American Review,* Spring, 1972.

Morton, W.L., *The Canadian Identity,* Toronto, 2nd edition, 1973.

Neatby, Hilda, "Canadianism," Canadian Historical Association, *Papers, 1956,* pp. 74-76.

Newman, Peter C. *The Distemper of our Times,* Toronto, 1968.

Newman, Peter C. "The Thawing of Canada," *The Atlantic Community Quarterly,* Vol. IX, 1971, pp. 219-228.

Park, Libbie and Frank, *Anatomy of Big Business,* Toronto, 2nd edition, 1973.

Pitfield, P. Michael, "Canada in the Seventies," April 1972, in *Canadian-American Relations—Towards a Better Understanding,* St. Lawrence University, New York, 1974.

Policies of the New Democratic Party, 1961-1973, Ottawa, 1974.

Porter, John, *The Vertical Mosaic,* Toronto, 1965.

Prang, Margaret E., "Nationalism in Canada's First Century," Canadian Historical Association, *Historical Papers, 1968,* pp. 114-125.

Preston, R.A., Canadian Historical Association, *Papers, 1956,* pp. 76-79.

The Progressive Worker, "Independence and Socialism in Canada: A Marxist-Leninist View," Vancouver, 1969.

Purdy, Al, ed., *The New Romans,* Edmonton, 1968.

Radosh, Ronald, *American Labour and United States Foreign Policy,* New York, 1969.

Renan, Ernst, "The Meaning of Nationality," in Hans Kohn, ed., *Nationalism,* New York, 1955.

Robarts, John, speech to the Progressive Conservative Advisory Conference on the Centennial Convention, in *Report of the Montmorency Conference,* 1967.

Roberts, Leslie, *C.D. The Life and Times of Clarence Decatur Howe,* Toronto, 1957.

Roblin, Duff, "A new national policy and Canadian nationalism," The W. Clifford Clark Memorial Lecture, *Canadian Journal of Public Administration,* 1973, pp. 542-56.

Rotstein, Abraham, *The Precarious Homestead,* Toronto, 1973.

Rotstein, Abraham, and Lax, Gary, editors, *Getting it Back: A Program for Canadian Independence,* edited for the Committee for an Independent Canada, Toronto, 1974.

Royal Institute for International Affairs, *Nationalism,* London, 1939.

Russell, Peter, ed., *Nationalism in Canada,* Toronto, 1966.

Schwartz, Mildred A. *Public Opinion and Canadian Identity,* Berkeley and Los Angeles, 1967.

Shorter Oxford English Dictionary, "Nation," Vol. II, Oxford, 1964, p. 1311.

Smiley, Donald V., "Canada and the Quest for a National Policy," *Canadian Journal of Political Science,* Vol. VIII, March 1975, pp. 40-62.

Smith, Denis, *Bleeding Hearts . . . Bleeding Country,* Edmonton, 1971.

Smith, Denis, *Gentle Patriots: A Political Biography of Walter Gordon,* Edmonton, 1973.

Spencer, R.A., *Canada in World Affairs 1946-1949,* Toronto, 1959.

Stalin, J.V., *Marxism and the National Question,* in *Works,* Vol. 2, Moscow, 1953.

Stock, Brian, "A culture in search of an economy" in *The Times Literary Supplement,* London, October 26, 1973, pp. 1311-13, part of an issue on "Canadian Writing Today."

Swanson, Roger Frank, ed., *Canadian-American Summit Diplomacy 1923-1973,* Toronto, 1975.

Sweetenham, John Alexander, *McNaughton,* Vol. 3, Toronto, 1969.

Sykes, Philip, *Sellout: The Giveaway of Canada's Energy Resources,* Edmonton, 1973.

Teeple, Gary, ed., *Capitalism and the National Question in Canada,* Toronto, 1972.

Trudeau, Pierre Elliott, *Conversations with Canadians,* Toronto, 1972.

Trudeau, Pierre Elliott, *Federalism and the French Canadians,* Toronto, 1968.

Trudeau, Pierre Elliott, *Transcript of Questions and Answers at the Prime Minister's Accountability Session,* Liberal Party Convention, November 20, 1970.

Underhill, Frank H., *In Search of Canadian Liberalism,* Toronto, 1960.

Underhill, Frank H., *The Image of Confederation,* Toronto, CBC Publications, 1964.

Urquhart, M.C. and Buckley, K.A.H., editors, *Historical Statistics of Canada,* Cambridge and Toronto, 1965.

Watkins, Melville H., "Economic Nationalism," *Canadian Journal of Economics and Political Science,* Vol. XXXII, 1966, pp. 388-392.

Weisskopf, Thomas E., *American Economic Interests in Foreign Countries: An Empirical Survey,* Center for Research on Economic Development, The University of Michigan, Discussion Paper 35, Ann Arbor, Michigan, 1974.

Woytinsky, Emma S., *Profile of the United States Economy,* New York, 1967.

SECONDARY SOURCES

Abella, Irving M., *Nationalism, Communism and Canadian Labour*, Toronto, 1973.

Agee, Philip, *Inside the Company: CIA Diary*, London, 1975.

Aitken, H.G.J., "Defensive Expansionism: The State and Economic Growth in Canada," in W.T. Easterbrook and M.H. Watkins, eds., *Approaches to Canadian Economic History*, Toronto, pp. 183-221.

d'Allemagne, Andre, *Le Colonialisme au Quebec*, Montreal, 1966.

Atwood, Margaret, *Survival*, Toronto, 1972.

Avakumovic, Ivan, *The Communist Party in Canada*, Toronto, 1975.

Babcock, Robert H. *Gompers in Canada*, Toronto, 1975.

Barnet, Richard J. and Muller, Ronald E., *Global Reach*, New York, 1974.

Baum, Daniel Jay, *The Banks of Canada in the Commonwealth Carribean—economic nationalism and multinational enterprises of a medium power*, New York, 1974.

Beard, Charles, *An Economic Interpretation of the Constitution of the United States*, New York, reprinted 1960.

Berlin, Isaiah, "Two Concepts of Liberty," in *Four Essays on Liberty*, New York, 1969.

Brazeau, Jacques, "Les nouvelles classes moyennes," in Fernand Dumont and Jean-Paul Montminy, eds., *Le pouvoir dans la societe canadienne-francaise*, Laval, Quebec, 1966.

Brebner, John Bartlet, *North Atlantic Triangle*, Carleton Library Edition, Toronto, 1966.

Cairns, Alan C. "National Influences on the Study of Politics," *Queen's Quarterly*, Vol. 81, 1974, pp. 333-347.

Cairns, Alan C., "Political Science in Canada and the Americanization Issue," *Canadian Journal of Political Science*, June 1975, Vol. VIII, pp. 191-234.

Caloren, Fred, "Layoffs, Shutdowns, and Plant Closures in Ontario: The Economics of Misery," *Our Generation*, Montreal, Vol. 10, No. 4, pp. 61-75.

Centrale des Enseignants du Quebec, *Ecole et lutte de classe au Quebec*, 1974.

Creighton, Donald, *Empire of the St. Lawrence*, Toronto, 2nd edition, 1956.

Culhane, Claire, *Why is Canada in Vietnam?*, Toronto, 1972.

Deverell, John and the Latin American Working Group, *Falconbridge: Portrait of a Canadian Mining Multinational*, Toronto, 1975.

Drache, Daniel, ed., *Quebec—Only the Beginning*, Toronto, 1972.

Drache, Daniel, "Rediscovering Canadian Political Economy," Canadian Political Science Association, *Papers, 1975*.

Dumont, Fernand, *La vigile du Quebec*, Montreal, 1971.

Emmanuel, Arghiri, *Unequal Exchange: A Study of the Imperialism of Trade*, New York, 1972.

Fayerweather, John, *Foreign Investment in Canada*, Toronto, 1974.

Fayerweather, John, *The Mercantile Bank Affair: A Case Study of Canadian Nationalism and the Multinational Firm*, New York, 1974.

Forsey, Eugene, *Freedom and Order*, Collected Essays, Toronto, 1974.

Fowke, Vernon C., *The National Policy and the Wheat Economy*, Toronto, 1957.

Frank, Andre Gunder, *Capitalism and Underdevelopment in Latin America*, New York, 1960.

Frumhartz, Muni, *The unionization of white-collar workers*, Canadian Labour Congress, 1963.

Guindon, Hubert, "Social Unrest, Social Class and Quebec's Bureaucratic Revolution," *Queen's Quarterly*, Vol. 71, No. 1, 1964, pp. 150-162.

Hardin, Herschel, *A Nation Unaware*, Vancouver, 1974.

Hill, Christopher, *Puritanism and Revolution*, London, Panther Edition, 1968.

Horowitz, Gad, *Canadian Labour in Politics*, Toronto, 1968.

Kamenka, Eugene, ed., *Nationalism—The Nature and Evolution of an Idea*, Canberra, 1973.

Lee, Dennis, *Civil Elegies,* Toronto, 1968.
Litvak, Isaiah A. and Maule, Christopher, *Cultural Sovereignty: The Time and Reader's Digest Case in Canada,* New York, 1974.
Luxemburg, Rosa, *The Mass Strike and the Junius Pamphlet,* New York: Harper Torchbooks, 1971.
Macpherson, C.B., *Democracy in Alberta,* Toronto, 1953.
Macpherson, Kay and Sears, Meg, "The Voice of Women: A History" in Gwen Mathewson, ed., *Women in the Canadian Mosaic,* Toronto, 1976.
Magdoff, Harry, *The Age of Imperialism,* New York, 1969.
Mallet, Serge, *La Nouvelle Classe Ouvriere,* Paris, 1963.
McNaught, Kenneth and Bercuson, David J., *The Winnipeg Strike: 1919,* Toronto, 1974.
Mills, C. Wright, *The Power Elite,* New York, 1956.
Minogue, Kenneth, *Nationalism,* London, 1967.
Neufeld, E.P., *The Financial System of Canada,* Toronto, 1972.
Nyere, Julius K., *Freedom and Socialism,* Dar es Salaam, 1969.
O'Connor, James, *The Fiscal Crisis of the State,* New York, 1973.
Parti Quebecois, *Quand nous serons vraiment chez nous,* Montreal, 1972.
Peers, Frank, W., *The Politics of Canadian Broadcasting 1920-1951,* Toronto, 1969.
Penner, Norman, ed., *Winnipeg, 1919: The strikers' own history of the Winnipeg General Strike,* Toronto, 1973.
Pratt, Larry, *The Tar Sands,* Edmonton, 1976.
Reid, J.H., McNaught, Kenneth and Crowe, Harry S., *A Source Book of Canadian History,* Toronto, 1959.
Ricta, Radovan and associates, *Civilization at the Crossroads: Social and Human Implications of the Scientific and Technological Revolution,* New York, 1969.
Rioux, Marcel, *Les Quebecois,* Paris, 1974.
Scheinberg, Stephen, "The Indispensable Ally: Canadian Resources and the Cold War," Candian Historical Association, *Papers, 1975.*
Seguin, Maurice, *L'Idee d'independance au Quebec,* Trois Rivieres, 1968.
Siegel, Lenny, "AFL-CIA" in Steve Weissman *et al.,* eds., *The Trojan Horse: A Radical Look at Foreign Aid,* Palo Alto, Cal.: Ramparts Press, 1974, pp. 117-135.
Sieyes, Emmanuel Joseph, *What is the Third Estate?,* London, 1964.
Smiley, Donald, *Canada in Question: Federalism in the Seventies,* Toronto, 1972.
Taylor, Charles, *The Pattern of Politics,* Toronto, 1970.
Taylor, Charles, *Snow-job: Canada, the United States and Vietnam, 1954 to 1973,* Toronto, 1974.
Touraine, Alain, *The May movement: Revolt and reform,* New York, 1971.
Touraine, Alain, *The Post-Industrial Society,* New York, 1971.
Vernon, Raymond, *Sovereignty at Bay,* New York, 1971.
Warnock, John W. *Partner to Behemoth,* Toronto, 1970.

PAMPHLETS

A Canadian Voice—Does Labor Need a National Identity?, published by a group of Canadian workers at Vancouver, B.C., July 1967, Library, Department of Labour, Ottawa.
The Canadian Federation of Independent Business, *The Programmes and Objectives.*
Canadian Union of Students, *What Happened? A History,* Ottawa, no date.
Committee for an Independent Canada, *Why You Should Support the CIC,* Toronto, 1970.
Hutchison, Brian, *C.U.S. and Student Unionism,* Address to the XXXII Congress of the Canadian Union of Sudents, Guelph, Ontario August 28-September 4, 1968.

Hyde, Tony, *Economics: Large Questions, Short Answers*, Canadian Union of Students, Ottawa, 1968.
Leonard, Colin, *Relations with l'Union Generale des Etudieants du Quebec*, Canadian Union of Students, Ottawa, 1968.
Nationalism, Socialism and Canadian Independence, Canadian Dimension pamphlet, Winnipeg, no date.
Ray, Don I., *Political Thought of C.U.S.*, Ottawa, Canadian Union of Students, 1968.
Soward, F.H., "Canada in a Two-Power World," Canadian Institute for International Affairs, *Behind the Headlines*, Toronto, August 1948.

UNPUBLISHED ADDRESSES, PAPERS, LETTERS AND PRESS RELEASES

Barkway, Michael, Address to the Society of Industrial Editors, Toronto, November 14, 1957.
Barkway, Michael, "How Independent Can We Be?," Speech to the Liberal Party's Study Conference on National Problems, Kingston, Ontario September 1960.
Bonner, Robert W., Vice-Chairman, MacMillan-Bloedel, "The Future Role of Canadian Companies in International Trade," Address to the 15th Annual Business Conference, University of Western Ontario, London, Ontario, June 4, 1971.
Bulloch, John, President, Canadian Federation of Independent Business, "Incentives for What?," speech to the National Conference on Incentives, Halifax, May 28, 1975.
Canadian Association of University Teachers, Council Meetings, *Minutes*, 1968-1975.
Canadian Federation of Independent Business, Brief to the Commons Committee considering amendments to the Combines Investigation Act, 1975.
Canadian Union of Public Employees, Press Releases, 1972-1975.
Conrad, James R., Director of Policy and Research, Canadian Federation of Independent Business, Letter to the author, May 20, 1975.
Kinnear, David, President of T. Eaton Co., Speech to the Canadian-U.S. Committee of the Canada and United States Chamber of Commerce, News release by the Canadian Chamber of Commerce, Montreal, dated March 25, 1972.
Murray, J. Alex and LeDuc, Laurence, "Public Opinion and Current Foreign Policy Options in Canada," unpublished paper, University of Windsor, 1974.
Page, Robert, 1974-75, "Canadian Nationalism—Does it make the border more visible?," An Address to the Chicago Council on Foreign Relations April 18-19, 1975, Library of the Canadian Institute of International Affairs, Toronto.
Transcript of the program "Le nationalisme au Canada anglais," *Present national*, Radio Canada, 10 fevrier, 1975.

THESES AND COLLECTIONS

Armstrong, Hugh, *The Patron State of Canada: An Exploratory Essay on the State and Job Creation in Canada since World War Two*, M.A. Thesis, Department of Sociology and Anthropology, Carleton University, 1974.
Boyd, Maureen, *The Making of the Foreign Investment Reivew Act: Sources of Influence on Bill C-132*, Honours Essay, U.B.C., Department of Political Science, 1975.
Le Borgne, Louis, *La CSN et la question nationale, 1960-1973*, these de maitrise, Department de Science Politique, Universite du Quebec a Montreal, 1975.

Mellos, Koula, *Theories of Ideology in Advanced Capitalist Society,* Ph.D. thesis, Queen's University, 1974.

The Norman Mackenzie Papers, papers of the former President of the University of British Columbia, especially material related to the Massey Royal Commission and the Canadian-American Committee, both of which Mackenzie was a member of, U.B.C., Special Collections.

Penner, Norman, *The Socialist Idea in Canadian Political Thought,* Ph.D. thesis, Toronto, 1975.

Thakur, Rishee S., *Imperialism and Nationalism in the Caribbean: The Political Economy of Dependent Underdevelopment in Guyana,* M.A. thesis, U.B.C., Department of Political Science, 1976.

Wallace, Mary Elizabeth, *The Changing Canadian State: A Study of the Changing Conception of the State as Revealed in Canadian Social Legislation: 1867-1948,* Ph.D. thesis, Columbia University, 1950.

INTERVIEWS

Barkway, Michael, long-time Ottawa correspondent of *The Financial Post,* later publisher of *The Financial Times of Canada,* Montreal, May 27, 1975.

Catherwood, R.H., senior editor, *The Financial Post,* Toronto, May 14, 1975.

Lang, Ron, Legislative Director, Canadian Labour Congress, Ottawa, May 21, 1975.

Lewis, David, then Deputy Leader of the New Democratic Party, Ottawa, Christmas 1967, in connection with a study the author was then undertaking on Canadian defence policy.

Logan, Daryl, National Director, Committee for an Independent Canada, Ottawa, May 20, 1975.

Morris, Joe, President, Canadian Labour Congress, Ottawa, May 21, 1975.

Rotstein, Abe, co-founder of the Committee for an Independent Canada, Toronto, May 14, 1975.

Savage, Donald, executive secretary, Canadian Association of University Teachers, Ottawa, May 23, 1975.

Simon, Norm, publicity director of the Canadian Union of Public Employees, Ottawa, May 22, 1975.

LIST OF CHARTS, STATEMENTS AND TABLES

CHARTS

STATEMENTS

TABLES

INDEX